studies in jazz

Institute of Jazz Studies
Rutgers—The State University of New Jersey
General Editors: Dan Morgenstern and Edward Berger

1. BENNY CARTER: A Life in American Music, *by Morroe Berger, Edward Berger, and James Patrick, 2 vols., 1982*
2. ART TATUM: A Guide to His Recorded Music, *by Arnold Laubich and Ray Spencer, 1982*
3. ERROLL GARNER: The Most Happy Piano, *by James M. Doran, 1995*
4. JAMES P. JOHNSON: A Case of Mistaken Identity, *by Scott E. Brown;* Discography 1917–1950, *by Robert Hilbert, 1986*
5. PEE WEE ERWIN: This Horn for Hire, *as told to Warren W. Vaché Sr., 1987*
6. BENNY GOODMAN: Listen to His Legacy, *by D. Russell Connor, 1988*
7. ELLINGTONIA: The Recorded Music of Duke Ellington and His Sidemen, *by W. E. Timner, 1988; 4th ed., 1996*
8. THE GLENN MILLER ARMY AIR FORCE BAND: Sustineo Alas / I Sustain the Wings, *by Edward F. Polic;* Foreword *by George T. Simon, 1989*
9. SWING LEGACY, *by Chip Deffaa, 1989*
10. REMINISCING IN TEMPO: The Life and Times of a Jazz Hustler, *by Teddy Reig, with Edward Berger, 1990*
11. IN THE MAINSTREAM: 18 Portraits in Jazz, *by Chip Deffaa, 1992*
12. BUDDY DeFRANCO: A Biographical Portrait and Discography, *by John Kuehn and Arne Astrup, 1993*
13. PEE WEE SPEAKS: A Discography of Pee Wee Russell, *by Robert Hilbert, with David Niven, 1992*
14. SYLVESTER AHOLA: The Gloucester Gabriel, *by Dick Hill, 1993*
15. THE POLICE CARD DISCORD, *by Maxwell T. Cohen, 1993*
16. TRADITIONALISTS AND REVIVALISTS IN JAZZ, *by Chip Deffaa, 1993*
17. BASSICALLY SPEAKING: An Oral History of George Duvivier, *by Edward Berger;* Musical Analysis *by David Chevan, 1993*
18. TRAM: The Frank Trumbauer Story, *by Philip R. Evans and Larry F. Kiner, with William Trumbauer, 1994*
19. TOMMY DORSEY: On the Side, *by Robert L. Stockdale, 1995*
20. JOHN COLTRANE: A Discography and Musical Biography, *by Yasuhiro Fujioka, with Lewis Porter and Yoh-ichi Hamada, 1995*
21. RED HEAD: A Chronological Survey of "Red" Nichols and His Five Pennies, *by Stephen M. Stroff, 1996*
22. THE RED NICHOLS STORY: After Intermission 1942–1965, *by Philip R. Evans, Stanley Hester, Stephen Hester, and Linda Evans, 1997*
23. BENNY GOODMAN: Wrappin' It Up, *by D. Russell Connor, 1996*
24. CHARLIE PARKER AND THEMATIC IMPROVISATION, *by Henry Martin, 1996*

25. BACK BEATS AND RIM SHOTS: The Johnny Blowers Story, *by Warren W. Vaché Sr., 1997*
26. DUKE ELLINGTON: A Listener's Guide, *by Eddie Lambert, 1998*
27. SERGE CHALOFF: A Musical Biography and Discography, *by Vladimir Simosko, 1998*
28. HOT JAZZ: From Harlem to Storyville, *by David Griffiths, 1998*
29. ARTIE SHAW: A Musical Biography and Discography, *by Vladimir Simosko, 2000*
30. JIMMY DORSEY: A Study in Contrasts, *by Robert L. Stockdale, 1998*
31. STRIDE!: Fats, Jimmy, Lion, Lamb and All the Other Ticklers, *by John L. Fell and Terkild Vinding, 1999*
32. GIANT STRIDES: The Legacy of Dick Wellstood, *by Edward N. Meyer, 1999*
33. JAZZ GENTRY: Aristocrats of the Music World, *by Warren W. Vaché Sr., 1999*
34. THE UNSUNG SONGWRITERS: America's Masters of Melody, *by Warren W. Vaché Sr., 2000*
35. THE MUSICAL WORLD OF J. J. JOHNSON, *by Joshua Berrett and Louis G. Bourgois III, 1999*
36. THE LADIES WHO SING WITH THE BAND, *by Betty Bennett, 2000*
37. AN UNSUNG CAT: The Life and Music of Warne Marsh, *by Safford Chamberlain, 2000*
38. JAZZ IN NEW ORLEANS: The Postwar Years Through 1970, *by Charles Suhor, 2001*
39. THE YOUNG LOUIS ARMSTRONG ON RECORDS: A Critical Survey of the Early Recordings, 1923–1928, *by Edward Brooks, 2002*
40. BENNY CARTER: A Life in American Music, Second Edition, *by Morroe Berger, Edward Berger, and James Patrick, 2 vols., 2002*
41. CHORD CHANGES ON THE CHALKBOARD: How Public School Teachers Shaped Jazz and the Music of New Orleans, *by Al Kennedy;* Foreword *by Ellis Marsalis Jr., 2002*
42. CONTEMPORARY CAT: Terence Blanchard with Special Guests, *by Anthony Magro, 2002*

The *Annual Review of Jazz Studies* is published by Scarecrow Press and the Institute of Jazz Studies at Rutgers, The State University of New Jersey.

Authors should address manuscripts and editorial correspondence to:

The Editors, Annual Review of Jazz Studies
Institute of Jazz Studies
Dana Library, Rutgers, The State University
185 University Avenue
Newark, New Jersey 07102

Publishers should send review copies of books to this address, marked to the attention of the Book Review Editor.

Authors preparing manuscripts for consideration should follow *The Chicago Manual of Style,* 14th Edition. In particular: (1) manuscripts should be original word-processed copy; (2) except for foreign-language quotations, manuscripts must be in English; (3) *all* material (text, quotations, endnotes, author's biographical note) must be neat, *double-spaced,* left-aligned, and with adequate margins; (4) notes must be grouped together at the end of the manuscript, *not as footnotes* at page bottoms, following either of the two documentation styles (chapters 15 or 16 in *The Chicago Manual of Style,* 14th Edition); (5) author should append a two- or three-sentence biographical note, including current affiliation; (6) each music sample or complex table must be on a separate sheet in computer-copied, camera-ready form; in formatting examples and tables, authors should take into account that each item may have to be reduced to fit, with a caption, on a page of this size (4 × 6 inches; 10.5 × 16 cm.); (8) all text materials (but not the camera-ready examples) should be submitted both in hard copy and on a 3.5-inch computer diskette in Word for PC or Macintosh; (9) a cassette tape or CD of any examples transcribed or reproduced from recordings must be included to facilitate reading the paper and checking accuracy of transcriptions (a cassette is not necessary for printed music or examples composed by the author).

Authors alone are responsible for the contents of their article and for obtaining permission for use of material under copyright protection.

ANNUAL REVIEW OF JAZZ STUDIES 11 2000–2001

Edited by
Edward Berger
David Cayer
Henry Martin
Dan Morgenstern

The Scarecrow Press, Inc.
Lanham, Maryland, and Oxford
and
Institute of Jazz Studies
Rutgers—The State University of
New Jersey
2002

SCARECROW PRESS, INC.

Published in the United States of America
by Scarecrow Press, Inc.
A Member of the Rowman & Littlefield Publishing Group
4720 Boston Way, Lanham, Maryland 20706
www.scarecrowpress.com

PO Box 317
Oxford
OX2 9RU, UK

ISSN 0731-0641
ISBN 0-8108-4535-0

∞™ The paper used in this publication meets the minimum requirements of American National Standard for Information Sciences—Permanence of Paper for Printed Library Materials, ANSI/NISO Z39.48-1992.
Manufactured in the United States of America.

CONTENTS

PREFACE

This eleventh volume of the *Annual Review of Jazz Studies* is a double issue covering the two years of 2000 and 2001. Articles and reviews for the twelfth volume for the year 2002 are in preparation as this volume goes to press.

As our readers know, *ARJS* has published such double issues on special occasions when unusual opportunities presented themselves. Thus, *ARJS 9* (1997–1998) enabled us to publish the full texts and discussions of a panel cosponsored by two major academic societies, in addition to our usual collection of recent articles and reviews. This volume includes a special and extensive bibliographic section on jazz-related fiction by David Rife, growing out of his essay on the topic in *ARJS 10.*

It is especially fitting for *ARJS* to present such a bibliography because our publisher, Scarecrow Press, was founded by librarians and has long excelled at serving libraries and the public with bibliographic and related reference materials. Similarly, this issue introduces a regular feature, compiled by Keith Waters and Jason R. Titus, listing scholarly articles about jazz published in nonjazz journals. They will welcome notices of such articles from our readers. And, for the second time, we are concluding the volume with a listing of books received during the past year at the Institute of Jazz Studies at Rutgers, the State University, in Newark.

Our articles in this volume present important technical analyses of four major figures: Booker Little, Charlie Christian, Herbie Hancock, and Miles Davis. In addition to our usual photo gallery, there are seven book reviews which, collectively, span the history of the music.

ARJS welcomes comments and will publish, with permission, letters of general interest to our readership.

The Editors

OUT FRONT: THE ART OF BOOKER LITTLE[1]

Keith Waters and David Diamond

The career of trumpeter Booker Little was tragically brief. As trumpeter with Max Roach's Quintet, his earliest records date from 1958. Two years later Little began an extremely close musical relationship with saxophonist Eric Dolphy. Little's and Dolphy's work together culminated in a number of seminal studio recordings, including Dolphy's *Far Cry* and Little's *Out Front*, as well as in the series of live recordings taken from their July 1961 engagement at the Five Spot. Together with Dolphy, Little stood on the threshold of newer musical developments, but by October 1961 Little was dead of uremia at the age of 23. Although one of the most promising trumpet players on the musical landscape of the late 1950s and early 1960s, much of Little's promise went unfulfilled. During his three-and-a-half year recording history, however, Little left an important legacy of over twenty-five recordings and some two dozen compositions.

Little was an exact contemporary of Lee Morgan and Freddie Hubbard—all three were born in 1938—and his playing derived from the same hard bop tradition. Like Morgan and Hubbard, Little performed in a style characterized by long impressive lines, a mastery of difficult chord changes, and a swaggering technique. In contrast, though, Little's sound was darker, more refined, smoother, and less staccato-based than Morgan's or Hubbard's, probably a result of Little's classical conservatory training. Like Morgan and Hubbard, Little was deeply indebted to Clifford Brown, and he consciously struggled to escape from Brown's powerful influence and develop an individual sound.

Throughout Little's career, his compositions became increasingly exploratory and complex, quickly moving away from standard harmonic progressions and forms. Little cited Mingus and Ellington as major influences on his composition, and in Little's freer writing the influence of Dolphy is also apparent. Some of Little's later works also used unusual meters, no doubt a result of his extensive work with Max Roach, whose own improvisations and compositions explored irregular meters.

Following a biographical sketch, the essay examines the twin sides to Little's career, that of performer and composer. The analyses use transcriptions of his tunes and improvisations, and are divided into two sections. The first analytical section provides analyses and discussion of three of Little's trumpet solos (transcriptions follow the essay); the second section regards several of Little's compositions and presents distinctive aspects of his compositional style. The works represent a cross-section of Little's admittedly short career. Two compositions are taken from some of his earliest recordings—"Rounder's Mood" (from *Booker Little Quartet with Max Roach*), and "Larry-Larue" (Max Roach's *Deeds not Words*), both recorded in the fall of 1958. (See the appended discography for additional information on all recordings.) In addition, some of Little's last recordings will also be examined, including "Bee Vamp" (*Eric Dolphy at the Five Spot*), and "Victory and Sorrow," from his final recording session entitled *Booker Little and Friend*. The appendices contain a discography, a list of Little's compositions, and bibliography.

I. BIOGRAPHY

Born in Memphis, Tennessee, Little began playing trumpet at the age of twelve. He was born into a musical family: his mother was a church organist, his father played trombone in a church band, and his sister was for a time a member of the London Opera Company. Memphis in the early 1950s was a hospitable place for jazz. Little did some sessions with pianist Phineas Newborn, and Little's school, Manassas High, turned out a staggering number of jazz players: classmates included saxophonists George Coleman, Frank Strozier, and Hank Crawford, as well as pianist Harold Mabern. Coleman, three years older than Little, was an important mentor. "Jazz records were scarce in Memphis at that time," Little recalled,

> but there were a lot of guys who were interested in it. George Coleman was one. He was probably one of the most progressive people around town. . . . I was rather close to George because he was in the same high school. He was sharp enough to take things off records. I was fourteen or fifteen then and he sort of got me started.[2]

Little's musical association with Coleman and his classmates continued even after they all left Tennessee. Almost *en masse*, they migrated to Chicago during the mid-1950s: Mabern studied harmony with Ahmad Jamal, and Coleman relocated there in 1956. In 1955, Little, like Strozier, moved to Chicago in order to study at the Chicago Conservatory. Little majored in trumpet, minored in piano, and also studied composition, theory, and orchestration. His conservatory training was profoundly important both technically and musically. Although he developed a flawless technique, he was aware of the dangers of empty virtuousity:

> My background has been conventional . . . . A lot of guys, and I've been guilty of this too, put too much stress on the technical, and that's not hard to do when you've learned how to play in school . . . . Most of the younger guys, like myself, who started playing in school, they'd have the instructor driving at them, "Okay, you gotta have a big sound, you gotta have this and that." Consequently, if they came in sounding like Miles, which is beautiful for jazz, they flunked the lessons.[3]

In addition to providing a sure technique, Little's conservatory background affected his attitudes toward improvisation and composition. Exposure to the performance, theory, and composition of classical music clearly influenced his ideas about motivic development in improvisation and about writing:

> Those who have no idea about how "classical" music is constructed are definitely at a loss—it's a definite foundation. I don't think it should be carried to the point where you have to say this is this kind of phrase and this is this kind of development. Deep in your mind, though, you should maintain these thoughts and not just throw a phrase in without it answering itself or leading to something else.[4]

Despite his parents' wish that he become a classical player, the allure of Chicago's jazz world was nevertheless too intense. Ahmad Jamal, Johnny Griffin, John Gilmore, Clifford Jordan, Eddie Harris, and Gene Ammons were all based out of the city. While still a student, Little played some gigs with Johnny Griffin and, with some of his Memphis colleagues, played around town with drummer Walter Perkins's band MJT+3. Little and Sonny Rollins both lived at the YMCA—they each practiced in its basement—and Rollins introduced Little to Max Roach. Roach called the nineteen-year-old trumpeter for a recording date, made in June of 1958. Little's first recording, on *Max Roach+4 on the Chicago Scene*, featured primarily standards, including "Stella by Starlight," "My Old Flame,"and "Stompin' at the Savoy." In his third year of study, at the age of nineteen, Little left the conservatory and became a regular member of Roach's quintet.[5] A recording of the group's performance at the Newport Jazz Festival in July of 1958 was released by EmArcy records and included the standards "Love for Sale," "A Night in Tunisia," and "Tune Up."

As the trumpeter with Roach's group, Little thus followed his idol Clifford Brown. Along with Roach and Little, the band included Little's Memphis schoolmate George Coleman on saxophone and Art Davis on bass. But there Roach's band departed from the traditional quintet instrumentation. In lieu of piano, the group included Ray Draper on tuba. The pianoless quintet gave Little an opportunity for three-horn writing of trumpet, tenor, and tuba, heard in his composition "Larry-Larue" (*Deeds, Not Words*). In October of 1958, Little recorded under his own name as a leader. The recording, released as *Booker Little Quartet with Max Roach*, kept the same personnel as Roach's group, with the exception of pianist Tommy Flanagan replacing tubist Ray Draper. In the more traditional setting, Little mixed standards with original compositions, including his "Rounder's Mood," reminiscent of Dizzy Gillespie's "Woody 'n' You."

After relocating to New York, Little took a leave of absence from Roach's group, and freelanced, working with Slide Hampton, Sonny Stitt, Ed Schaugnessy, Teddy Charles, Mal Waldron, and Abbey Lincoln. He probably made only two recordings during 1959.[6] The following year he reunited with several of his Memphis colleagues. He did one record with Frank Strozier; another recording, *Downhome Reunion*, assembled a host of the Memphis players: Strozier, George Coleman, trumpeter Louis Smith, pianist Phineas Newborn and his brother guitarist Calvin Newborn, bassist George Joyner (Jamil Nasser), and drummer Charles Crosby. In 1960 Little also released a second album under his own name, this time a quartet consisting of Tommy Flanagan, bassist Scott LaFaro, and drummer Roy Haynes.[7] Showing an increased interest in writing and composition, Little contributed all of the compositions for the album with the exception of the ballad "Who Can I Turn To?"

Little's association with Eric Dolphy, beginning in 1960, marked an important turning point in his career. The two formed perhaps an unlikely combination, this pairing of the conservatory-trained twenty-two year old from Memphis and the older L.A. saxophonist who had spent the late 1950s playing with Chico Hamilton and Charles Mingus. There was something of a dissonance between Little's traditional hard-bop pedigree and Dolphy's emerging status as an important figure of the avant garde. Dolphy's involvement with the "New Thing" was being established by his December 1960 performance on Ornette Coleman's *Free Jazz* and Dolphy's later work with Coltrane. Although critics later were sometimes eager to compare Dolphy/Little with Ornette Coleman and Don Cherry, the correspondence was somewhat forced. Plainly Little's recordings with Dolphy maintained a stronger and conscious sense of jazz tradition than did Coleman's, and they relied more on fixed forms and improvisation over traditional harmonic progressions. Little himself assessed Coleman and addressed their differences:

> Ornette has his own ideas about what makes what and I don't think it's proper to put him down. . . . I have more conventional ideas about what makes what then [sic] he does, but I think I understand clearly what he's doing, and it's good. It's an honest effort. . . I do think what Ornette's doing is part of what jazz will become.[8]

A strong alliance with tradition is apparent on Dolphy's recording *Far Cry*, Little's and Dolphy's first collaboration.[9] The first side, for example, featured a loose suite in homage to Charlie Parker; the first composition, pianist Jaki Byard's "Mrs. Parker of K.C. (Bird's Mother)," was based upon a traditional twelve-bar blues structure. Nevertheless, "Mrs. Parker" shows subtle changes in the musical landscape: we hear the rhythm section of bassist Ron Carter and drummer Roy Haynes breaking up the time during the first chorus of Little's solo before they move into a more traditional walking 4/4. Little, too, seems encouraged occasionally to play outside the harmonic structure, but his unerring technical and rhythmic accuracy contrasts with Dolphy's freer and looser rhythmic conception. The work with Dolphy thus shifted Little's position from a traditional hard-bop player of the Clifford Brown school into a different camp. He was certainly aware of this newer position, although he understood that it stood somewhere in the mean between tradition and the newer developments. In acknowledging his altered aesthetic stance, he interestingly described it with a political metaphor. "My background," he noted, "has been conventional and maybe because of that I haven't become a leftist, though my ideas and tastes now might run left to a certain degree."[10]

But although Little here described the musical left, not the political left, the musical atmosphere *was* becoming overtly political in some quarters. Several recordings on which he participated as a sideman during 1960–61 represented the incipient civil rights movement and the African consciousness of the early sixties.[11] Little recorded again with Roach, although now Roach's recordings voiced repugnance toward South Africa's apartheid system on *We Insist! The Freedom Now Suite*, which included Roach's composition "Tears for Johannesburg"; Roach developed similar themes in his compositions "Garvey's Ghost," "Praise for a Martyr," and "Man from South Africa" from the album *Percussion Bitter Sweet*. Roach's use of irregular meters such as 5/4 and 7/4 originate in these recordings and intersected with his interest in African culture. These recordings also featured Roach's future wife, vocalist Abbey Lincoln, whose own album *Straight Ahead*—with its composition "African Woman"—symbolized African cultural awareness.[12] Little played also on John Coltrane's *Africa/Brass*, arranged and conducted by Dolphy. While less manifestly political, *Africa/Brass* similarly expressed the burgeoning interest in African culture.

Roach's *We Insist!* and Lincoln's *Straight Ahead* were released by Candid Records, a short-lived subsidiary of Cadence Records managed by producer/writer Nat Hentoff. Hentoff hired Little to record an album for Candid; Little was to choose his sidemen, and write the compositions and arrangements. For *Out Front*, his third recording as a leader, Little selected Dolphy, Roach, pianist Don Friedman, and trombonist Julian Priester. The recording was done in two dates (March 17 and April 4, 1961), with bassist Art Davis playing the former session, Ron Carter the latter. Little's sophisticated compositions show a concern with dissolving the distinctions between written and improvised passages, an approach derived from his compositional idols Ellington and Mingus. Its minor mode compositions, such as "Moods in Free Time" and "Man of Words," score two horns beneath the trumpet solo, and display also some of the temperament of the Miles Davis/Gil Evans collaborations, predating the impressionism of Herbie Hancock's *Maiden Voyage*. Little's compositional and arranging techniques are far removed from a loose jam session approach; they make use of metric shifts, sections in half-time, composed passages for horns without rhythm section, and horn scoring beneath the improvisations. Consciously, Little attempted to explore the interaction and tension between consonance and dissonance, as well as between straight-ahead playing and freer textures. "Moods in Free Time" alternates meters, beginning in 3/4, moving to 4/4, 5/4, then 6/4. "Hazy Hues" and "A New Day" both make use of 5/4 meter, demonstrating Roach's influence on Little. Throughout, the album is carefully crafted and arranged.

Out Front was the first of a projected two-record contract with Candid. For the second project Little was to provide the orchestration for a record which featured Coleman Hawkins in a "modern" setting; it was never completed. But with *Out Front*, Little seemed to be aware that he was finding a distinctive playing and compositional voice, and he stated shortly after that "I think I've found the way I want to play on my instrument and now I'd like to concentrate on the sound I'd like to build around it." He nearly disavowed all his previous work: "I don't think there's very much of my work prior to these Candid dates that expresses how I feel now about what I want to do."[13]

Sadly, there was little time left for him to pursue his individual path. Little was suffering from health problems, including arthritis, which made it painful for him to play. In the summer of 1961, Dolphy and Little assembled a band for a stint at the Five Spot. The rhythm section consisted of Mingus alumnus Mal Waldron on piano, bassist Richard Davis, and Ornette Coleman's drummer, Ed Blackwell. The band lasted no longer than the Five Spot gig, but the July 21 performance was recorded by Rudy van Gelder and subsequently released in three volumes. In contrast to the careful and complex arrangements of Little's *Out Front*, many of the compositions were based on rather simple forms that served as vehicles for extended soloing. Mal Waldron's "Fire Waltz" was a 16-bar AABA form, and Dolphy's "The Prophet" was based on a 32-bar AABA structure. Although performing mostly original compositions, the band did record Jimmy van Heusen's standard "Like Someone in Love." Little's tune "Bee Vamp" was probably the most harmonically and formally complex, and we even hear the rhythm section once losing the form during Little's solo in the alternate take version. While the rhythm section functioned conventionally, both Dolphy's and Little's solos ventured outside the chord changes. Little, too, seems frequently to abandon the eighth-note post-bop language and tap into Dolphy's irregular phrasing and flurry-of-notes approach.

Little entered the studio once more before his death, recording his fourth album as a leader, *Booker Little and Friend*. The sextet included saxophonist George Coleman and trombonist Julian Priester; the rhythm section consisted of Don Friedman on piano, Reggie Workman on bass, and Pete LaRoca on drums. With the exception of the standard "If I Should Lose You," all the compositions were Little's own. His intricate "Victory and Sorrow" is characteristic of his writing style, incorporating unusual harmonic progressions amidst more traditional patterns. His playing on the recording was completely assured, if perhaps more traditional than his recordings with Dolphy.

Booker Little died on October 5 of uremia, a kidney disease that affects the blood. His death cut short a prodigious talent. Interviews with Little reveal him as an extremely articulate and intelligent individual, certain in his musical direction despite his young age. Nat Hentoff's obituary in *Metronome* read:

> [O]f all the hundreds of jazz musicians I've known, some of them fairly well, Booker had the clearest view of himself and of those with whom he had to deal. . . . In the past year, he had not only decided where he wanted to go but he had also done the hard, self-testing work that proved to him he had the techniques

> and imagination to make the trip. Booker had a rare capacity—rare in any art—to be thoroughly lucid about what he was doing without his exceptional intelligence getting in the way of his emotions when he was actually bringing the music into being.[14]

II. IMPROVISATION

Little's improvisations have recently begun to attract analytical attention. Paul Berliner's book *Thinking in Jazz* examines Little's approach to motivic structure with several transcribed solos.[15] David Aagberg provides a partial transcription to Little's solo on "Booker's Blues," and illustrates characteristic figures, such as the double-neighbor figure, with which he negotiates the chord changes.[16] Warren Gale analyzes a transcription of Little's solo from the 12-bar blues "Mrs. Parker of K.C." (from Dolphy's *Far Cry*), indicating emphasized pitches and repeated rhythmic gestures. His analysis leads Gale to conclude that:

> Little has demonstrated perhaps the most prodigious technique in jazz on the B-flat trumpet to date. Not many trumpeters accomplished such total command of the instrument in terms of speed and dexterity of fingering, or the originality of harmonic and melodic conception.[17]

Little, although still very young, had developed an extremely individual and distinct sound. His tone was extremely controlled, dark, and always without edge. While negotiating phrases technically difficult—or impossible—for most players, his sound remained centered. The smoothness and liquidity with which his notes connect suggest an extremely fine wind control. In contrast to many trumpet players, Little always sounded focused in the upper register, and he never seemed to tire during a solo.

His control allowed Little a wide range of possibilities for expression. The half-valves and grace notes he often used were clean, each with its own fully intended and supported tone. The same can be said for each note of Little's amazingly even and clear double-time phrases: his finger technique was complete. Vibrato was relatively narrow and fast, and he was able to vary its speed for added intensity. Finally, his staccato articulation effectively punctuated selected phrases without disturbing his tone.

Little's solos frequently used recurring motives as formal signposts. Yet, instead of being mechanically repetitious, these motives are often transformed: they become shifted within the bar when they return, and are frequently compressed or stretched.[18] In his solo on "Rounder's Mood"—a virtuosic statement in the hard-bop idiom—several motives figure prominently. (The solo transcriptions are appended to this essay. In order to facilitate comparison, the two choruses are aligned one above the other.) The most important of these is the motive labeled "a," bracketed in the transcription. This is a double-neighbor figure around E♭ linked to a descending E♭ minor arpeggio, played over E♭-7 A♭7. It appears in the A sections of the composition: it is stated in the first chorus at mm. 5–6, and returns in the identical place at mm. 5–6 of the second chorus, now placed within a shorter phrase. Motive a also returns in the analogous spot in the second A section of both choruses, at mm. 29–30. In contrast to Motive a at mm. 4–5, however, the motive is shifted over one beat: F5 now appears on the fourth, instead of the third beat.[19]

Motive b fulfills a similar function. Initiated by a double-neighbor figure around A♭4 and followed by an ascending scale to B♭5, it occurs first at mm. 10–12. There it is launched on the fourth beat; B♭ is reached on the downbeat of m. 12. Likewise, Motive b recurs in the second chorus (mm. 11–12), but it is shifted over two beats, and B♭ is reached in the middle of m. 12. Motive b returns at mm. 27–28 of both choruses, again stated over F-7 (♭5) B♭7. In the first chorus, the initiating double-neighbor figure is reversed—following the two sixteenth notes, the motive begins with the upper, instead of the lower, neighbor. Note that in the first chorus at mm. 27–28, Motive b begins on the third beat; in the second chorus, the motive starts on the downbeat of m. 27. Thus, although Little states Motive b four times, each instance *begins on a different beat in the measure*: Mm. 10–12 (beats 4 and 1), and mm. 27–28 (beats 3 and 1). This exhibits Little's extreme flexibility with repeated material.[20]

The third motive identified here, Motive c, serves to signal the start of the bridge. In both choruses it begins on the downbeat of m. 17, but is stated in a different register each time. In the first chorus, Motive c begins with B♭5; in the second chorus, it begins an octave lower. The brief motive is in both instances part of a longer phrase, and in the first chorus Motive c yields to a double-time run, while in the second chorus the phrase moves to D♭6, the highest pitch of the solo. Both of these longer phrases help delineate the bridge as the climactic section of the extroverted solo.

Little's solo on "Rounder's Mood" exemplifies traditional hard bop practice. The harmonic progression encourages the soloist to handle the changes with somewhat standardized bop lines. His later solos, though, went beyond these traditional strategies, especially in his work with Dolphy. In "Bee Vamp," the somewhat static harmonies give Little more rhythmic flexibility, a flexibility that was undoubtedly in response to Dolphy's influence.

Too, much of "Bee Vamp" is played with a straight-eighth feel for the 8-bar modal sections by the rhythm section, and this feel alternates with the swing 4/4 of the bridge and the interior 4-bar segments of the A section. During the modal sections, Little frequently abandons bebop figures in favor of motives that displace and obscure the beat. These motives consist primarily of sixteenth-note runs and sustained pitches that begin and end away from the primary metric beats. For example, Little avoids all four beats of the measure at mm. 5–7 of the third chorus. (See the appended solo transcription, which again aligns the five choruses for convenience.) Again, mm. 29–32, second chorus, the melody changes pitch on the upbeats, and the run in m. 31 ends strongly a sixteenth note *prior* to the third beat of the measure.

Although Little loosens his rhythmic approach during "Bee Vamp," his solo nevertheless uses recurring motives that highlight the form of the piece. Nearly every 8-bar B♭ modal section refers to the first five notes of the B♭ minor scale, with particular emphasis on the rising tetrachord (C-D♭-E♭-F), consisting of the second through fifth scale degrees.[21] This is indicated as Motive d, and motivic structure is now defined only by pitch, not by rhythmic structure. Little improvises the head for these modal sections. The recurring Motive d, first appearing in these improvised "head" sections, then is reused throughout the solo, and appears in descending form within mm. 29–32 of the second and third choruses. In each instance of Motive d, the ninth of the B♭ harmony—C—is strongly emphasized.

Other motives recur in the shorter, nonmodal sections of "Bee Vamp." Motive e (which closely resembles Motive b from "Rounder's Mood") appears in the 4-bar contrasting sections of A. At mm. 9–10, Motive e occurs in the second and fourth chorus. Initiated by a double-neighbor figure around F, it is metrically shifted each time, beginning on the downbeat of m. 9 in the second chorus, and shifted to the second beat of m. 9 in the fourth chorus. The same motive reappears at the second A section of the third chorus, at m. 37.[22]

Additionally, within the bridge recurs Motive f. This brief motive is defined by the descending leap from G to D; it is stated at m. 21 in the second chorus, and m. 25 in the third chorus. Likewise, the bridge also features Motive g, which appears at mm. 26–27 of the second and third chorus. In both instances Motive g is part of a larger phrase. It is nested within a longer phrase in the second chorus and begins on the fourth beat of m. 26; and it initiates the phrase in the third chorus of m. 26. Typical for Little, Motive g is metrically displaced upon its return.[23] Both Motive f and g are more characteristic of the hard-bop idiom, and emphasize the bop orientation of the bridge in contrast to the more exploratory modal sections.

To a certain extent, Little's solo on "Victory and Sorrow" (*Booker Little and Friend*) relates more closely to the eighth-note phrasing of "Rounder's Mood" than to the freer playing of "Bee Vamp." Indeed, some of the motives recall those of "Rounder's Mood." The "Victory and Sorrow" solo opens with a motive resembling "Rounder's" Motive a, especially the pitches of a descending E♭ minor triad. (This is indicated in m. 2 as Motive a′ in the transcription of "Victory and Sorrow.") The motive is expanded at m. 30 in both the first two choruses. Note the identical motivic relationship between these two choruses which lasts for two entire measures. Another significant motivic relationship—labeled motive h—occurs between m. 4 of the second and third chorus, m. 8 of the third chorus, and m. 12 of *each* chorus. Although slightly varied in each instance, this Motive h begins each of these measures with E natural, serving as a signpost to the A-7 D7 (or D7) harmony.

In addition, Little's solo shows linear connections that control larger musical spans. On the surface, Little often chromatically fills out a whole step through eighth-note motion: the consecutive eighth notes that begin the second chorus (F-E-E♭) provides one example of many. At mm. 8–9 of the 1st chorus, Little projects this same motion, connecting C-B-B♭, but now this motion is embellished and is stated at the level of the half note. Example 1a shows the connection of these nonadjacent pitches.

Examples 1a and 1b: "Victory and Sorrow," 1/2-step connection

Similarly, an even longer-range connection appears in mm. 11–13 of the 1st chorus. Example 1b indicates that the pickup to m. 11 states the descent of F-E-E♭ on the eighth note level, and this motion is reversed and stated at the level of the complete measure: downbeats of mm. 11–13 connect E♭-E-F.

The unusual 13-bar bridge of "Victory and Sorrow" is somewhat static harmonically, affording Little more opportunity for rhythmic invention and motivic development, in contrast to the even flow of eighth notes used elsewhere. This development is especially pronounced in the second and third choruses at the bridge (mm. 17–29), and it delineates this B section from the A sections.

In these two choruses, Little sets up a fascinating motivic correspondence, based upon the pitches C, A, and G. The phrase which begins at m. 18 in the second chorus emphasizes A4 and G4, using C as an anacrusis to those pitches. There C is metrically subordinate to A and G. But at the analogous spot in the third chorus, Little reverses the relationship: C6 is metrically emphasized between mm. 18–22, while G5 and A5 become subordinate to C.

The analytical observations here offer only a beginning point for understanding Little's profound musical and creative achievements. A fundamental component to his improvisations stems from his use of recurring motives within solos. Moreover, he reuses these motives with complete flexibility—they recur metrically displaced, expanded, and contracted. In Little's freer solos, such as "Bee Vamp," motives are stripped of their rhythmic identity and are based solely upon pitch content. In "Victory and Sorrow," his improvisations create linear relationships with nonadjacent pitches; these operate across longer musical spans at both the half-note and the measure level.

Like a number of other jazz players—Jimmy Blanton, Charlie Christian, Scott LaFaro—Little's career was cut short by an early death. And like those players, Little was becoming recognized as one of the preeminent players on his instrument at the time of his death in 1961. Although earning the questionable distinction of being included in a 1977 anthology entitled *Neglected Jazz Figures of the 1950s and Early 1960s* (New World 275), Little has now attracted wider interest critically and musically. In 1986 Terence Blanchard and Donald Harrison recreated the Dolphy/Little Five Spot date at the New York club Sweet Basil, recorded with the original rhythm section of Mal Waldron, Richard Davis, and Ed Blackwell, and released in two volumes as *Eric Dolphy & Booker Little Remembered* (ProJazz CDJ681). Trumpeter Dave Douglas's recording *In Our Lifetime*, released in 1995 (New World/CounterCurrents 80471-2), is a tribute to Little's compositions and playing. We can hope that Little's legacy as a trumpeter continues to be brought into sharper focus.

III. COMPOSITIONS

> My approach to playing has been to find a sound around my sound and then write. Writing is a special thing with me. I want to play, but I am very interested in writing because I hear so many things for others.[24]

Despite its brevity, it is possible to trace an arc to Little's compositional development. In his earliest recordings, Little's compositions made use of a

Woody 'n' You Mm. 1–8	M. 1 G$^{\varnothing}$	2 C7	3 F$^{\varnothing}$	4 Bb7	5 Eb$^{\varnothing}$	6 Ab7	7 DbM7	8
Rounder's Mood Mm. 1–8	Dbmaj7	Gb-7 B7	F$^{\varnothing}$	Bb7	Eb-7	Ab7	Ab-7	Db7
Rounder's Mood Mm. 9–16	GbM7 M. 9	G$^{\varnothing}$ C7 10	F$^{\varnothing}$ 11	Bb7 12	Eb7#11 13	Ab7 14	DbM7 15	16

Figure 1: Comparison of A section to Gillespie's "Woody 'n' You" with Little's "Rounder's Mood"

number of standard harmonic and melodic practices of hard-bop, but by his final recordings he had merged these devices with less conventional harmonic progressions and modality. One element that strongly defined Little's writing style throughout his career was an atypical approach to form. None of the works examined here exhibits a standard 32-bar structure. "Rounder's Mood" comprises a 40-bar ABA form: "Larry-Larue," a 36-bar ABAC; "Bee Vamp," a 48-bar ABA, and "Victory and Sorrow" is a 45-measure ABA. All abandon the 4 × 8 measure matrix typical of jazz and popular song standards. Even Little's blues tune, "Booker's Blues," appends an 8-measure tag to the 12-bar blues, creating a repeating 20-measure form.[25]

Little's frequent use of ABA structures suggests an interest in compositional and formal symmetry. Thus, "Rounder's Mood" (from *Booker Little Quartet + Max Roach*) demonstrates two identical 16-measure A sections surrounding the 8-bar bridge in a symmetrical format: A (16 mm.) B (8 mm.) A (16 mm.).

Harmonically, "Rounder's Mood" is perhaps indebted to Dizzy Gillespie's "Woody 'n' You," sharing the same key of D♭ and many of the same harmonic moves. This relationship is present but veiled in the A sections. Figure 1 aligns the A sections of both compositions. Gillespie's tune begins on the half-diminished chord a tritone away from D♭, while Little's m. 1 begins on D♭ (I), and his m. 9 begins on G♭ (IV). But by m. 3 (and 11), however, Little's descending fifths progression aligns somewhat with Gillespie's.

Certainly, Gillespie's fascination with the half-diminished chord in the A section to "Woody 'n' You" is not as evident in Little's composition. But in the bridge section to "Rounder's Mood," shown in Figure 2, Little creates an even closer resemblance to Gillespie's work.

Figure 2 shows that the progressions are very similar. Both are organized through a harmonic arrival on Gb in the fourth measure of the bridge, and

Woody 'n' You (Bridge)	Ab-7 Db7			Gb	Bb-7 Eb7			Ab7
Rounder's Mood (Bridge)	Ab-7 Db7	A-7 D7	Ab-7 Db7	GbM7	Eb7	B-7 E7	Eb-7	Ab7

Figure 2: Comparison of bridge to Gillespie's "Woody 'n' You" with Little's "Rounder's Mood"

on Ab in the last measure. In the second and sixth measures of the bridge, Little inserts embellishing ii-V substitutions up a half-step (A-7 D7, and B-7 E7), substitutions frequently inserted by players in those measures in "Woody 'n' You."

"Larry-Larue," recorded in the fall of 1958 on Roach's *Deeds, Not Words* recording, is another early work of Little's. With the rhythm section, it is written for three horns, a medium to which Little would return in his later recordings *Out Front* and *Booker Little and Friend*. However, Roach's unusual instrumentation featured not only trumpet and tenor saxophone, but tuba. In "Larry-Larue," the trumpet is given the melody, and the tenor and tuba provide contrapuntal accompaniment below. Example 2 provides the harmonic progression to "Larry-Larue."

m. 1-6	G-7(b5)	Gbmaj7	F7 B9(#11)	Bb9 Bb(b9)	Eb-7	Ab7
m. 7-12	D-7	G7	Db-7	Gb7	C-7	F7
m. 13-18	Bbm		E7#11		Eb-7	Ab7
m. 19-24	G-7(b5)	Gbmaj7	F7 B9(#11)	Bb9 Bb(b9)	Eb-7	Ab7
m. 25-30	D-7	G7	Db-7	Gb7	C-7	F7
m. 31-36	Bbm	Abm	G-7	Gbmaj7	Bbmaj7	

Example 2: "Larry-Larue," harmonic progression

While the 32-bar ABAC form is found in the popular song repertoire—"All of Me" and "Back Home in Indiana" provide two examples—the ABAC of "Larry-Larue" forms a 36-bar structure. The 12-measure A sections are followed by 6-measure B or C sections. Not only is the unusual length of the sections difficult for the soloists to negotiate, but the harmonic structure—with its relentless ii-V sequences—is equally taxing.

Clearly, Little's circular harmonic progressions make for an ambiguous tonal center. The melody and the progression of the first six measures seem to suggest D♭ major: the melody is almost entirely diatonic to D♭, and following the chromatic slides of mm. 1–3 (G-7♭5 G♭maj7 F7), the harmonic progression of the following three bars (B♭7 E♭-7 A♭7) strongly suggests D♭ major. In addition, the final two measures of the B section (mm. 17–18) contain a ii-V progression (E♭-7 A♭7) which also implies a return to D♭.

The harmony of D♭ major, though, *never* appears. Its promise at m. 7 is thwarted, and the ii-V slippage at mm. 7–12 brings about a harmonic and melodic arrival on B♭ minor at the beginning of both B sections (mm. 13 and 31), the first conclusive cadence so far.

More surprising, though, are the final two measures of the composition, which conclude on B♭ major before returning to the top of the form each time. Thus, while the opening measures of the composition imply both D♭ major and B♭ minor, these keys are abandoned at the end of the composition, which makes an unsuspected move to B♭ major. The entire composition makes abundant use of the ii-V progressions of the hard bop harmonic vocabulary, but its tonal center is decidedly more ambiguous than many compositions written at the end of the 1950s.

The melodic structure of "Larry-Larue" is equally fascinating. Rather than a series of hard bop clichés over the rapid harmonic pacing, the legato melody line connects across the *entire* first eighteen bars of the form. Example 3 shows that the skeletal pitches of the melody create a large scale stepwise line which arches across the first eighteen measures of the tune.

With Example 3, the stemmed notes show the stepwise ascent from C to G♭ at mm. 1–5. This ascent then reverses itself and begins to descend by m. 7. The related melodic sequences which follow—mm. 8–9, 9–10, 11–12, 13–14—create a compound melody of thirds, eventually bringing the lower pitch into prominence. (The compound melody is indicated by up-stems and down-stems in Example 3.) So by mm. 12 and 15, B♭ becomes the focal pitch, emphasized by duration and metric placement. This B♭ then yields to B at m. 18, the final measure of the B section, before reconnecting with the opening pitch of C at the return of the A section.

Example 3: "Larry-Larue," stepwise line, mm. 1–8

In addition to this large scale stepwise construction of the melody, we can also see another interesting compositional detail that suggests a sense of compositional symmetry. As Example 3 shows, the melodic structure at mm. 1–4 progresses from C to F. Example 4 shows that this is mirrored at the end of the composition: the skeletal ascent of the opening four measures (C-D♭-E♭-F) is mirrored by the literal descent of the closing four measures (F-E♭-D♭-C). The melody of the opening and closing four measures thus forms a retrograde relationship, and illustrates Little's heightened sense of compositional design and control.

Example 4: "Larry-Larue," melodic retrograde, mm. 1–4, 33–36

Little's compositions recorded in 1961, the last year of his life, have some marked differences from his earlier works. For example, in "Bee Vamp" (*Eric Dolphy at the Five Spot, vol. 1*) there is a turn to modality, and much of the composition is given over to eight-measure sections written over a B♭ pedal point. Additionally, Little improvises the melody over these sections, while the rhythm section vamps, staying constant, becoming the composed element. Despite the single repeated bass pitch of B♭, the pianist articulates two pairs of chords: these are shown in Example 5a. Each chord is a transposition of the same intervallic structure (this structure is often referred to as Maj7#5: in this case, the four successive chords are A♭maj7#5, D♭maj7#5, C♭maj#5, G♭maj7#5.) The example shows the use of extended pedal point which would come to be characteristic of modal compositions throughout the decade of the 1960s. The accompanimental chords shown in Example 5a reveal that the sense of a single modality is abandoned, since the four chords use all 12 chromatic pitches. (However, the transcription to the solo of "Bee Vamp" shows Little often adhering to the pitches of B♭ melodic minor in both ascending and descending forms above the B♭ pedal point.)

Little's interest in modality may have been inspired by Miles Davis, whose *Kind of Blue* recording appeared in 1959, or perhaps by John Coltrane's early modal explorations. Little himself performed on Coltrane's *Africa/Brass*. ("Bee Vamp" was composed, though, before many of Coltrane's more celebrated modal outings.) Yet Little was unwilling to succumb completely to modal organization, and the straight-eighth modal sec-

Example 5a: "Bee Vamp," B♭ pedal point chords

tions of "Bee Vamp" alternate with sections that revisit characteristic bebop progressions over a swing feel. Nested within each of the A sections is a 4-bar section that recalls the first four measures of Charlie Parker's "Blues for Alice." Similarly, the 8-bar bridge is based upon a simple bebop motive over a more traditional harmonic progression. (See solo transcription at the end of the article for chord changes.)

Formally, "Bee Vamp" exhibits ABA symmetry on several levels. Example 5b shows that, in the larger sense, the ABA design is made up of 20+8+20 measures for the entire 48-measure tune. And on the smaller level, another ABA scheme (indicated in the lowest line of Example 5b as "aba") is nested within each 20-measure A section: two eight-measure Bb pedal sections surround the four-measure "Blues for Alice" ("BFA") section. Thus, ABA structures govern both the overall form of the 48-bar work, and provide an interior aba form within the interior of the A sections.

A			**B**	**A**		
Mm. 1-8	9-12	13-20	21-28	29-36	37-40	41-48
Bb pedal	"BFA"	Bb pedal	Bridge	Bb pedal	"BFA"	Bb pedal
a	**b**	**a**		**a**	**b**	**a**

Example 5b: "Bee Vamp," ABA form and nested aba form (BFA = "Blues for Alice changes)

Since the trumpet improvises the melody in the B♭ pedal "a" sections, the work is partly spontaneous. In stark contrast is Little's composition "Victory and Sorrow," from his final album *Booker Little and Friend*. "Victory and Sorrow" is fully arranged for three horns (trumpet, trombone, tenor) with rhythm section. The tune is undoubtedly the most intricately conceived of the works examined here. Its formal design is indicated in Example 6a. Like "Rounder's Mood," and "Bee Vamp," the composition is an

A			**B** (13 mm.!)	**A**		
Mm. 1-8	9-12	13-16	17-29	30-37	38-41	42-45
Whole-tone	Half-time	4/4	Latin	Whole-tone	Half-time	4/4
	(C# min)		(F-Eb)	4/4	(C# min.)	

Example 6a: ABA form to head of "Victory and Sorrow"

ABA form, and the 45-measure work incorporates two 16-measure A sections with a (highly unusual) 13-measure bridge. The "head" of the tune is somewhat different from the solo sections: the head alternates tempo and rhythmic feel while solos are accompanied by a swinging 4/4.

Additionally, the A section harmonies are altered from head to solos. In fact, one of the most arresting aspects of the opening melody and accompaniment is its reliance on the whole-tone scale. Example 6b shows a non-rhythmicized version of the introduction and the following eight measures of the opening A section. Note that between mm.1–4 the three horns use whole-tone planing exclusively, and this parallel movement is maintained in the accompanying voices in mm. 5–8. This whole-tone construction is abandoned in the second half (mm. 9–16) of the A section (not shown in Example 6b), which shifts from four measures of half-time in C# minor (mm. 9–12) to a 4/4 swing feel in mm. 13–16. The 13-bar bridge asserts a Latin feel, alternating F maj7 and E♭7.

Example 6b: "Victory and Sorrow," harmonic planing

With its title "Victory and Sorrow"—and tempo shifts—it is quite possible that Little considered the work as programmatic: he explicitly described a similarly titled work, "Strength and Sanity," in programmatic terms.[26]

What is important to acknowledge, though, is Little's use of pitch and musical resources outside of the hard-bop tradition; these stand cheek-by-jowl along more conventional jazz harmonic and melodic devices. As Example 6b shows, harmonic planing gives one example of Little's use of these nontraditional resources, and in his brief introduction to "Victory and Sorrow" Little incorporates major triad planing (using C, D♭, E♭, F, and G♭ major triads) prior to the whole-tone parallelism of the A section.

Despite the rhythmic change at m. 9 when the rhythm section moves from 4/4 to a half-time feel, Little melodically links the two sections through the use of a half-step motive. The brackets above the staff in Example 7 show that the prominence of E♭-E-E♭ in the 3-bar phrase at mm. 6–8 carries across to the next four bars, which similarly emphasize those pitches, now indicated as D# and E over the C# minor harmony. Interestingly, too, at the arrival of F# minor in the final two bars of the A section (mm. 15–16), the inner voice motion given to the tenor saxophone again restates those pitches.

Example 7: "Victory and Sorrow," melodic connection (E and E♭/D#) over sections

Once the head is stated, another new aspect of the piece appears: entirely new changes for the A section. These A section blowing changes have at best only a tenuous relationship to the A section in the head of the composition. As indicated in Example 8, chord roots at the odd-measured measures in mm. 1–6 are in a whole-step relationship (Eb-F-Db), perhaps recalling the whole-tone melodic construction of the opening.

M. 1*	2	3*	4	5*	6	7	8	9
Eb-7		**F7**	A-7-D7	**Dbmaj7**		C7	D7	Eb-7

Example 8: "Victory and Sorrow," whole-step relationship (E♭-F-Db) at mm. 1, 3, and 5 of A section solo changes

In addition, despite a straight-ahead 4/4 feel, the harmonic progression for the A section solos only occasionally makes use of typical bop progressions. Throughout the A section, there is a struggle for tonal priority between E♭ and F, and this makes the tonal center ambiguous. E♭-7 begins both 8-bar phrases of the A section (see Example 8, mm. 1 and 9)—and is the final chord of the composition—but is not necessarily perceived as the tonal center. Instead, Eb is heard as a lower neighbor harmony to the F7 of m. 3 (and m. 11). Eb-7 also ends the A section (mm. 15–16), but again is cast as a lower neighbor chord to the F tonal center of the entire bridge. Example 9 shows the harmonic progression for the bridge. While it oscillates between Fmaj7 and E♭7, the E♭ is made harmonically and metrically subordinate to F.

End of A	**Bridge**							**(2nd A)**
Mm. 15-16	17/18	19/20	21/22	23/24	25/26	27	28/29	30
Eb-7	Fmaj7	Eb7	Fmaj7	Eb7	Fmaj7	Eb7	Fmaj7	Eb-7

Example 9: Harmonic progression of bridge to "Victory and Sorrow" (Eb vs. F)

There is frequently a sense of cadential arrival following dominant chords, but these dominant chords resolve "upward" rather than down by fifth or half-step. The cadential arrival on Eb-7 at m. 9 provides an example (see Example 8): E♭-7 is preceded by C7 and D7 at mm. 7–8.

Example 10 includes the formal designs for five of Little's compositions from *Out Front*, including "We Speak," "Quiet Please," "Moods in Free Time," "Hazy Hues," and "A New Day."[27] The example provides letters for formal sections of the compositions, the number of measures for those sections, and (where applicable) changes of meter. By their metric shifts, their irregular phrase lengths in both the written and improvised sections, and their use of irregular meters, these compositions show Little as an innovative jazz composer, consciously attempting to develop complex and advanced formal structures.

Clearly, Little's legacy lies in his contributions both as a player and as a composer. It may be that—while a master improviser—his real innovations are in the compositional realm. As a composer Little was obviously interested in writing works that were more than just serviceable vehicles for improvisation. The compositions examined here all show careful attention to compositional craft and detail, and a powerful interest in crafting forms outside of the 32-bar template. Although all the works were written within a short time span, we may still see a development in Little's works. His earliest compositions ("Rounder's Mood" and "Larry-Larue") rely on the harmonic progressions of the late-1950s hard-bop vocabulary. Yet at times these works, particularly "Larry-Larue," are harmonically ambiguous, and display astonishing melodic relationships. In the later two works ("Bee Vamp" and "Victory and Sorrow"), more forward looking harmonic and melodic resources are used alongside traditional methods. "Bee Vamp" is a

"We Speak"
Head: Intro (6 mm.) A (8) B (6) A (8) C (6) D (8) E (8 mm. ½ time)
Solos: A (8) B (6) A (8) C (6)

"Quiet Please"
Head: Intro (21: 8 mm. ½ time + 8 + 5 mm. ½ time)
A (7 mm.: 4 + 2 mm. of 6/4) A (7) B (5)
Solos: 10 + 5 (1/2 time) + 10

"Moods in Free Time"
Head: Intro (8 mm.; 3/4 meter) A (6 mm: 3 + 3; 4/4 meter) B (17 mm.: 8 + 3 + 6; 5/4 meter) A (6) C (6 mm.; 6/4)
Solos: C (18 mm.; 6/4 meter)

"Hazy Hues"
Head: Intro A (9 mm.; 5/4 meter) B (10; 5/4) A (9; 5/4 + 1 m. 2/4) C (15: 7 + 8; 5/4)
Solos: A (8 mm.; 5/4) B (8 mm.; 3/4) A (8 mm.; 5/4)

"A New Day" (5/4 meter)
Head: Intro (4) A (12: 3+3+3+3) B (13: 2+2+3+3+3)
Solos: A (12: 3+3+3+3)

Example 10: Other formal structures from *Out Front*

relatively early excursion into modality whose 8-bar pedal sections alternate with standard harmonic progressions; "Victory and Sorrow" employs triadic and whole-tone planing in its melody, and its blowing changes use somewhat atypical cadential devices. Finally, his compositions from *Out Front* reveal extremely forward looking formal designs. Little's compositional devices—complex forms, irregular section lengths, harmonic ambiguity, a harmonic language that makes use of bop as well as both modality and more unusual progressions—were sustained and developed throughout the 1960s by other composers, most notably Wayne Shorter. For Little, though, all these features added up to a uniquely individual and highly innovative compositional voice.[28]

Booker Little's Solo on "Rounder's Mood"

from "Booker Little 4" Blue Note CDP84457 2

transcribed by David Diamond

a chorus comparison

21
Eb7 Bmin7 E7 Ebmin7 Ab7
21
Eb7 Bmin7 E7 Ebmin7 Ab7
A
25
DbMaj7 Gbmin7 Cb7 Fm7(b5) b Bb7
A 2:40
25
DbMaj7 Gbmin7 Cb7 Fm7(b5) b Bb7
29
Ebmin7 a Ab7 Abmin7 Db7
29
Ebm7(b5) a Ab7 Abmin7 Db7
33
GbMaj7 Gm7(b5) C7 b Fm7(b5) Bb7
33
GbMaj7 Gm7(b5) C7 Fmin7 Bb7
37
Ebmin7 Ab7 DbMaj7
37
Ebmin7 Ab7 DbMaj7 DbMaj7

Booker Little's Solo on "Bee Vamp" (alt. take)

from "Eric Dolphy at the Five Spot Vol. 1"
Prestige OJCCd-247-2

transcribed by David Diamond
a chorus comparison

9
FMaj7
Emin7
A7
Dmin7
G7
Cmin7
F7
e
3
13
B♭min7
d
5

17
21
EbMaj7
B
:35
Amin7
D7
Abmin7
Db7
Gb7(#11)
1:19
f
g
1:54
2:40
3

EbMaj7
Amin7
D7 Abmin7
Db7
Gb7(#11)
f
g
Bbmin7
A
:41 d
1:27
d (descending)
2:02
2:48

FMaj7
Emin7
A7
Dmin7
G7
Cmin7
F7

Bbmin7
3
d
41
45

Booker Little's Solo on "Victory and Sorrow"
from "Booker Little and Friend"
Bethlehem CD 20-40102
transcribed by David Diamond
a chorus comparison
1. A 2:37
2. A 3:12
3. A 3:49
A' 2:43
A' 3:21
A' 3:57
E♭min7
F7
Amin7
D7alt
D♭Maj7
C7
D7

FMaj7
B
2:51
E♭7
very sharp
3
B
3:28
FMaj7
E♭7
B
4:05
FMaj7
E♭7
FMaj7
3
E♭7
3
FMaj7
E♭7
FMaj7
E♭7
3
3
FMaj7
E♭7
FMaj7
3
FMaj7
E♭7
3
FMaj7
3
FMaj7
E♭7
3
FMaj7
E♭min7
A
3:05
a (extended)
E♭min7
F7
3
E♭min7
A
3:41
a (extended)
E♭min7
F7
E♭min7
A
4:17
E♭min7
F7
3

Amin7
D7alt
D♭Maj7
C7
D7
E♭min7
A
4:25

APPENDIX I: BOOKER LITTLE DISCOGRAPHY

1. *Max Roach Plus Four On the Chicago Scene* (June 1958), EmArcy MG-36132.
2. Max Roach Plus Four: *Max Roach at Newport* (July 6, 1958), EmArcy MG-36140; EmArcy SR-80010.
3. Max Roach Quintet: *Deeds, Not Words* (September 4, 1958), Riverside RLP 12-280; RLP-1122. Rereleased as RS3018 and as OJCCD-304-2.
4. *Booker Little 4* (October 1958), United Artists UAL4034 and 5034. Rereleased by Blue Note CDP 7 84457 2.
5. Max Roach Quintet: *Award Winning Drummer* (November 25, 1958), Time T70003. Rereleased as *Max Roach,* Bainbridge: BT-1042 and BCD 1042.
6. Max Roach: *The Many Sides of Max* (September 22, 1959), Mercury MG20911and 60911. Rereleased on Trip 5599.
7. *Bill Henderson* (October 27, 1959), VJ-1015 and 1016.
8. Slide Hampton: *Slide Hampton and his Horn of Plenty* (late 1959/early 1960), Strand S1006.
9. Frank Strozier: *Fantastic Frank Stozier* (February 2, 1960), VJ-362 and VJLP 1007. Reissued as *Waltz of the demons* Affinity 49. Rereleased with #29 as Booker Little, *Looking Ahead*, Affinity 753.
10. *The Soul of Jazz Percussion* (c. Spring 1960), Warwick W5003. Reissued as Donald Byrd: *Music of the Third World*, TCB Records: TCB1004.
11. Booker Little (April 13 and 15, 1960), Time 52011. Rereleased as Bainbridge BCD1041.
12. Teddy Charles New Directions With Guest Stars: *Jazz in the Garden of the Museum of Modern Art* (August 25, 1960) Warwick W2033.
13. Booker Little and Booker Ervin, *Sounds of the Inner City*, TCB 1003.
14. Max Roach: *We Insist! The Freedom Now Suite* (August 31 and September 6, 1960), Candid CD-8002 and CS-9002. Rereleased as Columbia JC 36390.
15. Eric Dolphy: *Candid Dolphy* (October 1960-April 1961). Contains selections/alternate takes from #21 and #22. Candid CCD 79033.
16. The Jazz Artists Guild: *Newport Rebels* (November 1, 1960), Candid 79022.
17. Young Men From Memphis: *Downhome Reunion* (early 1959), United Artists 4084 and 5084.

18. Eric Dolphy: *Far Cry* (December 21, 1960), New Jazz NJLP-8270. Reissued on Prestige: PRT 7747.
19. Eric Dolphy: *Magic*. Prestige P-24053. Sides 1 and 2 originally issued as *Far Cry*; Sides 3 and 4 as Ron Carter: *Where?* (June 20, 1961), New Jazz 8265.
20. Eric Dolphy: *Here and there* [n.d.], Prestige: PRST 7382. (Contains selection from #25.)
21. Abbey Lincoln: *Straight Ahead* (February 22, 1961), Candid 8015 and 9015
22. Booker Little: *Out Front* (March 17 and April 4, 1961), Candid CD 9027
23. John Coltrane: *Africa Brass* (May 23 and June 7, 1961), Impulse! A(S)6 CSD 1431.
24. John Coltrane: *The Africa Brass Sessions, Vol. 2* (May 23 and June 7, 1961), ABC AS-9273.
25. *Eric Dolphy at the Five Spot* (vol. 1) (July 16, 1961), New Jazz 8260. Rereleased as Prestige 7611, New Jazz OJC-133, Prestige VDJ-1504.
26. Eric Dolphy: *At the Five Spot,* vol. 2 (July 16, 1961), Prestige 7294. Rereleased as Prestige 7836, Prestige VDJ 1525.
27. Vols. 1 and 2 rereleased as *Eric Dolphy at the Five Spot* (includes alternate take of "Bee Vamp"). Prestige OJCCD-133-2, OJCCD-247-2.
28. *Eric Dolphy At the Five Spot, vol. 3.* (July 16, 1961), Prestige PRT-7334. Reissued as *Eric Dolphy & Booker Little Memorial Album*. Prestige OJCCD-353-2 (P-7334).
29. Max Roach: *Percussion Bitter Sweet* (August 1–9, 1961), Impulse A-8. Rereleased as Impulse GRD-122.
30. Booker Little Sextet: *Booker Little and Friend* (August or September 1961), Bethlehem BCP-6061. Rereleased with #9 as Booker Little, *Looking Ahead*, Affinity 753.

Anthologies:

Introspection: Neglected jazz figures of the 1950s and early 1960s. 1977. New World Records NW 275. Includes Booker Little Sextet, "We speak" and "Strength and Sanity," originally from *Out Front*.

When Malindy sings. 1977. New World Records NW 295. Includes Abbey Lincoln, "When Malindy Sings," originally from *Straight Ahead*.

The Jazz Trumpet: Volume 2: Modern time. 1983. Prestige P-24112. Includes Max Roach, "Larry-Larue," originally from *Words, Not Deeds*.

The Message: 14 Jazz Masterpieces from the Affinity Catalog. Affinity CD Pro 1. Includes "If I Should Lose You," originally from *Booker Little and Friend*.

Jazz 'Round Midnight. Verve 513-461-2. Includes "There's No You," originally from Max Roach, *The Many Sides of Max*.

Time Records, Vol. 8, Jazz Series. Time 8. Includes "Variations on the Scene" and "Gandolfo's Bounce," originally from Max Roach, *Award Winning Drummer*.

Eric Dolphy, *The Complete Prestige Recordings*. Prestige 4418-2. Contains complete recordings of *Far Cry* and *Live at the Five Spot,* volumes 1–3.

APPENDIX 2: BOOKER LITTLE COMPOSITIONS

(Number following title indicates recording no. from Appendix 1 above)

1. Aggression (26)
2. Bee Tee's Minor Plea (11)
3. Bee Vamp (25)
4. Booker's Blues (29)
5. Booker's Waltz (27) (Same composition as The Grand Valse and Waltz of the Demons)
6. Calling Softly (29)
7. Cliffwalk (16)
8. The Confined Few (12 and 13)
9. Dungeon Waltz (4)
10. Forward Flight (29)
11. Gandolfo's Bounce (5)
12. The Grand Valse (11) (Same composition as Booker's Waltz and Waltz of the Demons)
13. Hazy Hues (22)
14. Jewel's Tempo (4)
15. Larry-Larue (3)
16. Life's a Little Blue (11)
17. Looking Ahead (Also titled Molotone Music, 29. Same composition as Cliffwalk.)
18. Man of Words (22)
19. Matilde (29)
20. Minor Mode (2)
21. Minor Sweet (11)
22. Moods in Free Time (22)

23. A New Day (22)
24. Opening Statement (11)
25. Quiet Please (22)
26. Rounder's Mood (4)
27. Strength and Sanity (22)
28. Victory and Sorrow (29)
29. Waltz of the Demons (9) (Same composition as The Grand Waltz and Booker's Waltz)
30. We Speak (22)
31. Witchfire (10, *The Soul of Jazz Percussion* only, and 13)

APPENDIX III: BOOKER LITTLE BIBLIOGRAPHY

Aagberg, David. "Booker Little's Trumpet Solo On 'Booker's Blues.'" *Down Beat* 61, no.12 (December 1994): 74–75.

Berliner, Paul. *Thinking in Jazz: The Infinite Art of Improvisation*. Chicago and London: University of Chicago Press, 1994. (Transcription and analysis of "W.K. Blues," "Minor Sweet," and others.)

Gale, Warren. "Eight Advanced Analyses of Jazz Trumpet Improvisations from 1927–1960." D.M.A. thesis, California State/Hayward, 1988. (Transcription and analysis of "Mrs. Parker of K.C.")

Hentoff, Nat. Booker Little Obituary. *Metronome* 78, no.12 (December 1961): 11.

Kerschbaumer, Franz. "Booker Little: Seine Improvisations und Kompositionstechnik." *Jazzforschung* 14 (1982): 9–60. (Includes solo transcriptions or lead sheets for "My Old Flame," "A Night in Tunisia," "Minor Mode," "You Stepped Out of a Dream," "Milestones," "Jewel's Tempo," "Things Ain't What They Used to Be," "Bee Tee's Minor Plea," "Cliff Walk," "Miss Ann," "Strength and Sanity," "Bee Vamp," and "Booker's Waltz.")

Levin, Robert. "Booker Little." *Metronome* 78, no.10 (October 1961): 32–34.

Monti, Pierre-Andre. *Booker Little Discography*. Sierre, Switzerland: Jazz 360, 1983.

Saul, Alan. Booker Little Discography. http://farcry.neurobio.pitt.edu/Discographies/Booker.html

Walker, Malcolm. "Booker Little: Discography." *Jazz Monthly* 12, no. 5 (1966): 13; 12, no. 8 (1966): 26; and 13, no. 2 (1967): 27.

Obituary. "A Talent Cut Down—A Promise Unfilled." *Down Beat* 28, no. 23 (November 9, 1961): 11.

NOTES

1. A version of this paper was given as a Roundtable presentation at the Institute of Jazz Studies, Rutgers University, in September 2000. The authors

would like to thank Paul Berliner, Alan Saul, and Don Sickler for their comments and suggestions. In order to avoid any potential copyright infringements in this essay (in accordance with the policy of the *Annual Review of Jazz Studies*), musical examples have been "de-rhythmicized": that is, they are given without rhythmic values.

2. Quoted from the interview by Robert Levin, "Booker Little," *Metronome* 78, no. 10 (October 1961): 33. The interview is one of the most substantive of Little's in print.
3. Ibid., 32.
4. Ibid., 33.
5. David Wild's entry on Booker Little in the *New Grove Dictionary of Jazz* incorrectly states that Little received a B.M. degree in 1958.
6. There may have been three recordings. It is unclear whether *Slide Hampton and His Horn of Plenty* was made in late 1959 or early 1960.
7. Wynton Kelly replaces Flanagan on piano for two compositions. Chronology is a little unclear for this record: the sleeve for the original recording gives the dates April 13 and 16, 1960; Time Records elsewhere provided the date of July 11, 1960. See Malcolm Walker's discography in *Jazz Monthly* 12, no. 5 (1966): 13.
8. Levin, "Little," 34.
9. Amazingly, Dolphy recorded *Far Cry* on the same day that he participated on Ornette Coleman's *Free Jazz* record. Coleman's record was done on the morning of December 21, 1960; *Far Cry* was done later that afternoon.
10. Levin, "Little," 32.
11. For further examination of these social currents, see Robert K. McMichael, "'We Insist—Freedom Now!': Black Moral Authority, Jazz, and the Changeable Shape of Whiteness," *American Music* 16, no. 4 (Winter 1998): 375–416.
12. Both *We Insist!* and *Straight Ahead* are also notable for the presence of Coleman Hawkins on tenor saxophone, still attempting to stay in the musical vanguard nearly forty years after he began his career. In an amusing 1961 interview in *Down Beat*, Hawkins discussed his current work, stating, "You know, I've been making records with Max Roach and Eric Dolphy and them cats lately. . . . They hit this chord and all the time they got this other thing goin' down there. . .then they say, 'Go, you got it, Bean.' Got what? What the hell can you get? What can you play between these two things? But it's interesting. That's what music is—interesting. That's what music's all about anyway. Finding those things; the adventure." From "In Between, the Adventure," *Down Beat* (April 13, 1961): 15.
13. Levin, "Little," 33.
14. Nat Hentoff, Booker Little Obituary, *Metronome* 78, no. 12 (December 1961): 11.
15. Paul Berliner, *Thinking in Jazz: The Infinite Art of Improvisation* (Chicago and London: University of Chicago Press, 1994).

16. David Aagberg, "Booker Little's Trumpet Solo on "Booker's Blues,'" *Down Beat* 61/12 (December 1994): 74–76.
17. Warren Gale, "Eight Advanced Analyses of Jazz Trumpet Solos" (D.M.A. thesis, California State/Hayward, 1988), 118. See Chapter 9 for Gale's discussion of Little.
18. Paul Berliner makes a similar analytical point in his discussions of Little in *Thinking in Jazz*, op. cit.
19. Motive a undergoes a pitch alteration at m. 29 of the first chorus as well: instead of beginning with D natural, it begins with E♭.
20. In m. 28 of the second chorus, too, the motive tops out at C♭ instead of B♭, lending variety to the sound. Motive b also returns at m. 35 of the first chorus.
21. Interestingly, this tetrachord is identical to the one stated in the opening and closing four bars of the melody to "Larry-Larue." This is probably a fallout from Little's attraction toward writing compositions which strongly emphasize D♭ major and B♭ minor, keys he obviously felt extremely comfortable improvising in.
22. Careful listeners will also hear Motive e as something of a surprise at the beginning of the third chorus, over the B♭ minor harmony. In fact, the rhythm section drops the last 12 bars of the second chorus (the * at m. 36 of the second chorus indicates where the rhythm section loses these bars and reverts to the top of the next chorus). Little, though, is correct at m. 37, playing Motive e (see m. 1 of the third chorus), but quickly adapts to the rhythm section's mistake. This probably motivated the choice of this version of "Bee Vamp" as the alternate take.
23. Motive g also is used at mm. 23–24 of the second chorus.
24. Obituary, "A Talent Cut Down—A Promise Unfilled," *Down Beat* 28, no. 23 (November 9, 1961): 11.
25. "Booker's Blues," from his *Victory and Sorrow* recording, is not examined here, but a partial transcription and analysis may be found in David Aagberg's article in the Woodshed section of *Down Beat*. See "Booker Little's Trumpet Solo on 'Booker's Blues,'" *Down Beat* 61, no.12 (December 1994): 74.
26. See the liner notes to *Out Front*.
27. This example is indebted to Franz Kerschbaumer's article "Booker Little: Seine Improvisations und Kompositionstechnik," *Jazzforschung* 14 (1982): 9–60.
28. Quite possibly, Little's most adventurous compositions were never recorded. Little wrote a three-part suite for Max Roach's group, entitled "The Battle," "The Defeat," and "The Long Blue Hereafter." As described by bassist Ray McKinney, its first movement was free-form, organized only by a set group of notes given to the horns. See "The Drummer Most Likely to Succeed," *Down Beat* 28, no.7 (March 30, 1961): 20–21.

METRIC DISPLACEMENT IN THE IMPROVISATION OF CHARLIE CHRISTIAN

Clive Downs

1. INTRODUCTION

In this article my aim is to explain how Charlie Christian created the effects of metric displacement that are evident in his solos. Metric displacement is defined more precisely below, but in essence it is an effect in which the underlying meter of a piece of music is challenged. My strategy will be to attempt to define ten categories of musical devices which can be observed in these solos and which serve to produce the metric displacement effects in them.

1.1 The Puzzle of Metric Displacement

There seems to be powerful rhythmic "drive" in Christian's playing. Sleeve notes and comments in books of transcriptions are intriguing—they hint at the way this effect was produced but do not explain it. For example, Avakian and Prince (1955, 181) observe: "His improvisations sound simple and effortless, but, when analyzed, prove complex, and daring in their exploration of musical principles"; Fox (1964, 28) says "the interesting points are too numerous to mention" of his solo on "Solo Flight."

I suggest that the rhythmic drive of Christian's solos is, in part, created by metric displacement. In this paper I shall try to solve this puzzle and to show in detail how this effect is produced. We should acknowledge, though, that effects like this are, in the end, subjective; one listener may hear a certain passage and perceive that the meter is displaced, but another person may fail to do so. To look at it another way, many listeners might agree that Christian's solos sound metrically displaced, but perhaps they would not be able to define exactly how that effect had been produced.

1.2 Analysis of Solo Style in Jazz

Owens (1974, 271) comments that although there was an extensive bibliography of jazz, there was little analysis of the favorite melodic figures used by great soloists. In the quarter century since then, much more analysis of jazz musicians' style has been published, but there is still little analysis of the rhythmic features of soloists' style.

Waters (1997, 20) suggests that, although in the last fifteen years we have seen much theoretical, analytical, and instructional material about jazz improvisation, almost all has been concerned with harmonic and melodic issues, while neglecting rhythm. Finkelman (1997, 159) argues that jazz research increasingly focuses upon the formulas that soloists use. Surprisingly, an early critical commentary on jazz (Sargeant 1938, 88) did give equal attention to rhythm as it did to melody, and used (or possibly introduced) the term "polyrhythm" into the discussion of jazz styles.

1.3 Biographical Sketch

For readers not familiar with the artist, it may help to provide some biographical background. Charles Christian is often acknowledged as one of the most influential guitarists in the history of jazz. He played with Benny Goodman, Lionel Hampton, Lester Young, and many other leading musicians of his era, and died at 25. Our knowledge of his life and career is based on a limited number of accounts (Downs 2000). Ellison (1959, 7–8) describes his schooldays with Christian, the guitarist's musical education, his family, and his musical influences. Feather (1977, 5) recounts Christian's early career (as related by Mary Osborne), including playing with Al Trent's band in Bismarck, North Dakota.

John Hammond (1981, 223) writes of how he heard Christian for the first time in Oklahoma and arranged the famous audition with Benny Goodman. He recalls Christian's career with Goodman, his eventual illness and death. Blesh (1971, 161) tells of the musical culture of Oklahoma City at the time of Christian's childhood, and his early musical development. Barney Kessel (1982, 72) relates how he met Christian and played with him. Grosz and Cohn (1980) report their research into the date and place of Christian's birth, his burial, and family. Arnold (1994), in a publication produced on the tenth anniversary of the Charlie Christian festival, collects reminiscences of several Oklahoma City residents who knew Christian.

He recorded in the studio, predominantly with Benny Goodman small groups and big bands, but also with Lionel Hampton and other well-known artists. We also have recordings from jam sessions with Thelonious Monk, Kenny Clarke, and others. Compositions he recorded are mainly popular standards or original compositions based on the 12-bar blues or on familiar 32-bar chord sequences such as that of Fats Waller's "Honeysuckle Rose."

He was a soloist of great imagination. In the studio recordings and on airchecks with the Goodman bands, his solos are generally limited to one or two choruses. In the jam sessions recorded at Minton's Playhouse, Monroe's, and other venues, he could improvise over extended choruses, yet sustain great inventiveness. As Max Harrison wrote:

> . . .the beautiful guitar solos on "Swing to Bop," "Up on Teddy's Hill," and "Stompin' at the Savoy" do not tell us anything new about the way Christian's jazz is organized. But, as we listen to him play chorus after chorus, his seemingly inexhaustible power of invention overwhelms us, and it is, of course, as with Parker, the vehicle of everything else his music contains (McCarthy et al. 1968, 46).

1.4 Previous Analysis of His Style

Several studies of Christian's style have been published in books and theses and are also to be found in liner notes. Spring (1980; 1990) studied Christian's use of melodic formulas. Schuller's (1989, 562) analysis of Swing Era styles includes several transcriptions and a general discussion of the guitarist's style. Finkelman (1993; 1997) has written about Christian's use of melodic formulas and other features of his style. The studies of Spring and Finkelman, the most thorough, have focused in the main on harmonic and melodic aspects of Christian's style.

Many critics have remarked on the subtlety of Christian's phrasing. For example, Hansen (1998):

> . . . compared to many contemporary guitarists, Charlie was not a particularly fast player. He did play with imagination, drive, and energy, however, which is always more effective than raw speed. Much of that drive is a product of phrasing.

Although several critics comment in general terms on rhythmic features of his style, there has been little detailed analysis of rhythmic aspects of Christian's playing.

1.5 Phrasing

In this paper I will examine phrasing in some detail. In particular, I will consider phrasing in the sense of where phrases start and end, and how long they are. Phrasing is a term that tends to be used loosely by critics, and musical dictionaries often fail to give a precise definition. For instance, Sadie (1986, 663) offers:

> A term adopted from linguistic syntax and used for short musical units of various lengths; a phrase is generally regarded as longer than a motif but shorter than a period. . . . As a formal unit, however, it must be considered in its polyphonic entirety, like "period", "sentence," or even "theme."

For consistency, in the analyses that follow I have used a definition of "phrase" that is as rigorous as possible. My aim is a definition precise enough that a computer program could be written to automatically detect the start and end of each phrase. In the music examples that follow, phrases will be identified which conform to the definition given here.

Intuitively, we regard a phrase as a unit of melody that has some coherence. The rules that I would use to detect a phrase are:

(a) a phrase is a sequence of pitches in which there are no (notated) rests of an eighth note or greater;

(b) a rest of an eighth note or greater marks the end of a phrase, except for rules (c) and (d);

(c) when a rest has the effect of syncopation, it does not mark the end of a phrase. For instance, in Example 1.1(a), the quarter-note rest in bar 1, with the C preceding it, has the effect of syncopation. The eighth-note rests in bar 2 similarly combine with the C pitches they follow in producing a syncopation. Therefore, they function to give a syncopation rather than to separate phrases. To clarify this, consider a less syncopated version of the same phrase in Example 1.1(b).

Example 1.1(a): Good Enough to Keep (Air Mail Special)

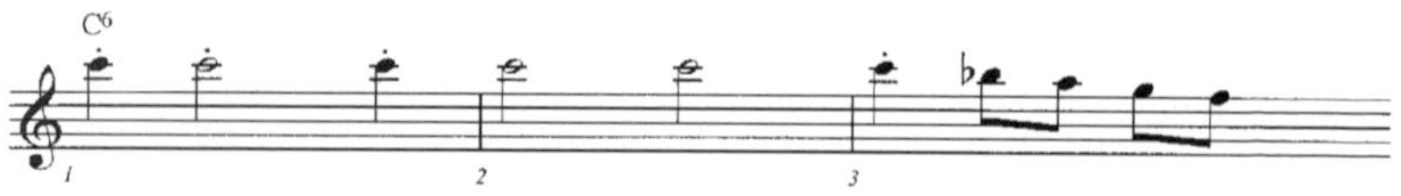

Example 1.1(b): Good Enough to Keep (Air Mail Special)

(d) when a rest of an eighth note or more separates from another phrase a sequence of notes that lasts for three beats or less, that sequence does not form a separate phrase; instead, it is considered part of that same phrase. For instance, in Example 1.2, the sequence of notes in bar 27 is separated from the A natural in bar 26 by a rest of a quarter note. However that sequence (bar 27) lasts less than three beats, so it is considered to form the end of the phrase starting half way through bar 25.

Example 1.2: I Found a New Baby

To establish a phrase's length in the comments below, I have simplified matters by treating each phrase as though it lasted a whole number of bars. Let us count the final bar of a phrase as a whole bar if the final note of the phrase extends to the first beat of the bar or further. Thus the phrase in Example 1.3 lasts three bars; its final note extends to the first beat of the third bar. We count the first whole bar of the phrase as the bar in which the first note of the phrase occurs, except if it occurs on the last beat of the bar.

Example 1.3: Benny's Bugle

We should acknowledge that this analysis of a phrase is to some extent dependent on the transcription on which it is based. A transcription always involves some interpretation. For instance, a section of a solo might be notated as two bars of consecutive eighth notes in one transcription, but in another with some eighth-note rests or ghosted notes. Such variation could clearly affect the way one parses a solo into phrases and the way phrases are categorized in the system described below. (Nevertheless, it would still be of value to have an objective and exact means of identifying phrases in a single transcription!)

1.6 Outline of Devices Which Create Metric Displacement

Each of the rhythmic devices described here adds interest to the improvisation by creating a kind of ambiguity in the metric structure. Christian uses at least ten devices, and for each type I have presented two examples from his solos to illustrate how the device is used. Where possible I have drawn one example of each type from those identified by other authors. This is to help support my argument and make it less likely my analysis is a biased, personal one.

I have tried to be as precise as possible in defining the categories. My aim is to produce a definition precise enough that a computer program could be written to automatically detect all instances of the device by searching a database of digitized Christian solos.

These are the ten types:

1. Metric displacement by contour
2. Metric superimposition
3. Metric displacement by phrase starting point
4. Displaced motivic repetition
5. Metric displacement by patterning
6. Long sequences of eighth notes
7. Long phrases of mixed texture
8. Irregular phrase length
9. Hypermetric displacement
10. Phrase ending peculiarities

Each of these is examined in the following ten sections.

Many transcriptions of Christian's solos have been published (Downs 1993; 2000). All examples used here are taken from the complete transcriptions of Leo Valdés (Valdés 2000). Discographical details, including conventions for identifying take numbers, follow Valdés's Internet discography (Valdés 2000).

2. METRIC DISPLACEMENT

In his dictionary entry on "beat," Kernfield (1988, 85) describes how "turning the rhythm (or beat or time) around" is a practice in which a soloist superimposes another meter on the basic meter of a piece. Several effects can be created (according to Folio 1995):

(a) time-signature variation: where the meter of the improvisation appears to be in a different time-signature to that of the ensemble (e.g., 3/4 against 4/4);

(b) out-of-phase: where the meter of the improvisation appears to be in the same time-signature as the ensemble, but the bar-lines it implies occur at different points to it;
(c) tempo variation: where the soloist plays faster or slower than the ensemble; Kernfield refers to Charlie Parker's fondness for this practice, and Collier (1988, 595) suggests that Parker was influenced by Christian in this respect.

A soloist can achieve these effects by several methods, including accents, phrasing, or the contour of the line. Waters (1997), in his study of Herbie Hancock's piano solos, distinguishes several methods which soloists use to create metric displacement. Each will be described in detail as we review examples from Christian's solos.

2.1 Metric Displacement by Contour

This section examines phrases with a contour that displaces the underlying meter. Contour refers to the way in which the direction of a melodic line rises and falls and to the peaks and lowest points of such lines. Although some jazz critics have attempted to analyze contour in jazz improvisation (e.g., Porter's [1985, 76] discussion of Lester Young), its study is as yet underdeveloped (Marvin's [1995] examination of this subject indicates its complexity). In this section we shall examine only a very specific type of contour.

Several critics have commented on the importance of contour in Christian's improvisation. Fox (1964, 22) discusses his solo on "Shivers":

> . . . it is interesting to look at the shape of Charley's solo—just the way it looks on the page. A comparison with many great pieces of classical music will show similar outlines—the rise and fall of melody. The rules of great music—after all—apply to all kinds.

Schuller (1989, 572) writes that:

> the larger contours of his lines are so pleasing to our ears because they consist of a flowing alternation of rising and falling shapes. Moreover, these alternations are generally cast in almost classic symmetrical proportions, very much in the classic sense of arsis and thesis. A surging rising figure (arsis) will invariably be resolved by a relaxing falling one (thesis).

Again, some of these comments are frustrating because they tend to be very generalized and lack specific examples.

2.1.1 "Breakfast Feud" [Columbia matrix: CO 29259-1, December 19, 1940]

Avakian and Prince (1955, 185), in a perceptive note on Christian's solo on this composition, observe:

> [He] shifts the metric accent from the normally strong first beat to the secondary third beat, thereby creating the illusion that he is starting his phrase on a pick-up from the previous chorus when in reality he is starting on the first beat of the chorus. He molded the contour of this phrase so that melodic peaks also occur on the accented third beats.

Avakian and Prince refer to Christian's solo on take-1 of the earlier studio recording (there were at least two sessions, December 19, 1940, and January 15, 1941), issued in an edited version on LP and now available in its original, complete version on CD. (See details in Section 4 below.) As can be seen in Example 2.1.1, at bar 5 (the first bar of the solo, and fifth in the 12-bar structure of the composition), the C natural on beat three is the highest point of the melodic line in the bar (and, indeed, in the phrase that begins the solo). The contour of the phrase rises over beats one and two, and peaks at beat three, falling to beat four. It suggests that Christian moves the perceived down beat to C.

Example 2.1.1: Breakfast Feud

2.1.2 "Flying Home" [Columbia matrix: WCO-26132-A, October 2, 1939]

Halfway through bar 20 of the guitar solo is a phrase similar to the example of Avakian and Prince (section 2.1.1). It has a similar contour; in this case, it starts on beat three of the bar (instead of rising to it), but the peak of the phrase occurs on the C natural with which it starts (Example 2.1.2). It is interesting to note also that the contour peaks on beat 3 of both measures 22 and 23 as well, therefore reinforcing the metric displacement.

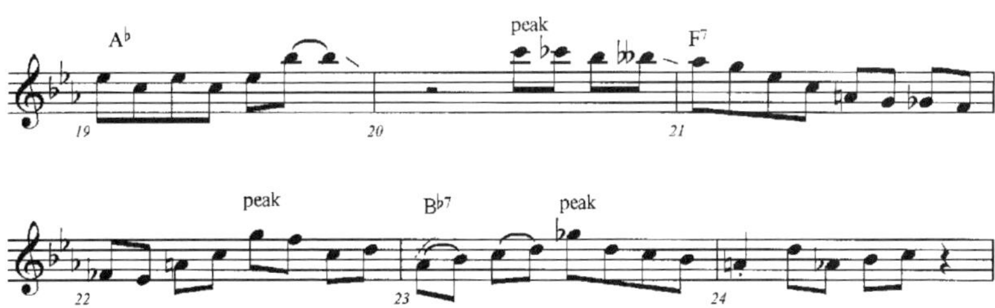

Example 2.1.2: Flying Home

2.2. Metric Superimposition

Metric superimposition can be defined as an effect in which the melodic line suggests a meter with a different time-signature to that of the ensemble. This device has often been used by improvisers and is found also in jazz and popular song compositions. An example often quoted is that of "three against four," i.e., a figure repeated at three-beat intervals in a piece in 4/4 time, thus suggesting 3/4 meter.

Kernfield (1995, 31) notes that this device has been used by jazz soloists at least since the 1920s. Sargeant (1938, 88) refers to it as one example of "polyrhythm," so evidently it was recognized before Christian's time.

2.2.1 "Good Enough to Keep" ("Airmail Special") [Columbia matrix: CO 29943-2, March 13, 1941]

Fox (1964, p. 14), in one of the earliest published albums of notated Christian solos, points out that the passage at the start of the bridge (bars 16 through 18 of the solo) consists of a rhythmic figure repeated four times, at three-beat intervals, thus superimposing a triple meter on the underlying 4/4 meter (Example 2.2.1). In fact, the first occurrence starts with a syncopated note that is half a beat longer than its repetitions.

Example 2.2.1: Good Enough to Keep (Air Mail Special)

2.2.2 "Topsy" ("Swing to Bop") [jam: May 12, 1941]

In a passage in the extended solo on "Topsy" recorded at Minton's Playhouse, a three-beat motif is repeated over the basic 4/4 meter (Example 2.2.2). On this occasion, the motif is repeated four times, again suggesting a triple meter contrasting with the 4/4 of the ensemble. This passage occurs in the sixth chorus of the first guitar solo.

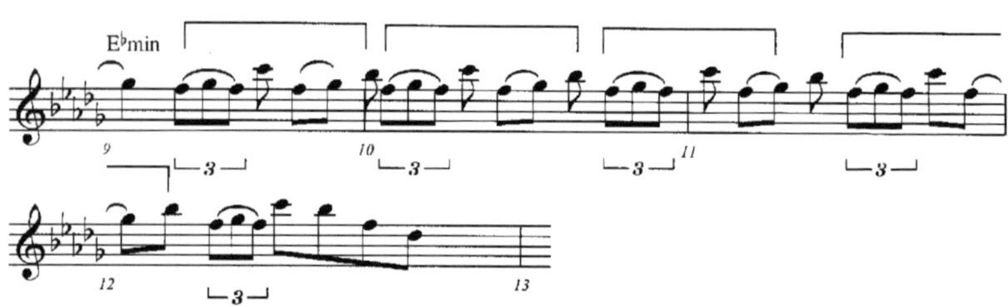

Example 2.2.2: Topsy (Swing to Bop)

2.3 Metric Displacement by Phrase Starting Point

Waters (1997, 22) describes a type of metric displacement termed "grouping structure." By this, he means that where a melodic line begins (or ends) can create a conflict with the underlying metric structure. A line that starts on a weak beat (2, or 4, in common time) is "out of phase" with the basic meter. Let us refer to this device as "metric displacement by phrase starting position" to make the meaning more specific.

There are numerous examples of Christian using this device in his solos. As far as I know, this aspect of his playing has never before been identified in the literature. He often starts phrases on the third beat of the bar, or with a "pick-up" on the second beat. On listening to these phrases, there seems to be an ambiguity about where the bar begins; it seems as though the phrase in question could be starting on the first beat of the bar (or with a pick-up on the last beat of the preceding bar).

2.3.1 "Flying Home" [Aircheck: October 16, 1939]

In this solo (Example 2.3.1)—he recorded many versions of this composition—Christian plays a phrase in the bridge, at bar 20, which starts with a B-flat on the second half of beat two; the phrase continues through to bar 22.

This placing of the phrase creates an ambiguity, as it seems as though the B-flat could lie on the second half of the last beat of the preceding bar, and the B-double flat (enharmonic A-natural) on the first beat of the bar. Undoubtedly this effect is strengthened by the harmonic anticipation implied by the A-natural falling on a strong beat, implying the F7 chord of the following bar.

Example 2.3.1: Flying Home

2.3.2 "The Sheik of Araby" [aircheck: April 26, 1940]

This solo (Example 2.3.2) is from an aircheck of a composition for which there are three known versions by Christian (one a studio recording and two from radio broadcasts). A phrase in the second eight-bar section, at bar 11, starts halfway through the bar, on beat three, and the phrase continues until the start of bar 14. Thus this phrase again creates a tension against the underlying meter, shifting the meter by two beats, and suggesting that the start of the bar may be on beat three of bar 11.

Example 2.3.2: The Sheik of Araby

2.4 Displaced Motivic Repetition

This device is another feature of Christian's playing that, to my knowledge, has not been identified before in discussions of his style. The device is another means of displacing meter described by Waters (1997). It occurs when a melodic figure is repeated, but starts at a different point in the bar. Pitches in the figure may be identical when it is repeated, or may differ, while the figure simply retains the same contour.

2.4.1 "Ida, Sweet as Apple Cider" [aircheck: April 14, 1941]

Example 2.4.1(a) shows bars 24 to 25 of the guitar solo, one of Christian's most interesting and driving improvisations. Bar 24 starts with a motif that begins on an F-natural and continues for three beats (with the pitches F–B–A–G–G-flat–F). This motif is then repeated, starting on the second half of beat three of bar 24, but altered to fit the change of harmony from G7 to C7. Its contour remains the same, some pitches are altered. In fact, some harmonic anticipation is involved as well, since the B-flat on beat four of bar 24 suggests the C7 following.

Example 2.4.1(a): Ida, Sweet as Apple Cider

There is some ambiguity additional to the displaced repetition, because the F on the second half of beat three could be heard as belonging to the end of the first occurrence of the motif and to the beginning of its second occurrence. Following Waters's example, a normalized version of this passage (i.e., with the motif repeated but with no displacement) is shown in Example 2.4.1(b).

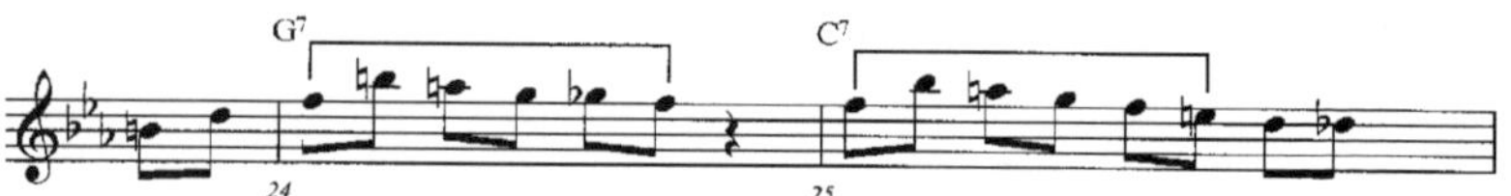

Example 2.4.1(b): Ida, Sweet as Apple Cider (normalized version)

2.4.2 "Stompin' at the Savoy" [jam: May 1941]

A further example of displaced motivic repetition occurs in the first chorus of the first guitar solo on this jam recorded at Minton's Playhouse, in a version released on many LPs. In a phrase referred to by Finkelman (1993, 191) as an example of a long sequence of consecutive eighth notes, the motif that begins the phrase starts on beat four of bar 16—bracketed in the transcription, Example 2.4.2(a)—and extends over the next five pitches. Its contour is such that its first five pitches descend, then the final pitch rises. This motif then recurs starting on the last beat of bar 17, and continues through bar 18. It recurs again, starting on beat two of bar 19. While the pitches and some intervals vary each time to fit the chord and the register, the contour remains the same. Each occurrence starts at a different point in the bar. Again, a normalized version is shown in Example 2.4.2 (b).

Example 2.4.2(a): Stompin' at the Savoy

Example 2.4.2(b): Stompin' at the Savoy (normalized version)

2.5 Metric Displacement by Pattern

A further type of device identified by Waters (1997) is displacement by pattern. A pattern formed either by a rhythmic feature or by melody is repeated, but at a point in the bar different from its first occurrence.

2.5.1 "Tea for Two" [jam: September 24, 1939]

On the second solo of a piece Christian recorded only once, a motif of three pitches in a rising contour is repeated nine times over four bars (the pattern shown bracketed in Example 2.5.1). The grouping of three eighth-note pitches sets up an interesting tension against the duple time of the composition and the accompaniment. At the beginning of bar 20, the motif even crosses the bar line. The whole tone pattern in bars 17 to 18 on which it is based has since the 1940s been widely used in jazz. Christian used whole-tone color quite sparingly.

Example 2.5.1: Tea for Two

2.5.2 "Up on Teddy's Hill" [jam: May 1941]

In this extract from the fourth chorus of the solo, a motif of three notes in a rising contour is repeated six times over three bars (the motif crossing the bar line twice). This pattern is shown by brackets in Example 2.5.2, and one can see that the perfect fourth interval is quite prominent.

Example 2.5.2: Up on Teddy's Hill

2.6 Long Sequences of Eighth Notes

Several critics have drawn attention to Christian's use of long phrases consisting of eighth notes. Avakian and Prince (1955, 185), in perhaps one of the first technical discussions of his style, point out "the unusual length of his melodic lines, consisting of even and clearly executed *eighth notes*." Collier (1981, 292) refers to Christian's "long lines of relatively uninflected *eighth notes*." (Italics added.)

It would be possible to search all the solos and count the frequency of phrases made up of consecutive eighth notes, extending over four, five, six bars and so on. For now, let us include in this category sequences of consecutive eighth notes that extend through at least four complete bars.

2.6.1 "Breakfast Feud" [Columbia matrix: CO-29512-4, January 15, 1941]

Collier (1989, 292) comments that on this solo, Christian plays:

> . . . a run of uninterrupted eighth notes from bar three into bar eight. Strings of eighth notes this long would be rare even in a piano solo.

This solo is on a 12-bar blues and starts half way through bar 4 of the 12-bar structure (after the ensemble), continues to the end of the chorus, and on into a further complete 12-bar chorus. This section, shown in Example 2.6.1, includes four complete bars (4 to 7) with consecutive eighth notes. The sequence begins at bar 4 (bar 8 of the first 12-bar chorus) and continues through to beat two of bar 8 (the last bar of the chorus). This solo was edited, with others from alternate takes—some from a different date—into a composite track issued on LP, but it is now available in its original form on CD).

Example 2.6.1: Breakfast Feud

2.6.2 "Breakfast Feud" [Columbia matrix: CO-29512-3, January 15, 1941]

In a further version of the same composition, we can see (Example 2.6.2) a sequence of five complete bars of consecutive eighth notes (bar 12 of the preceding chorus, then bars 1 through 4 of the next chorus).

Example 2.6.2: Breakfast Feud

It may be that this device works as follows. A "normal" phrase, in which there are a variety of note lengths, tends to reinforce the meter because the patterns the notes form are usually consistent with the strong and weak beats. A sequence of consecutive eighth notes does not reinforce the normal metric structure, and thus creates ambiguity. However, this effect will depend on the contour of the phrase, as Example 2.6.3 illustrates.

2.6.3 "Shivers" [Columbia matrix: WCO-26354-A, December 20, 1939]

In this example, the phrase starting at beat four of bar 8 continues through six bars of consecutive eighth notes. However, the contour of the phrase is such that the meter is not displaced. Bars 9, 10, and 11 each start with a four-note motif that is rather similar (labeled in Example 2.6.3 as motif x). This repetition, starting each time on beat one, seems to reinforce the underlying meter of the performance.

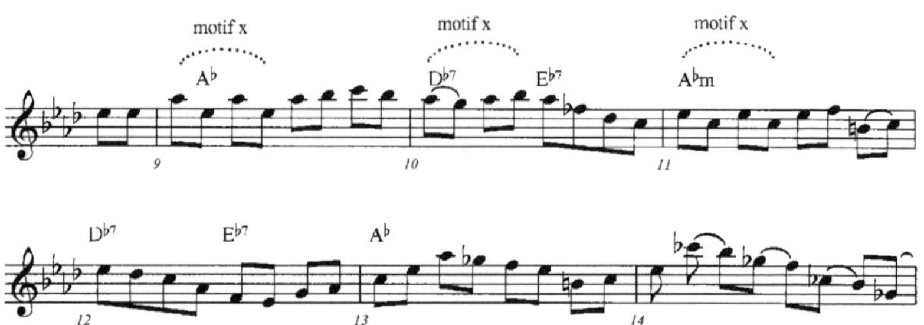

Example 2.6.3: Shivers

2.7 Long Phrases of Mixed Texture

Several commentators refer to Christian's use of long phrases. Williams (1970, 286) notes how Christian played "long, flowing bursts of lyric melody," while Feather (1961, 240) observes that he was "capable of unusually long phrases." We can identify many occasions where Christian played phrases made up of eighth notes, plus notes of rather longer duration. Let us focus upon phrases of at least six bars length—again a somewhat arbitrary definition.

In his sleeve notes Carriére (1992) comments on the "Tea for Two" solo:

> . . . the coherence with which he expresses his generally very long musical ideas. Note especially the bewildering lines he develops from the outset of the second chorus of his opening solo, and again during the final 16 bars of his second solo.

The word "bewildering" is very apt; those phrases that span four or more bars tend to disorient us from the underlying metric structure. We listen to them intently to see where they go.

2.7.1 "Named it Yet" [Victor matrix: BS-042942-1, October 13, 1939]

In this improvisation (Example 2.7.1) on the paradoxically titled "Haven't Named it Yet," the last phrase of the solo starts on beat one of bar 26 and continues through to bar 31 (the end of the solo). Thus the phrase extends over six bars. There are eighth notes and quarter notes in the phrase.

Example 2.7.1: Haven't Named It Yet

2.7.2 "Flying Home" ("Homeward Bound") [Columbia matrix: WCO 26132-B, October 2, 1939]

In this version of the tune, recorded many times by Christian with Goodman, a phrase in the middle-eight, starting on bar 17 (Example 2.7.2) lasts for the whole eight bars. It includes eighth notes, quarter notes and triplets. It was quite common for Christian to use long phrases in the middle-eight, as Hansen (1998) has pointed out.

Example 2.7.2: Flying Home (Homeward Bound)

2.8 Irregular Phrase Length

A number of critics have commented upon Christian's phrasing. Lee (1996, 128) states

> His solos . . . are deceptively lyrical, since as one comes to know them one begins to perceive all manner of subtleties. His sense of cross rhythm and phrase structure, in particular are remarkable.

As with rhythm in general, there is, in the jazz literature, perhaps less discussion about phrase length than about motifs, formulas, and harmonic features of solos. Gridley (1978, 314) suggests that it was in the bop era that soloists started to play phrases of lengths other than two- or four-bars.

In his analysis of Lester Young's solos, Porter (1985, 76) observes that Young sometimes used phrases lasting an unusual number of bars—three, five, or six—rather than the more predictable two or four. It has been said (e.g., Ellison, 1959, 8) that Christian was influenced by Young, and we can speculate that this aspect of Young's phrasing accounted in part for this influence.

2.8.1 "Benny's Bugle" [Columbia matrix: CO 29030-1, November 7, 1940]

Spring (1980, 26–29) points out that Christian tended to use phrases of varying length and that often phrases did not match the length of the underlying harmonic structure. Phrases often extended over the transitions between changes in the harmony. He analyzes "Benny's Bugle" as an interesting example and contrasts it with a solo by Eddie Durham. Durham's phrases tend to last even numbers of bars (e.g., two or four), whereas Christian's are of odd numbers of bars and vary greatly in length. The phrases and the solo transcription are shown in Example 2.8.1.

Example 2.8.1: Benny's Bugle

Table 1 gives the start-points, end-points, and length of phrases in the solo. My analysis of phrases is a little different from Spring's, but the overall conclusion the same. Phrase one of the solo is three bars long. This is followed by a seven-bar phrase, extending to the end of bar 10. Chorus two starts with a single-bar phrase, followed by another, then a three-bar phrase, and finally an eight-bar phrase. The last phrase, described by Spring:

> starts on beat three of measure three and continues almost right to the end of the 12 measures with only a few resting places along the way (112).

Clearly, these phrases extend over the harmonic changes of the composition.

2.8.2 "I Found a New Baby" [Columbia matrix : CO 29514-1, January 15, 1941]

The solo on the first take of this studio recording shows great variation in phrase length. In the bridge, there is a single long phrase, which begins at the first bar of the section and continues until its last bar (bar 24). There are three other "long" phrases (between four and six bars length). Table 2

Chorus	Phrase	Length (entire bars)	Start and end bars
1	1	3	1-3
1	2	7	4-10
2	3	1	1
2	4	1	2-3
2	5	3	3-5
2	6	8	5-12

Table 1: Phrase structure in "Benny's Bugle"

Phrase	Length (entire bars)	Start and end bars	Notes
1	2	1-2	
2	6	2-7	starts on 'weak' bar
3	1	8	
4	3	9-11	
5	5	12-16	starts on 'weak' bar
6	8	17-24	bridge
7	3	25-27	
8	4	28-31	starts on 'weak' bar
9	2	32-33	

Table 2: Phrase structure in "I Found a New Baby"

shows the position and lengths of phrases, also indicated by phrase marks in the transcription (Example 2.8.2).

Several of the phrases in this example contain eighth-note rests that create syncopation, instead of marking the end of the phrase. To illustrate how the syncopation does not mark the end of the phrase, Example 2.8.3 is

Example 2.8.2: I Found a New Baby

Dm

Example 2.8.3: I Found a New Baby (normalized version of phrase 2, first three bars)

shown in a "normalized" form. In this version, the contour and sequence of pitches are precisely the same as the original, and there are no rests.

In this section, we have been mainly concerned with the length of phrases. Of course, improvisers have many choices about how they phrase. They can vary where a phrase starts, where it ends, and how long it is. In the following section, let us turn to the positioning of phrases.

2.9 Hypermetric Displacement

Most of the types of metric displacement we have looked at so far work mainly at the level of the bar (what may be called a "surface" level). Waters (1997, 29) points out that there can be different levels of metric displacement, including one which works at the broader metric structure of a composition. For example, many "standards" have an AABA structure, with eight bars in each A or B section, and often four-bar sections within these. We can visualize these as in Figure 1, where each "bar" divided by a barline represents a four-bar section. In each section there are four whole notes corresponding to the four bars.

At a surface level, a phrase that starts on beat four of the bar may displace the meter of that bar. A solo can have features that produce a similar effect at this broader level. As a phrase may start on beat four and create surface level displacement, so a motif that occurs at bar four of the first A section, and is repeated in bar five of the section (shown in diagrammatic form in Figure 2), may create metric displacement at a higher level. Indeed there can be numerous hierarchical levels of metric displacement. For example, at a 4-bar level, a "hypermetric downbeat" will normally occur at

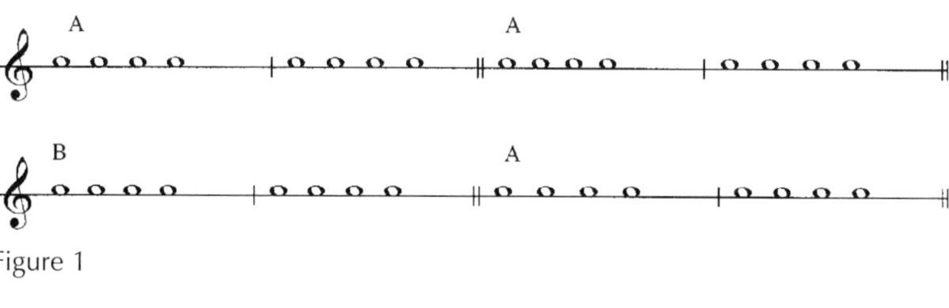

Figure 1

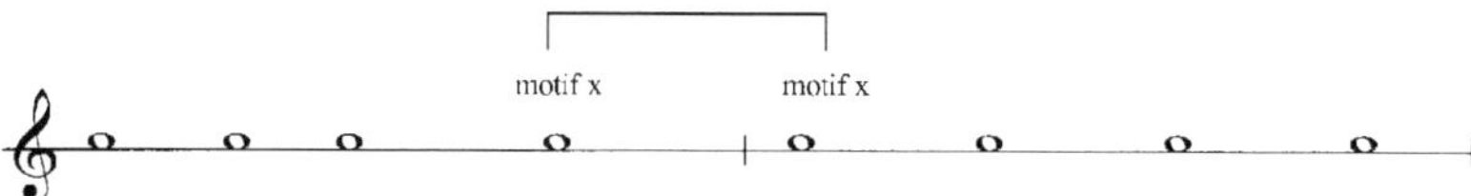

Figure 2

bars 1, 5, 9, etc. At a yet higher level, one can even regard a 32-bar composition as a single repeated "hypermeasure."

Waters identifies features like this in the solo of Herbie Hancock he analyzes. He describes, as I understand it, two ways in which a soloist can create this type of displacement. First, as in the example just cited, the soloist can leave a "strong" bar weak and start a phrase on a weak bar. This effect is reinforced if the pattern of a tacit strong bar followed by a phrase starting on a weak bar is repeated in the next section of the solo. Second, the soloist can play a motif on a "weak" bar and repeat the motif shortly after on a bar in the following section. The repetition sets up a pattern which bridges the structure of the composition. (Waters presents an example in Herbie Hancock's solo which demonstrates this effect: a motif played on bar 11 of a 12-bar blues repeated at bar 1 of the next chorus.)

It seems that this type of displacement was not an innovation of Hancock's era. Kernfield (1988, 88), in his discussion of "turning the rhythm (or beat) around" describes how Charlie Parker was said to be able to start playing at bar 11 of a 12-bar blues and create the illusion that he was starting at bar one. Collier (1988, 595) suggests that Christian placed his phrases so they did not align with the structure of the composition. Collier gives no examples, but Spring (1980, 26-29) in the analysis referred to in section 2.8, points out how some phrases in the "Benny's Bugle" solo do not match the position and length of the underlying harmonic structure and tend to extend over the changes in harmony.

So far I have not been able to find examples in Christian's solos of the precise types of hypermetric displacement described by Waters. In theory, it would be possible to search for such instances by computer. However, I believe that the way that Christian used phrases that started and ended in positions which conflicted with the underlying structure, as referred to by Spring and Collier, is a type of hypermetric displacement and is illustrated in the following examples.

2.9.1 "I Found a New Baby" [Columbia matrix: CO 29514-1, January 15, 1941]

We can return to this solo, already discussed in 2.8.2, to see one example of hypermetric displacement (Table 2). Phrase 5 starts on a "weak" bar, i.e., the last bar of the four-bar section at the beginning of the second eight (the second A section). The phrase in question extends over the boundary between the two four-bar sections of the A section (finishing at bar 16). Indeed phrase 8 on the same solo is placed in a similar way, since it starts on bar 28 (the last bar of the four-bar section of the third A section) and extends to the last but one bar of the chorus.

To reinforce a point made already, it can be argued that some phrases seem not to be displaced, even though they start just before the hypermetric downbeat. For example, consider phrase 5: bar 12, at the beginning of the phrase, sounds rather like a pick-up (anacrusis) to bar 13 (i.e., the regular hypermetric downbeat). Contrast phrase 8 with phrase 5. Phrase 8 starts in a similar position, i.e., one bar before the hypermetric downbeat, but *does* sound displaced. Surely the reason for the difference is that the pattern of notes in bar 28 of phrase 8 is echoed in bar 29 and thus bar 28 does not sound like a pick-up. Rather it sounds like the beginning of the phrase.

This is a subtle difference, and it would be quite complex for a computer program to detect such differences.

2.9.2 "Dinah" [aircheck: December 16, 1939]

One can see that the phrase shown in Example 2.9.2 begins just before the start of bar 28 and continues on to the end of bar 29. Thus the phrase spans the end of one 4-bar section and the start of the next (including a change of chord, from A-flat to Eb7, at the start of the second 4-bar passage of this, the final 8-bar section of the composition).

Example 2.9.2: Dinah

2.10 Phrase-ending Peculiarities

Collier has argued that bop soloists, and Christian in particular, tended to end phrases in unusual points in the bar.

> . . . the boppers . . . had a tendency to place the final eighth note of a fast figure on the second half of the fourth beat, instead of on the first beat of the

succeeding bar, a practice particularly evident in the work of Christian (Collier 1988, 596).

> . . . jazz players normally ended their figures on the first or especially third beat of a measure; Christian habitually ended on the second half of a beat, often the fourth beat, the weakest point in the measure (Collier 1981, 345).

I am not sure to what extent this specific way of ending phrases is peculiar to Christian. On the other hand, I suspect it was a characteristic of his style to end phrases rather unusually. It is more difficult to pin down exactly what these phrase endings have in common. Ending a phrase on a weak beat is perhaps not peculiar to Christian; it may be simply a feature of a more general idiom of playing. The value of the note with which the phrase ends could be more a peculiarity of Christian. In Collier's example (Example 2.10.1), the phrase ends on a dotted quarter-note, and perhaps it is partly because of this that the ending sounds rather unusual. Another possibility is that contour may play a role, for example, if a phrase peaks at its end.

Example 2.10.1: Seven Come Eleven

2.10.1 "Seven Come Eleven" [Columbia matrix: WCO 26286-A, November 22, 1939]

Collier (1981, 34) comments:

> "The . . . phrase begins at a peak in the middle of the second beat of the fourth measure, and runs through the next measure, ending on the fourth beat.

The long note with which the phrase ends perhaps gives a sense of pause rather than of completion that sometimes comes at the end of a phrase (Example 2.10.1). This impression is perhaps reinforced by the suspension created by the D-flat pitch against the A-flat harmony.

Example 2.10.2: Seven Come Eleven

2.10.2 Example 2.10.1: Seven Come Eleven"Seven Come Eleven" [aircheck: May 28, 1940]

In this radio broadcast of a tune that occurs many times in the Christian discography, we find a further example of a phrase ending on the fourth beat of the bar. On this occasion, the phrase begins at bar 21 and continues through bar 23 ending in a short note (an eighth note) (Example 2.10.2). One may also note that both bars 21 and 22 emphasize beat 4 through contour, duration, and repetition.

3. DISCUSSION AND CONCLUSIONS

The solos considered here are a small sample from Christian's complete output. I have highlighted only two examples of each device in this article. It would be useful to identify further examples of each to provide greater confidence that this analysis applies to Christian's work in general. Given that the total number of solos is not that great and that all are transcribed and available in digital format, it is quite feasible that a computer program could be written to automatically search out every example of each device outlined above. The only condition for this is that each device has been specified precisely enough for a search to be programmed. A similar condition applies to the definition of phrase. I believe these conditions have been met, and so such a search is in principle possible.

Our discussion has looked at individual aspects of solos in isolation, and as such has been rather artificial. Of course, in reality any single feature of a solo exists as a part of the whole solo and works within that larger context. We have not tried to explain the whole solo here; instead we have focused on small segments of solos.

I believe that the types of displacement outlined above go some of the way to explaining the sense of drive and interest created by the solos. However, they by no means provide a complete explanation. In particular, I feel there is much to do with contour in the solos and that we have only scratched the surface of that subject.

4. LPS AND CDS ON WHICH SOLOS CAN BE FOUND

Tables 3 and 4 give details of albums on which can be found the solos discussed above.

Example	Title	Date	Matrix (take)	CD issue(track/segment)	LP issue (disk/ track)
1.1	Good Enough to Keep (Air Mail Special)	March 13, 1941	CO 29943-2	CK 40846	CL 652
1.2	I Found a New Baby	January 15, 1941	CO 29514-1	CK 40846	
1.3	Benny's Bugle	November 7, 1940	CO 29030-1	JUCD 2013 (8f)	
2.1.1	Breakfast Feud	December 19, 1940	CO 29259-1	JUCD 2013 (9)	CL 652
2.1.2	Flying Home	October 2, 1939	WCO 26132-A	CK 45144	
2.2.1	Good Enough to Keep (Air Mail Special)	March 13, 1941	CO 29943-2	CK 40846	CL 652
2.2.2	Swing to Bop	May 12, 1941	(jam)	600135	
2.3.1	Flying Home	October 16, 1939	(aircheck)	MJCD 24 (17)	
2.3.2	The Sheik (of Araby)	April 26, 1940	(aircheck)	MJCD 40 (18)	
2.4.1	Ida, Sweet as Apple Cider	April 14, 1941	(aircheck)	VJC-1021-2	
2.4.2	Stompin' At the Savoy	May/June 1941	(jam)	600135	
2.5.1	Tea for Two	September 24, 1939	(jam)	ARCD 19168	G 30779

Table 3: CD and LP issues of music examples. Continues on next page.

Example	Title	Date	Matrix (take)	CD issue(track/segment)	LP issue (disk/ track)
2.5.2	Up on Teddy's Hill	May 1, 1941	(jam)	600135	
2.6.1	Breakfast Feud	January 15, 1941	CO 29512-4	JUCD 2013 (14)	G 30779 (D1)
2.6.2	Breakfast Feud	January 15 1941	CO-29512-3	JUCD 2013 (15)	
2.6.3	Shivers	December 20 1939	WCO-26354-A	CK 45144	
2.7.1	Haven't Named it Yet	October 12, 1939	BS-042942-1	AMSC 612	
2.7.2	Flying Home (Homeward Bound)	October 2, 1939	WCO 26132-B	MJCD 24 (8)	
2.8.1	Benny's Bugle	[see 1.3]			
2.8.2	I Found a New Baby	[see 1.2]			
2.8.3	I Found a New Baby	[see 1.2]			
2.9.1	I Found a New Baby	[see 1.2]			
2.9.2	Dinah	December 16, 1939	(aircheck)	VJC-1021-2	
2.10.1	Seven Come Eleven	November 22, 1939	WCO 26286-A	CK 40846	
2.10.2	Seven Come Eleven	May 28, 1940	(aircheck)	MJCD 40	

Table 3: concluded

Catalog no.	Title	Label
AMSC 612	Lionel Hampton All Star Sessions, v. 2	Avid
ArCD 19168	Something old, something new, something borrowed, something blue.	Arbors
CK 40846	Charlie Christian - The genius of the electric guitar	Columbia
CK 45144	The Benny Goodman Sextet featuring Charlie Christian	Columbia
JUCD 2013	Benny Goodman The rehearsal sessions 1940-1941 featuring Charlie Christian	Jazz Unlimited
MJCD 24	Charlie Christian Volume 1 1939	Masters of Jazz
MJCD 40	Charlie Christian Volume 3 1939-1940	Masters of Jazz
MJCD 74	Charlie Christian Volume 7 1941	Masters of Jazz
VJC-1021-2	Solo Flight Charlie Christian with the Benny Goodman sextet	Vintage Jazz Classics
600135	Charlie Christian/Dizzy Gillespie 1941 historical performances	Vogue
CL 652	Charlie Christian with the Benny Goodman Sextet and Orchestra	Columbia
G 30779	Solo Flight: The genius of Charlie Christian	Columbia

Table 4: Compact disks and LPs

REFERENCES

Arnold, Anita G. 1994. *Charlie and the Deuce.* Oklahoma City: Black Liberated Arts Center.

Avakian, Al, and Bob Prince. 1955. Notes to Columbia LP CL652, *Charlie Christian with the Benny Goodman Sextet and Orchestra.* Reprinted in Williams, Martin T., ed. 1980. *The Art Of Jazz: Ragtime To Bebop.* New York: DaCapo.

Ayeroff, Stan. 1979. *Charlie Christian.* New York: Consolidated Music.

Blesh, Rudi. 1971. *Combo: USA.* Philadelphia: Chilton. [Chapter: "Flying Home"].

Carriére, Claude. 1992. Notes to Masters of Jazz CD MJCD 24, *Charlie Christian Complete Edition:Vol 1.*

Collier, James L. 1981. *The Making of Jazz.* London: Macmillan.

———. 1988. "Jazz: Section V: Bop and Modern Jazz." In Kernfeld, Barry, ed. *New Grove Dictionary Of Jazz.* New York: Grove's Dictionaries of Music, pp. 595–596.

———. 1989. *Benny Goodman and The Swing Era.* London: Oxford University. Chs. 22, "The Sextet," and 20 "The Columbia Band," pp. 288–294, 262–267.

Downs, Clive G. 1993. "An Annotated Bibliography of Notated Charlie Christian Solos." *Annual Review of Jazz Studies* 6: 153–186. Published in updated, revised version on website Valdés (2000).

———. 2000. *A Charlie Christian Bibliography.* Published on website Valdés (2000).

Ellison, Ralph. 1959."The Charlie Christian Story." *Saturday Review* 41 (May 17, 1958): 42. Reprinted *Jazz Journal*, 12, no. 5 (1959).

Feather, Leonard. 1961. *The Book of Jazz.* London: The Jazz Book Club.

———. 1977. *Inside Jazz.* New York: Da Capo.

Finkelman, Jonathan. 1993. "Charlie Christian, Bebop, and the Recordings at Minton's." *Annual Review of Jazz Studies* 6: 187–204.

———. 1997. "Charlie Christian and the Role of Formulas in Jazz Improvisation." *Jazzforschung/Jazz Research 27:* 159–188.

Folio, Cynthia. 1995. "An Analysis of Polyrhythm in Selected Improvised Jazz Solos". In E. W. Marvin and R. Hermann. *Concert Music, Rock, and Jazz Since 1945: Essays and Analytical Studies.* Rochester, NY: University of Rochester.

Fox, Dan, ed. 1964, reprinted 1988. *The Art of the Jazz Guitar: Charley Christian.* New York: Regent Music.

Gridley, Mark C. 1978. *Jazz Styles.* Prentice-Hall.

Grosz, Marty, and Lawrence Cohn. 1980. *The Guitarists* (booklet and memo accompanying *Giants of Jazz* LP set.). Alexandria, Virginia: Time-Life.

Hammond, John. 1981. *John Hammond: On Record.* Harmondsworth: Penguin. Pp. 223–228, 231–233.

Hansen, Garry. 1998. *Charlie Christian: Legend of the Jazz Guitar.* Internet site: http://www3.nbnet.nb.ca/hansen/Charlie/

Kernfield, Barry. 1988. "Beat." In Kernfeld, ed. *New Grove Dictionary of Jazz*. New York: Grove's Dictionaries of Music.

——. 1995. *What to Listen for in Jazz*. New Haven: Yale University Press.

Kessel, Barney. 1982. "On Charlie Christian: Barney Kessel." *Guitar Player*, March 1982.

Lee, Edward. 1996. *Jazz: An Introduction*. Rev. ed. London: Kahn & Averill.

Marvin, Elizabeth West. 1995. "A Generalization of Contour Theory to Diverse Musical Spaces: Analytical Application to the Music of Dallapiccola and Stockhausen." In E. W. Marvin and R. Hermann. *Concert Music, Rock, And Jazz Since 1945: Essays and Analytical Studies*. Rochester, NY: University of Rochester.

McCarthy, Albert, Alun Morgan, Paul Oliver, and Max Harrison. 1968. *Jazz On Record: A Critical Guide to the First 50 Years: 1917–1967*. London: Hanover.

Owens, T. 1974. Charlie Parker: Techniques of Improvisation. Ph.D. diss., University of California at Los Angeles.

Porter, Lewis. 1985. *Lester Young*. Boston: Twayne.

Sadie, S., ed.. 1986. *The New Grove Dictionary of Music and Musicians*. London: Macmillan. (Vol. 14).

Sargeant, Winthrop. 1938, reprinted 1975. *Jazz: Hot and Hybrid*. New York: Da Capo.

Schuller, Gunther. 1989. *The Swing Era: The Development of Jazz, 1930–1945*. New York: Oxford University Press. Pp. 562–578.

Spring, Howard A. 1980. The Improvisational Style of Charlie Christian. MFA thesis. York University.

Valdés, Leo. 2000. *Solo Flight: The Charlie Christian Web Site*. Internet site: http://home.elp.rr.com/valdes/.

Waters, Keith 1997. "Blurring the Barline: Metric Displacement in the Piano Solos of Herbie Hancock." *Annual Review of Jazz Studies* 8: 19–37.

Williams, Martin. 1970. *Jazz Masters in Transition, 1957–69*. New York: Macmillan.

ACKNOWLEDGMENTS

I am most grateful to Leo Valdés for making available to me transcriptions of solos referred to above, and for his kind permission to use copies of sections of these in this article. A related paper, based on this research, was presented at the University of Jyväskylä Summer Jazz Conference, June 2000, in Jyväskylä, Finland. My thanks are due to those who kindly commented and made suggestions on an earlier draft of this paper and on my conference presentation: Christopher Beeston, Fabian Holt, Leo Valdés, Keith Waters, and Patrick Zemb.

Also I thank this journal's reviewers for their comments on the submitted draft. As ever, my grateful thanks go to Maureen Stallard, too.

SUPERIMPOSITION IN THE IMPROVISATIONS OF HERBIE HANCOCK

David Morgan

Jazz musicians have long been fascinated with making their improvised lines more chromatic, a tendency that intensified noticeably during the 1960s. At the time, some artists abandoned chord progressions and song forms as bases for improvisation and chose instead to use the motives, the modality, or even the feeling of the theme as a point of departure. This trend came to be known as avant-garde or free jazz. For those not ready to abandon these conventions, there were two options: expand the chromaticism of the song forms themselves or improvise more chromatically against the traditional diatonic structures. The first option resulted in jazz compositions that are tonal but not in a single key. From the second option came improvised lines that transcend the underlying harmonic framework. Superimposition is a significant method for creating such lines.

Superimposition is the technique by which an improviser plays a melody implying a chord, chord progression, or tonal center other than that being stated by the rhythm section. It has been identified as the primary means for achieving chromaticism in jazz after 1960.[1] It is an extension of the concept of substitution, the technique in which both the rhythm section and the soloist are working from the same alternate chord changes. Important innovators in the use of superimposition include the pianists Lennie Tristano, Paul Bley, McCoy Tyner, and Herbie Hancock. Hancock's pervasive use of superimposition while pianist for the Miles Davis Quintet from 1963 to 1968 contributed significantly to the increasing chromaticism and abstraction of Davis's music. The mid-1960s quintet of Davis, Hancock, Wayne Shorter on saxophone, Ron Carter on bass, and Tony Williams on drums is best known for its influential studio albums featuring original music, yet in live performance the quintet continued to rely on a small repertory of standards, blues, and Davis originals recorded by previous incarnations of the group. The recycling of this well-known repertory of standards invites comparison of Hancock's performances with those of his predecessors in Davis's band, especially Red Garland and Wynton Kelly, and their playing provides a context for Hancock's melodic vocabulary and its comprehension. The clear tonal and metrical structures of these selections make them ideal vehicles for both the application and perception of superimposition.

By the time Hancock joins the Davis band in 1963 he is a stellar hard bop pianist with several recordings under his belt and is emerging as an original voice, particularly in his handling of rhythm. His playing evolves significantly during his tenure with Davis. His comping becomes less dense and less active behind the other soloists, and left-hand comping and block chord techniques are gradually eliminated in his own solos. A decreased reliance on fast licks leads to a more deliberate melodic approach. This evolution was certainly facilitated to some extent by his colleagues. Tony Williams was a vocal proponent of free and nonformulaic improvisation, and recorded evidence suggests that Wayne Shorter's more advanced melodic ideas influenced Hancock. Davis himself takes some credit:

> . . . one time I told him that his chords were too thick, and he said, "Man, I don't know what to play some of the time." "Then Herbie, don't play nothing if you don't know what to play. You know, just let it go; you don't have to be playing all the time!" . . . that was the only thing I had to tell him, except to do it slow sometimes rather than so fast. And not to overplay; don't play nothing sometimes, even if you sit up there all night. Don't just play because you have eighty-eight keys to play.[2]

By his sophisticated use of superimposition Hancock clears a creative space for himself, working simultaneously with the vocabulary of mainstream jazz and the aesthetic principles of free jazz. While he generally maintains the integrity of the underlying song form in his solos, Hancock and his section mates disguise these forms to such an extent that the uninitiated may not recognize this relationship but rather experience the improvisations as free form. Bassist Buster Williams explains:

> Playing with Miles, I learned how to keep a structure in mind and play changes so loosely that you can play for some time without people knowing whether the structure is played or not, but then hit on certain points to indicate that you have been playing the structure all the time. When you hear those points being played, you just say, "Wow! It's like the Invisible Man. You see him here and then you don't. Then all of a sudden you see him over there and then you see him over here." And it indicates that it's been happening all the time.[3]

Hancock's freedom within the song forms can be construed as a critique of free jazz. A. B. Spellman reminds us that

> [Ornette] Coleman and [Cecil] Taylor were the first two musicians to appear on the scene during that time who placed themselves totally outside the mainstream and who had the temerity to suggest that all the assumptions of hard and cool bop would have to be overhauled and reassembled before the music could move forward.[4]

While Hancock's live recordings with Davis challenge mainstream assumptions as well, they also suggest that plenty of progress could still be made within the song forms. Throughout these performances the listener is confronted by passages in which the relationship of Hancock's improvised lines to the underlying harmony goes out of focus. The ubiquity of superimposition imposes a new set of demands on the listener, requiring complete familiarity with both the harmonic rhythm of the song forms and the melodic conventions of the jazz of the 1950s.

Hancock's solo on Cole Porter's "All of You" from *The Complete Live at the Plugged Nickel*, serves as the focus of this article.[5] A brief consideration of the structure of "All of You," Davis's transformation of it into a jazz vehicle, and a Red Garland improvisation over the form, is followed by analysis of Hancock's improvisation. The article concludes with additional examples of superimposition from Hancock improvisations, along with some thoughts on the significance of superimposition in Hancock's playing, which can serve as a filter through which we play, hear, and analyze jazz today.

"ALL OF YOU"

Cole Porter's "All of You" is a 32-bar ABA´C tune written for the 1955 Broadway show *Silk Stockings*.[6] Example 1 juxtaposes a transcription of the original cast recording version of the tune above a transcription of Davis's first recorded version of the tune.[7] Porter's original is a very attractive and well-constructed tune. Among the striking aspects of the melody are the recurring motive comprising an accented upper neighbor and its resolution in dotted half/quarter rhythm first heard in m. 1, the suggestion of mode mixture by the lowered sixth degree in mm. 3 and 19, and the gradual attainment of the climax in mm. 25–26.

The 1956 Davis version significantly transforms the original. Certain changes to harmony and voice leading are relevant to the forthcoming analysis. Root movement by fifth is more predominant in the new version; the upper-neighbor motive first heard in mm. 1–2, originally harmonized by tonic harmony embellished by an accented $^6_4$, is now harmonized by the stronger iiø7-V-I. The mode mixture of the original is more pervasive in

Example 1: "All of You" theme. Staves 1–2: Original cost recording (*Silk Stockings,* RCA, 1955); staves 3–4: Miles Davis rendition (*'Round About Midnight,* Columbia, 1956). *Continued on next page.*

Davis's version, including the use of iiø7 in many spots in the tune and Davis's lowering of the melody's C naturals to C flats in mm. 14–15. In contrast, Davis effects a satisfying harmonization in m. 7 by changing C♭ to C. In mm. 23–24, Davis's transformation of the melody's B♭s to C naturals provides a smoother preparation for the climax in mm. 25–26. Paul Chambers's bass line also alters the original. For example, in mm. 26–27

he resolves the raised fourth scale degree, A natural, up to B♭ instead of down to the original's G, thereby creating a more satisfying line while correcting the direct octaves of the original.

Red Garland's elegant solo in this 1956 version exemplifies the sort of formulaic improvisation typical of the mid-1950s.[8] Example 2 is a transcription of Garland's solo, which consists of two choruses over the form

Example 2: Red Garland's solo on "All of You" (*'Round About Midnight,* Columbia, 1956). *Continued on next page.*

of the tune followed by a sixteen-measure vamp. (For the sake of space and clarity only the improvised line is provided without left-hand comping and additional voices in the right hand. Note that slurs in the transcription not indicating ties or triplets mark voice-leading connections, and that circled noteheads identify thematic pitches. The chord symbols reflect the basic underlying harmony; symbols in parentheses are those suggested by the improvised line.) Garland paraphrases the theme extensively and his lines employ stepwise and arpeggiated motion with oc-

casional chromatic embellishment. Most noteworthy are the smooth linear connections when underlying chords change: sevenths resolve down to thirds of chords whose roots are a fifth away, and many of the voice-leading connections found in the theme are simply embellished in the solo.

Hancock's solo on "All of You," (Disc 3, Track 1, solo starts at 9:06), consists of three choruses over the form of the tune followed by a 132-measure vamp. Example 3 is a transcription of the right-hand lines over

Example 3: Herbie Hancock's solo on "All of You" (*Live at the Plugged Nickle,* December 22, 1965. *Continued on next two pages.*

the three choruses over the form. (Once again, slurs in the transcription not indicating ties or triplets mark voice-leading connections, and circled noteheads identify thematic pitches. Chord symbols above the staff reflect the basic underlying harmony, while chord symbols below the staff indicate upper-structure harmonies and progressions implied through superimposition.)

Example 3 *continued; concluded on next page.*

Listen to the recording a few times before referring to the transcription. If you are familiar enough with Porter's theme and with the bop style, you will notice that the relationship of Hancock's improvised lines to the underlying harmony fluctuates. If you are less experienced, you will probably hear the solo as a swinging free improvisation, loosely based in E♭, with coherence provided by motivic recurrence and development. Ideally, the solo

Example 3 *concluded.*

should be apprehended on both levels simultaneously. Hancock himself suggests that this is the point:

> what I was trying to do and what I feel they were trying to do was to combine—take all these influences that were happening to all of us at the time and amalgamate them, personalize them in such a way that when people were hearing us, they were hearing the avant-garde on one hand, and they were

> hearing the history of jazz that led up to it on the other hand—because Miles was that history. He was that link. We were sort of walking a tightrope with the kind of experimentation we were doing in music, not total experimentation, but we used to call it "controlled freedom."[9]

The solo contains a variety of uses of superimposition, including side slips, superimposition of bop formulas, superimposed quotation, the simultaneous superimposition of pitch and meter, and superimposed sequences of fragments and formulas. A "normal" version may often be inferred from a superimposed passage, and extensive listening to post-1960 jazz leads to the ability to hear superimposed material in terms of a normalized version. Where applicable, I will suggest a normalized version of superimposed passages. Keep in mind, however, that just as there are a number of possible superimposed versions of any given "normal" passage, there is often ambiguity about *the* normal version of a superimposed passage.

Side slipping is defined as a "half step up or down movement away from what is given melodically or harmonically."[10] The frequent application of this procedure makes the semitone the most common interval of superimposition. Side slips generally function as large-scale chromatic neighbors of the following inside material. Examples 4 and 5 demonstrate two instances of side slips in the solo, along with normalized versions of the passages. In Example 4, the arpeggiated A triad starting on the offbeat of two of m. 12

Example 4: Side slip, mm. 12–13

Example 5: Side slip, mm. 30–31

of the solo is a semitone lower than the underlying harmony, B♭7. Here, the prolonged A resolves to the pitch B♭ on the downbeat of m. 13. The passage beginning on the downbeat of m. 30 and going through beat three of m. 31, shown in Example 5, is a lengthier superimposition of A7 material over a B♭7 chord. The second half of the line can also be interpreted as a B♭7 altered scale, the seventh mode of C♭ melodic minor ascending, a common mode mixture in modern jazz. Side slips often suggest such dual harmonic interpretations. The side slip finally resolves to the pitch B♭ on the third beat of m. 31.

Bop and hard bop improvisers make extensive use of recurrent melodic ideas, often referred to as "formulas" or "licks." Hancock draws from this shared vocabulary as well, but often gives their presentation an ironic twist: he frequently undermines their harmonic implications by inserting them at pitch levels in conflict with the underlying progression. The solo contains several examples of this procedure.

Mm. 51–52 feature a ii-V-I formula of a type invaluable to the jazz improviser because it implies the tonal center so clearly. The primary characteristic of this formula, here in G major, is that it outlines the chromatic descent from the root of the supertonic chord, A, to its 7th, G, that resolves to the 3rd of the dominant, F#. Hancock contradicts the strong tonal implications of this formula by using it at the "wrong" pitch level. The formula implying Am7-D7 in G major is superimposed over the underlying progression Fø7-B♭7. The passage and a normalized version are shown in Example 6.

Example 6: Superimposed formula, mm. 51–52

Example 7, from the beginning of the third beat of m. 68 through the third beat of m. 69, shows the superimposition of another common ii-V-I formula. In this formula, here played in the key of G♭ major, the third degree of the supertonic seventh chord, C♭, is reinterpreted as the seventh of the dominant, and resolves to the third of the tonic, B♭. This ii-V-I formula is superimposed in the midst of a mixed-mode passage in E♭ major. The last note of the for-

Example 7: Superimposed formula, mm. 67–69

mula, B♭, is immediately reinterpreted as $\hat{5}$ in E♭ major, and in retrospect the D♭s and C♭s in m. 69 are heard as the characteristic mixture notes, #9 and ♭9, of the B♭7 chord. Such dual implications show how skillfully Hancock embeds his outside playing—often initially startling—within the established chord progression. The harmonic implications of this superimposition are not as extreme as the superimposition of G major material in the context of E♭ major, since G♭ major is the relative major of E♭ minor, the parent key of Fø7. Nonetheless, the passage from the beginning of m. 67 through the third beat of m. 69 clearly suggests G♭ major, not E♭ major or minor. Also of interest in this passage is the fact that the ii-V-I formula is rhythmically displaced, beginning and ending on the third beat rather that on downbeats.

Measures 21–22 contain yet another common formula, played here in the key of G major. This ii-V-I formula in G major includes a chromatic descent from the root of the supertonic chord, and is superimposed over the underlying iiø7-V-I progression in E♭ major. Perhaps Hancock's most brilliant stroke in these harmonically complex bars is that he embeds inside material within outside playing. Specifically, while playing in G major, he manages to preserve the thematic connection between $\check{4}$ and $\hat{3}$—circled G# and G— of the underlying E♭ major. This passage, along with a normalized version, is shown in Example 8.

Example 8: Superimposed formula, mm. 21–22

Despite the pervasive use of superimposition, or perhaps to balance it, Hancock paraphrases the theme throughout his solo. He is often very playful in his use of paraphrase, as at the beginning of his second chorus. In m. 33, the thematic pitch A♭ begins the second chorus on the offbeat of one, preceded by the thematic pick-up notes E♭, F, and G. Instead of resolving as expected to G, the A♭ ascends to A natural on the downbeat of m. 34. A natural is 5 of the D minor pentatonic traversed in m. 34. Jazz analysis would typically rationalize this as the #11 of the E♭ major chord and be done with it. In this context, however, the A natural is an especially striking dissonance, since its arrival defeats our assumption that the A♭ will resolve down to G as it does in the tune and as it does previously in this solo. Hancock's play on our expectation creates a new one, that the chromatic ascent begun by A♭-A will continue. It does, reaching B♭ on the downbeat of m. 36.

This B♭ marks the beginning of one of the most striking passages of superimposition in the solo. B♭, root of the underlying B♭7 chord in m. 36, serves simultaneously as the third of Hancock's superimposed G♭ major triad. The melodic formula initiated in m. 36 to express the G♭ triad is reiterated twice, each time transposed down a whole step, stopping on the D major triad traversed in the second half of m. 38. This D major triad "resolves" to the superimposed G major formula heard from the end of m. 39 through m. 40. The G-major segment might be heard as resolving another issue as well. The G5 on beat 4 of m. 40, while locally coming from the F♯ 5s of mm. 38–39, is also the long-lost G expected in m. 34 after A♭fi. Hancock even recalls the thematic A♭5 in m. 40 where the pitch functions briefly as a chromatic passing tone to G.

Initially, the superimposed triads in mm. 36–40 are heard as being inside, specifically as upper structure triads implying mixture.[11] The material in mm. 38–40, however, is dissonant against the underlying changes. Adding to the sense of progressive disorientation created in mm. 36–40 is the metric superimposition that layers 5/4 in the solo meter over the tune's established 4/4.[12]

Jazz musicians have long indulged in the practice of inserting quotations from other sources into their improvisations. The sources of these quotations range from common children's songs such as "Pop Goes the Weasel" to Stravinsky's ballet scores. Such quotations are generally meant to amuse while demonstrating the musical knowledge and mental agility of the improviser. Hancock takes the practice to the next level. From m. 25 through the middle of m. 27, Hancock quotes a very common phrase that is found, among other places, in both Tadd Dameron's "If You Could See

Me Now" and Miles Davis's "Four." In Hancock's superimposed version of the phrase, extended sequentially through the downbeat of m. 29, the chord changes implied by the quotation, although in the key of E♭, contradict the underlying chord changes at this section of "All of You." Example 9 juxtaposes the chord changes and melody from mm. 25–28 of the theme above Hancock's improvised line at the analogous place in the form, as well as the chord changes and melody from the analogous spot in the theme of "Four." The melodic pattern established in m. 25 is transposed by semitone with slight variations through m. 28. The resulting ascending chromatic line comprising downbeat pitches B♭-B-C-D♭ resolves to the thematic C natural on the downbeat of m. 29. This passage illustrates an important consequence of Hancock's superimposed sequences: they often create voice-leading strands that conflict with those suggested by the underlying changes, yet, as in m. 29, ultimately reconnect with the underlying structure.

Example 9: Superimposed quotation, mm. 25–28

Hancock's superimposed, sequential approach to the C in m. 29 is an example of what jazz musicians often refer to as "landmarks"—the process of connecting goals in their solos by means other than expressing each underlying chord along the way. The concept of landmarks is useful for explaining why superimposed sequences work not just internally but in the larger context of the solo. Frequently, Hancock's melodic sequences begin with a pattern that, as initially stated, is consonant with the underlying changes and even emphasizes thematic pitches. Subsequent transpositions of the model stray from the underlying progression, until the end of the sequence returns the line to inside material and its thematic goal pitch.

The passage from mm. 45–49 is an illustration. Hancock connects the thematic B♭ on the downbeat of m. 45 to the thematic A♭ in m. 49. Rather than follow the I-vi-ii-V progression prescribed by the underlying changes he reaches the same destination via a cycle of ascending minor thirds. In m.

45, a melodic formula, essentially the same as that heard in m. 25, is played in the tonic. It is transposed to outline G♭ major in m. 46, A major in m. 47, then C major in m. 48. This sequence creates voice-leading expectations independent of the underlying progression, but ultimately tied to it. That is, downbeat pitches B♭-D♭-E-G—the last three members of superimposed harmonies—form an E diminished seventh chord that resolves to the underlying Fø7 in m. 49.

"IF I WERE A BELL" AND "ON GREEN DOLPHIN STREET"

Two additional examples from the *Plugged Nickel* collection further demonstrate Hancock's fascination with superimposition and his uncanny ability to flow naturally between inside material and superimposed material while retaining a relationship to the underlying theme. A typically bold yet ultimately logical passage is the first half of his third chorus on "If I Were A Bell" (Disc 4, Track 1, solo begins at 8:26). Example 10 juxtaposes Hancock's improvised line above the underlying melody and harmony of the theme. Like mm. 45–48 of the "All of You" solo, this passage is based on a cycle of ascending minor thirds, but now at the level of the phrase rather than the single measure. The opening four measures of the chorus, mm. 65–66, simply paraphrase the opening line of the theme in the home key of F major. In the following four measures, mm. 69–72, the first line is restated transposed up a minor third. This line, which clearly suggests the key of A♭ major, is superimposed over the underlying changes in F major. A strong relationship to the theme is maintained, however, since the C on the downbeat of m. 69 of the solo corresponds to the prominent C on the downbeat of m. 5 of the theme. The line at mm. 73–74 continues the process of transposition by ascending minor third, resulting in a line that implies the key of C♭ major superimposed over the underlying F major tonality. A prominent thematic pitch is embedded into this line as well, as the B♭ on the offbeat of two in m. 74 recalls the B♭ of the theme. The improvised line over the first two beats of m. 76 finally implies the home key of F major, but at this point in the form the underlying harmony has begun tonicizing the relative minor, D minor, and the improvised line seems displaced from the previous measure. The line from beat three of m. 76 through beat one of m. 78 is a side slip a semitone below the underlying harmony, implying C# minor over the underlying D minor harmony of m. 77. The improvised line finally works its way back into agreement with the underlying changes at the A major chord of mm. 79–80.

Example 10: Hancock's solo on "If I Were a Bell," mm. 65–80

Example 11 is from the beginning of Hancock's solo on "On Green Dolphin Street" (Disc 5, Track 4, solo starts at 10:50). His improvised line from m. 3 through m. 12 implies harmonies a whole step above the underlying changes: F minor material is superimposed over the E♭mi7 in mm. 3–4, G over F7 in m. 5, Gb over E in m. 6 and F over E♭MA7 in mm. 7–8. He continues superimposing F major material over the ii-V-I in Eb major in mm. 9–12. At mm. 13–15, where the underlying changes ascend by minor third to a ii-V-I in G♭ major, the improvised line simply slides up by semitone to provide *inside* G♭ major material. The motivic idea initiated in m. 7 continues in mm. 16-20, implying E Lydian material superimposed a semitone above the underlying E♭MA7 in mm. 17–18 and the E♭mi7 in mm. 19–20. The remainder of the chorus, mm. 21–32, consists of conventional bop material that fits the underlying changes.

Example 11: Hancock's solo on "On Green Dolphin Street," mm. 1–32

THE SIGNIFICANCE OF SUPERIMPOSITION

The types of superimposition in Hancock's improvisations—side slips, superimpositions of bop formulas, superimposed quotation, and superimposed sequences of fragments—are woven seamlessly through the fabric of thematic paraphrase and inside bop formulas, with meticulous attention to voice leading in both inside and outside material. Hancock synthesizes the conventional voice leading and thematic paraphrase heard in the improvisations of the previous generation of pianists like Garland and Kelly with new possibilities created by the incorporation of superimposition. In these improvisations we hear superimposed material skillfully connected to conventional inside lines, important details from the underlying progressions embedded into superimposed lines, thematic landmarks connected by superimposed sequences, and superimposition enhanced with rhythmic displacement. While remaining within the framework of the song forms, Hancock pushes the boundaries of tonality, testing his listener's abilities to understand longer-term voice-leading connections and maintain awareness of the underlying form.

Hancock's playing is, in a sense, a dialogue with seemingly opposing traditions. Many scholars have found that Henry Louis Gates's metaphor of signifyin(g) resonates with their own observations and intuitions about such dialogues in the process of jazz improvisation.[13] Robert Walser, for example, states that:

> the whole point of a jazz musician . . . playing a Tin Pan Alley pop song could be understood as his opportunity to signify on the melodic possibilities, formal conventions (such as the AABA plan of the 32-measure chorus), harmonic potentials, and previously performed versions of the original song.[14]

There is general agreement among both musicians and critics that jazz musicians need to have "roots," that they build upon the performances and recordings of their predecessors. For the jazz artist the issue centers on whether the tradition becomes the basis for innovation or remains simply an object of imitation. Gates addresses this issue when he differentiates between motivated and unmotivated signification. Motivated signification is critical, and actual parody, while unmotivated signification is homage, a pastiche.[15] Parody, according to Linda Hutcheon, "is one of the techniques of self-referentiality by which art reveals its awareness of the context-dependent nature of meaning, of the importance to signification of the circumstances surrounding any utterance."[16] Gates goes on to suggest that

> the most salient analogue for this unmotivated mode of revision in the broader black cultural tradition might be that between black jazz musicians who perform each other's standards on a joint album, not to critique these but to engage in refiguration as an act of homage. Such an instance, one of hundreds, is the relationship between two jazz greats on the album they made together, *Duke Ellington and John Coltrane*.[17]

He is not the only commentator to suggest that the signifying in jazz tends to be unmotivated. Hutcheon suggests that

> ironic "transcontextualization" is what distinguishes parody from pastiche or imitation. Modern jazz, for instance, is therfore probably not in itself parodic, though there do exist some parodies even in this, an art form that tends to takes itself very seriously.[18]

Hancock signifies on two seemingly contradictory traditions through his use of superimposition: he simultaneously pays homage to the mainstream tradition by borrowing its melodic clichés while parodying that tradition by displacing the same clichés tonally. Subjecting these archetypal formulas to tonal displacement shifts the focus of the improvisation from the licks themselves to the melody's constantly changing relationship to the harmonic background. Hancock is ultimately playing with and challenging the conventions of voice leading and tonality in general. By his ability to function within the parameters of mainstream jazz and free jazz simultaneously, especially his creation of new middleground voice-leading strands external to the underlying progression, Hancock broadens the range of technical and emotional possibilities of improvising on song forms.

There is to be found in these performances the foundation for an approach to improvisation that informs the ways in which we listen to and play jazz today. There is clearly an element of irony and self-awareness in Hancock's performances that is lacking in much of the jazz being recorded today, which has the surface characteristics of the jazz of the 1950s and 1960s, but is divorced from its original social and aesthetic context. While many of today's musicians are indeed very serious in their mission to recreate the past as a way of "preserving" it, hence engage in very little "ironic transcontextualization," others are continuing to explore the trails blazed in the 1960s. Thoughtful consideration of what Hancock and his peers were up to may enhance our capacity to appreciate the contributions of those improvisers of today who have assimilated the true lessons of the 1960s in developing their own voices.

NOTES

1. David Liebman, A Chromatic Approach to Jazz Harmony and Melody (Germany: Advance, 1991).
2. Miles Davis with Quincy Trope, *Miles: The Autobiography* (New York: Simon and Schuster, 1989), 275.
3. Paul F. Berliner, *Thinking in Jazz: The Infinite Art of Improvisation* (Chicago and London: University of Chicago Press, 1994), 340.

4. A. B. Spellman, *Four Lives in the Bebop Business* (New York: Limelight Editions, 1985), xi.
5. Miles Davis, *The Complete Live at the Plugged Nickel* (Sony CXK 66955, 1995). The *Plugged Nickel* collection is especially provocative because it contains all of the music played over the course of two nights—December 22 and 23, 1965—in a relaxed club setting in which the musicians are clearly willing to take more chances than in the studio or in concert.
6. Cole Porter, "All of You" (New York: Chappell and Co., 1954). *Silk Stockings*, Original Cast Recording (RCA 1102-2-RG, 1955).
7. Miles Davis, *'Round About Midnight* (Columbia CS 8649, Davis, 1956).
8. Other notable improvisations on "All of You" by pianists on Davis recordings include Wynton Kelly's solo from *In Person, Friday Night at the Blackhawk, Vol. 1* (Columbia CK 44257, 1961) and Hancock's solo from *The Complete Concert: 1964* (Columbia C2K 48821).
9. Berliner, 341.
10. Liebman, 173.
11. An upper structure triad is a major or minor triad stacked above a basic seventh chord, providing upper extensions above the basic chord tones. The resulting sonority generally suggests one of the modes of the three parent scales. For example, an upper structure major triad with a root a whole step above the root of the underlying dominant seventh chord—such as D/C7—provides the 9th, #11th, and 13th of the seventh chord. The resulting sonority, which can be abbreviated C7 USII, suggests Mode IV of G melodic minor ascending. An upper structure major triad whose root is a minor sixth above the root of the underlying dominant seventh—such as A♭/C7—provides the #9 and #5 of the seventh chord. The resulting C7 US♭6 suggests the C7 altered scale, Mode 7 of D♭ melodic minor ascending. Note that the chordal fifth is often omitted from the underlying seventh chord, especially if it contradicts the modal implications of the upper structure triad. The notion of upper structure triads provides a convenient shorthand to rather complex sonorities. For a detailed explanation of upper structure triads, see Mark Levine, *The Jazz Piano Book* (Petaluma, CA: Sher, 1989), 109–24.
12. See Keith Waters, "Blurring the Barline: Metric Displacement in the Piano Solos of Herbie Hancock," *Annual Review of Jazz Studies* 8 (1996): 19–37. Waters examines rhythmic displacement in Hancock's music using analytical strategies derived from the current music theory literature.
13. Henry Louis Gates Jr., *The Signifying Monkey: A Theory of African-American Literary Criticism* (New York: Oxford University Press, 1988). See Samuel A. Floyd Jr., "Ring Shout! Literary Studies, Historical Studies, and Black Music Inquiry," in *Black Music Research Journal* 11:2 (Fall 1991): 265–87; John P. Murphy, "Jazz Improvisation: The Joy of Influence," in *Black Perspectives in Music* 18.1: 2: 7–19; and Gary Tomlinson, "Cultural Dialogics and Jazz: A White Historian Signifies," in *Disciplining Music:*

Musicology and Its Canons, edited by Katherine Bergeron and Philip V. Bohlman (Chicago: University of Chicago Press, 1992), 64–94.

14. Robert Walser, "Out of Notes: Signification, Interpretation, and the Problem of Miles Davis," in *Jazz Among the Discourses*, edited by Krin Gabbard (Durham: Duke University Press, 1995): 165–88, 173.
15. Gates suggests that Ishmael Reed's *Mumbo Jumbo* is a parody of texts by Wright and Ellison and thus an example of motivated signifying, while Alice Walker's *The Color Purple*, which he interprets as an homage to Zora Neale Hurston, exemplifies unmotivated signifying (Gates, 217).
16. Linda Hutcheon, *A Theory of Parody* (New York: Methuen, 1985), 85.
17. Gates, xxvii.
18. Hutcheon, 12.

ELECTRIC MILES: A LOOK AT THE *IN A SILENT WAY* AND *ON THE CORNER* SESSIONS

Victor Svorinich

Between 1969 and 1975, Miles Davis went through the most productive period of his career. In no other seven-year span had he produced as many studio and live recordings. This was a time in Davis's career marked with experimentation and innovation. However, these directions were his most controversial and misunderstood.

Many of the uncertainties concerning Davis's work during this period derive from a lack of information associated with some of the sessions. In dates such as *In a Silent Way* and *On the Corner*, there was a considerable amount of postediting involved that limits the listener in hearing the entire performance. In fact, much of the music has never been released. Also, more commentary from the musicians would enable us to understand the processes better.

This paper seeks to provide resolution to some of the uncertainties regarding these two sessions. I present new information regarding the music, as well as session data associated with these dates. This information includes explanations from some of the musicians who collaborated with Davis in the making of *On the Corner*.

Another phase of Davis's career began as the end of the 1960s arrived. To many, this phase had been categorized as his "fusion" period. However, when listening to *In a Silent Way* and some of its predecessors, one can hear a gradual transformation. Although Davis introduced new elements and ideas that shaped this phase, it was not a revolution. The work he had done with the second "classic quintet" (1965–1968) up to the work on *In a Silent Way* was a period of evolution. There were even certain hints that suggested this phase had its roots in the late 1950s.

Although Davis's thoughts were constantly evolving, the *In a Silent Way* session featured new concepts and experiments. This study will not only examine some of these ideas but also try to get a better understanding of the entire session. Only a portion of the session has been available to the public. The master reels and other associated data provide a larger perspective and thus a better understanding of this session and some of the others of that particular era.

One of the largest influences in regards to the *In a Silent Way* session was keyboardist Josef Zawinul. Davis had first heard him in Cannonball Adderley's band: "I had heard Joe Zawinul playing electric piano on 'Mercy, Mercy, Mercy' with Cannonball Adderley, and I really liked the sound of the instrument and wanted it in my band" (Davis and Troupe 1989, 294). Davis had first used electric keyboards in late 1967 and during the *Miles in the Sky* and *Filles de Kilimanjaro* sessions in 1968. In addition to the electric piano, Zawinul's contributions as a composer significantly influenced *In a Silent Way*.

Zawinul's first recording session with Davis was on November 27, 1968. This session's work included Zawinul's compositions "Ascent," "Directions I," and "Directions II." Davis recalled, "I had called Joe Zawinul and told him to bring some music to the studio because I loved his compositions" (Davis and Troupe 1989, 294–95). About three months later, Zawinul assisted in the making of *In a Silent Way*.

Recorded on February 18, 1969, *In a Silent Way* had two earlier working titles. The first was "On The Corner," which was eventually used for an album in 1972. That title was also originally used for the song "Shhh/Peaceful." The second working title was "Mornin' Fast Train from Memphis to Harlem," which also was used for "Shhh/Peaceful." On session data sheets, that track title was also abbreviated as "Choo-Choo Train." By June 26, 1969, the album and song titles were finalized (Macero).

The session took approximately three hours. Two tracks, each approximately twenty minutes, appeared on the album. The first track, titled "Shhh/Peaceful," originally was approximately forty-six minutes long. The postproduction efforts of Teo Macero cut it down to eighteen minutes for the album version, which begins approximately four and a half minutes into "Shhh/Peaceful." The segment edited out is a loose jam that lays out the harmony and rhythmic texture for the upcoming solos. On the album, the piece starts with a D major chord presented by Zawinul (organ) and guitarist John McLaughlin. A pedal point bass line appears in D and the drums enter. This sets up an introduction passage with Herbie Hancock, Chick Corea, Zawinul, and McLaughlin playing freely over the underlying groove.

In the actual session, the jam starts with a four and a half minute opening segment. After this, a transitional passage appears, a part that returns after each solo. The passage starts with a seven-measure keyboard riff, suggesting F major, which repeats once (Example 1). Since there is no time signature on the original lead sheet, the composer's intention could have been for the riff to be played freely. When notated in time, the music

Example 1: "Shhh/Peaceful" by Miles Davis, transition

Example 2: "Shhh/Peaceful" transition

changes from 4/4 to 6/4 (m.4) to 5/4 (m.5) to 6/4 (m.6). After the riff, there is an eight-bar melody stated by Davis and McLaughlin (Example 2), which initiates a key change back to D; the jam then concludes with solos.

The album has Davis taking the first solo. Davis's solo was actually the last. In postproduction, it was placed first and then repeated at the end; in effect, it was actually repeated at the beginning. McLaughlin takes the first solo. As with the others, McLaughlin's solo on the session reel is the same as the album version. The only difference is an eighteen-second overdub just prior to his solo, which consists of a small segment of McLaughlin playing without drums behind him. The solo then proceeds into the next transitional passage at 7:53.

Wayne Shorter's solo is next, and then the transitional passage returns. This transition is the same as the previous ones with the exception of the guitar track being slightly raised in volume. The electric keyboard/guitar segment (as released on the album) comes next. It is a playful, interactive soloing sequence between McLaughlin and Corea with both soloists playing off each other freely.

The opening D major chord played by McLaughlin and Zawinul (organ) follows the keyboard/guitar solo, which is found on both the album and the session reels. The album version loops back to the beginning, and Davis's solo is repeated before the piece fades out. On the master reels, the transitional passage appears right after the opening D major chord; the introduction passage is performed; and Davis's solo is then presented for the first time.

The next track on the album is "In a Silent Way/It's About That Time." They are actually two different tracks that were pasted together during postproduction. On the album, "It's About That Time" is put in between two identical performances of "In a Silent Way."

"It's About That Time," a jam in F, also went through much postproduction editing. The most obvious is Davis's first solo, which is actually an excerpt from his second solo on the track. The excerpt can be found in measures 70–93 (or at 14:00–14:43).

Zawinul contributed "In a Silent Way" to the session. It is not certain whether he contributed to the writing of the edited transitional passage in "Shhh/Peaceful." Zawinul's composition had gone through various variations and rearrangements. Davis recalled:

> We changed what Joe had written on "In a Silent Way," cut down all the chords and took his melody and used that. I wanted to make the sound more like rock. In rehearsals, we had played it like Joe had written it, but it wasn't working for me because all the chords were cluttering it up (Davis and Troupe 1989, 294–95).

Two versions of "In a Silent Way" were recorded at that session. The unreleased version featured chord changes along with an underlying beat. These two elements gave the piece a bossa nova feel. A copyrighted lead sheet of "In a Silent Way" reveals the proposed chords (Example 3). Due to inaccessibility, it is not certain whether the chords in the bossa nova version are the same as on the lead sheet. Neither a copy of the track or the manuscript is available to the public. The song can only be heard on the original master reels.

The other version appeared on the record. As Davis noted, it is without chord changes. The melody is played freely over an E major chord. Similar to "Ascent," it is a tone poem that floats freely. Zawinul described "In a Silent Way" as "impressions of [his] days as a shepherd boy in Austria" (Zawinul 1971). It is likely that Davis had instructed the musicians to play the melody very freely since there is no underlying beat. (On the transcription, a 4/4 meter is included to suggest a general rhythm).

Example 3: "In a Silent Way" (1969) by Josef Zawinul

Example 4: "In a Silent Way" (1970), continued on next page

There is other evidence that suggests that the melody was written for a very loose, improvisational performance. Another version of "In a Silent Way," from Zawinul's album, *Zawinul*, was recorded on June 8, 1970 (Example 4). The melody is quite different than the version on *In a Silent Way*. The 1969 version has the melody being stated by McLaughlin, and then repeated by Shorter, then Davis. Each performance is nearly identical. The 1970 version has the melody being stated three times, all quite differently. In fact, all of the melodies stated are quite different than the 1969 version. The second melody also includes a short countermelody by flutist George Davis.

It can be argued that the three statements on the 1970 version could be heard as three separate sections. It is peculiar that though each section contained related phrases, none of them correspond to the original lead sheet. In fact, the chords do not match the chords on the lead sheet. Two conclusions could be

Example 4: concluded

made: the piece was reworked and Zawinul's (and, for that matter, Davis's) objective was for the piece to be played freely and open-mindedly.

On February 6, 1970, Davis recorded another version of "In a Silent Way," this time titled "Take It or Leave It" and credited to Zawinul (Example 5). According to Sony producer Bob Belden, it "is actually the middle section of 'In a Silent Way' [1970]" (Belden 1998, 138). There is quite a similarity to the middle section in Example 4), but it is not identical. Also, these tracks were recorded on completely different sessions. Nonetheless, there are enough similarities to validate the piece as another version of "In a Silent Way." As Belden pointed out, the closest rendition of "In a Silent Way" is the middle section of the 1970 version. The shape of both melodies is quite similar, especially from measure 5 until the end. Although the melody featured more ritardando in the 1970 version, the pitches are identical.

Example 5: "Take It or Leave It" (1970) by Josef Zawinul

Another revealing moment on "Take It or Leave It" is the remark Davis made at the end where he stated, "I wanna use that somewhere, Teo." Unfortunately, there is no evidence that Davis actually used the track els where. It was finally released as part of the *Bitches Brew* box set some thirty years later.

"In a Silent Way" has always been considered as one of the first "fusion" compositions. Davis recalled, "Today, many people consider Joe's tune a classic and the beginning of fusion. If I had left that tune the way Joe had it, I don't think it would have been praised the way it was after the album came out" (Davis and Troupe 1989, 294–95). Whether it resembles the traits of rock in any of its genres is another debated issue.

The session yielded two other pieces. One was a jam in B♭ titled "Ghetto Walk," which was actually recorded two days later, with Joe Chambers filling in for Tony Williams on drums. This song and "Shhh/Peaceful" were the tracks originally intended for the album. "Ghetto Walk" was finally cut out in favor of "In a Silent Way/It's About That Time" on June 26, 1969. It remains unreleased (Macero).

The other track is "Early Minor," a composition Zawinul brought to the February 20 session. A handwritten copy of the introduction still exists. It is a tone poem similar to "In a Silent Way" and other Zawinul compositions in which an extramusical idea serves to inspire the composition. However, it is not any type of variation of "In a Silent Way."

In a Silent Way was one of Davis's significant transitional phases. Aside from personnel and instrumentation changes, the actual music had changed. According to Belden:

> The momentum created by the quintet from *E.S.P.* to [*Filles de*] *Kilimanjaro* was to be satisfied in many ways. Some say *In a Silent Way* marked the beginning of the end for the "post-bop" tradition in jazz. Some pointed to the success of *Bitches Brew* (which was developed conceptually from 1967 onwards and was not a radical departure as it is often regarded) as a logical culmination (Belden 1997, 103).

In a Silent Way provided a key link between Davis's work with the quintet and his subsequent efforts: the idea of freedom. Although *In a Silent Way* sounded radical, many of its concepts were already being experimented with in his previous efforts. He had already been experimenting with vamps and open forms such as Shorter's "Masqualero" (1967) and his own "Country Son" (1968). He had previously used electric instruments on sessions such as *Filles de Kilimanjaro* (1968) and *Miles in the Sky* (1968). *In a Silent Way* evolved and expanded from these earlier concepts. The work on these sessions identified with the concept of freedom. He wanted to break down forms and chord progressions. He was searching for new methods of improvisation and new ways of expression. His explorations led to the record, *On the Corner*.

On the Corner has been one of Davis's most controversial albums. Bill Milkowski's first sentence in the compact disc liner notes states, " *On the Corner* offended and angered more people then any other album in Miles Davis's lengthy discography" (Milkowski 1993).

The purpose of this study is to look inside the music. It is not necessarily to reason with its controversy, but to consider it from an insider perspective. Much of the hostility associated with this album has come from critics and other outsiders whose criteria are based upon Davis's previous efforts and the trends of the era. Perhaps the most prolific of these critics is Stanley Crouch, who has been notoriously outspoken in respect to the later work of Davis. Among the most cited works of criticism is his article, "On the Corner: The Sellout of Miles Davis." If the title was not sufficient, he quoted the criticism Nietzche had given to Wagner as "the greatest example of self-violation in the history of art" (Crouch 1996, 898). Crouch's cynical view of *On the Corner* and other contemporary works by Davis in this article is primarily based upon contrasts to Davis's previous recordings.

Critics such as Crouch have taken the outsider perspective of judging and evaluating *On the Corner.* This is not to say that an outsider perspective cannot offer any insight, but it is also fruitful to evaluate the music through the minds of the musicians who had participated in it, in this case saxophonist David Liebman and, most particularly, Indian tabla player Badal Roy. Both of these musicians were young and inexperienced with the direction Davis was taking. It was not that they were outsiders in respect to music; both were trained musicians who had been performing for some time. In the case of Liebman, he had been exposed to jazz since he was a teenager. It is the fact that these musicians had never played with Davis before. From this standpoint, one can see how this music was perceived from outsiders working on the inside.

On the Corner was recorded on June 1 and 6, and July 7, 1972. One of the album's first controversies or misconceptions involved the instrumentation. It was first issued without any personnel credits. Davis's reasoning behind this was, "so now the critics have to say, 'What's this instrument, and what's this?' I told them [Columbia executives] not to put any instrumentation on" (Milkowski 1993). It is as though Davis knew the album would be panned. The personnel listing is still somewhat in question. When I asked Roy if the session producer, Teo Macero, played saxophone on the date (which is mentioned in the reissue liner notes), he mentioned that he did not, unless it was edited in afterward. When Liebman announced the lineup in *Downbeat*, Teo's name was not listed under the instrumentation (Morgenstern 1973).

In 2000, Bob Belden collected a more accurate account of the personnel. According to his research, sixteen musicians were used during the three sessions. Macero's name was not mentioned. The expanded roster includes sitarist Khalil Balakrishna, drummer Al Foster, and bass clarinetist Bennie Maupin (Belden 2000).

These sessions were part of yet another adventurous period in Davis's music. However the music is categorized, his vision had changed. He was listening to artists such as James Brown and Sly Stone; he was using more electric instrumentation such as electric keyboards and a wah-wah effect pedal for his trumpet; he was adding more and more musicians to his band, thus adding more and more textures; his ideas were growing.

This period in jazz (late 1960s to early 1970s) was also a changing scene. Rock and roll was in the American mainstream. Liebman noted, "The late sixties was the lowest time for jazz. We weren't thinking about getting work, but it was like, this was a place where we can take a place." Younger jazz musicians tried to incorporate much of the rock scene into their music. "When you're young, you want to be contemporary. You want to be 'now', and rock 'n' roll beat with jazz improvisation over it was now" (Liebman 1999). As Liebman (who was born in September 1946) pointed out, the jazz scene was changing. "Because of the gigs, it was happening whether you liked it or not" (Liebman 1999). Although Davis (born in 1926) was not as young as Liebman, he was always contemporary, as was the music of *On the Corner*.

Davis's modern musical approach had branched out to reach a younger audience. "I really made an effort to get my music over to young black people. They were the ones who buy records and come to concerts, and I started thinking about building an audience for the future" (Davis and Troupe 1989, 324). It is unclear whether or not he really was trying to reach a black audience. As even Davis had stated, "I have gotten a lot of young white people coming to my concerts after *Bitches Brew*" (Davis and Troupe 1989, 324). Davis played concert halls such as The Fillmore (East and West) that had a predominantly white audience. Both Liebman and Roy have mixed feelings about this issue as well. Liebman argued, "I don't think he reached any black audience." When I raised the question to Roy, he simply stated, "honestly, no" (Liebman 1999; Roy 2000).

It is even unclear if Davis was trying to reach any audience at all. When asked if he needed his audience Davis reacted, "They need me!" He was also asked how he felt about playing for black audiences. "They can take it or leave it" (Davis 1974).

Whatever Davis's motives were, the music was new and challenging. Liebman felt that *On the Corner* and other jazz efforts at the time "had an artistic thrust to it" (Liebman 1999). The music Liebman made with Davis (as well as his own groups) was more challenging than rock and roll. It was more about interaction, improvisation, and complex rhythms:

> With the sophistication of rhythms, divisions of rhythms, that a jazz drummer or bass player could do were *way, way* beyond what a rock musician would do. And harmonically, it's not even the same discussion. . . . In the vamps we would go into different keys and be more chromatic, and dress up the chords a little bit . . . [You had to] keep that kind of funky rhythm going. . . . Once you gave that beat up, you weren't being true to the music. The whole thing was the beat (Liebman 1999).

Along with the soloists, everything was improvised. There were no music charts during the session. When I asked Roy about the rhythms and if they were patterns as the case with Indian classical musicians, he stated:

> [They were] totally improvised from my mind. Even at this time, when we play Indian ten [time signature], one way of going that people have been

> doing for the last five thousand years, Indian sixteen, Indian seven is this way . . . but I made my own ten. I made my own groovy, funky ten. I made my own seven, my own nine (Roy 2000).

Roy was an interesting case in which an outsider had come to work on the inside. Roy came to this country in 1969 to pursue a doctorate in statistics. In order to support himself, he had taken various jobs in New York City:

> I used to play in an Indian restaurant in the downtown [Greenwich] Village, making fifteen dollars a night. Man, that was good money. I was working as a busboy making forty dollars a week. Here I am making fifteen dollars a night, six nights a week. John [McLaughlin] used to come and sit with me and play (Roy 1999).

Movie executives in that restaurant also spotted Roy. They asked him to perform five or ten minutes of Indian music with flutist Jeremy Steig in the Jimi Hendrix movie, *Rainbow Bridge.* After these two breaks, Roy found himself working in the studio with McLaughlin for the album *My Goal's Beyond* (1970), and later, *On the Corner*:

> I remember going to the studio fifteen, twenty days [all of his work with Davis]. Eventually, Teo [Macero] asked me, "would you like to join the band?" I said "sure." Even at that time, I wasn't that excited. I don't even hear what he wants to do. I wanted to do one thing in my mind; let me tune my drums, and do my groove. That's what Miles wanted. He didn't say what groove to play. He says, "play your thing. . . . Play like a nigger." And then I played whatever it is, funky four, eight or six, or whatever. I still remember one groove I started [sings a tabla groove in 8/8] . . . Herbie Hancock says, "oh, yeah," Boom. Miles pointed at me. Herbie started, McLaughlin, the whole band started. . . . I still remember we were playing for an *hour* (Roy 2000).

I asked Roy if he could elaborate on how Davis told him to "play like a nigger":

> He would not do much of rehearsals, and I am new to this country. . . . At that point, I did not even know the sound of a bass. . . . At that point, I couldn't even differentiate between a trumpet sound and a saxophone sound. . . . I did not know that Herbie Hancock was a superstar. I knew Miles was a superstar, but not Herbie Hancock or Jack DeJohnette (Roy 2000).

Jazz was not a large part of Indian life when Roy was growing up. Roy was brought up in Calcutta, and recalled that jazz shows were rare, unpopular events. "I remember when I was in high school . . . big band, Duke Ellington [came to perform]. Me and my brother were the only two Indian people sitting there with all these white guys sitting, even in India, like five hundred people there, all foreigners" (Roy 2000).

The idea that jazz did not have any particular influence on Roy brought an interesting perspective to the music on *On the Corner.* The music presented new aspects to the jazz world in which it combined ideas from different points of view. It was not following the generic formulas other artists were pursuing. Much of this output was classified as "fusion" and Davis's music (in particular, *On the Corner)* was being placed in this category. Liebman points out, "I couldn't call Miles 'fusion'. . . . Miles was more African-based, more . . . almost ethnic" (Liebman 1999). Many of the ideas Davis had incorporated were being heavily overused, thus flooding the market. As Liebman recalled, "As with everything, it gets to be too well known. It gets to be too common, watered down" (Liebman 1999).

Roy brought in a key element that made *On the Corner* sound fresh. It was this outsider approach that produced multiple elements in the music. When asked if there was something from his background that was incorporated in the music, Roy reflects:

> I felt one thing with the sound of tabla and the groove that I brought in. Miles definitely knew what to do with it. Definitely, I made him play differently. The whole band played differently (Roy 2000).

Roy's Indian background was quite different than other musicians working on this album. His training as a percussionist provided contrasts to the other members of the band, which made him work harder in order to associate with the music. When asked if he had ever played in musical forms such as vamps, he responded, "Nothing happened like that, no way near" (Roy 2000). Even the rhythmic patterns were not anything like the styles he had been used to. The only thing he was familiar with was Western scales and harmony (the tabla is a tuned instrument, thus making scales achievable):

> If Miles says, "tune your drum in A," I'd tune in A. . . . Even now, if I go to a gig, I take six drums. Especially with Ornette [Coleman], I bring *twelve* drums. If I see some kind of note changing, let's say my drum was in C, and C is really bothering the whole thing, I'll just play the bass drum. [I would] still groove with the bass drum. No tonal things coming out (Roy 2000).

For *On The Corner*, Roy was using major and minor scales and tuned his drums accordingly.

The tabla and other rhythmic instruments used in the session provided multiple colors (or timbres) that enhanced the harmonic vamp in the music. Without the various colors, the one- or two-chord vamp could become stale. As Liebman pointed out:

> Harmony becomes the least most important thing, and in this band, that's the case. In the sense, there are no direct harmonies. And a new element, at least new in its emphasis, would be color. So the element of harmony is less. And the music could become boring *if* you don't treat those elements just like you treat harmony (Liebman 1973).

Liebman has provided a key point that not only explains the function of the music but provides a possible link to its controversy. The idea of Davis abandoning the emphasis on harmony has given critics a view of oversimplification. In a *Downbeat* blindfold test, Stan Getz replied, "that music is worthless. It means nothing. There is no form, no content, and it barely swings. The soloists are playing a half tone below so it will sound modern, but there's nothing to build on or anything logical . . . nothing" (Getz 1973). Writer Bill Cole also commented on Davis's work of this period as "an insult to the intellect of the people" (Cole 1974, 165). This was a typical criticism of *On the Corner* and other Davis albums made at that time, when Davis was pursuing the less complicated ventures of rock music.

Of course, Davis knew harmony, but he was looking for different ways of making the music fresh. One of these ways was breaking down harmony and allowing more colors and new venues of improvisation. This was part of the concept behind Davis's earlier experiments such as modal jazz. Liebman added:

> When you go from chord to chord, say, your mind is made up for you by the tune, and that's something that's limiting and was explored for so many years . . . [but when you do not use chord changes] you have to treat other elements in a certain way, with the same kind of discretion and balance, like using a certain chord against a certain chord, you use a certain color against a certain color. And this is what Miles is such a *bitch* at, is being able to do that (Liebman 1973).

In addition to Liebman's description, color instruments also elaborated the harmony. In the case of instruments such as tabla and electric keyboards (of which Davis used three altogether on the session), there were instruments that produced both percussion and harmony.

Such people as Getz and Cole suggest that *On the Corner* was one big, disorganized clutter. In fact, Davis had specific visions with his band and communicated his leadership verbally, physically, and musically. In the case of Roy, he remembered, "[He] just pointed at me, the finger. Boom! You, Badal!" (Roy 2000). Liebman recalled verbal communication. "He'll talk to you, or sing something to you. He'll talk to you about the conception behind what you played or what you should play." Liebman also described musical communication towards the whole ensemble. "He always tells you to watch it, everybody should be keeping their eyes on it [a change in the music]. And when he's *playing,* not just when he's leading" (Liebman 1973).

Liebman and Roy had touched upon the idea of a working unit. It was not that the music was organized to spotlight Davis or any particular soloist. Davis was looking for a group sound, which explains why Davis did not play very much on the album. Liebman recalled:

> In order to control that tone and the tensions within it, what he actually does is he leads it, he actually brings it up and brings it down, just like a conductor does. He used to walk off the stage when he had a quintet because when he wasn't soloing there was nothing to do. Now he's up there leading the dynamics, in the sense of the rhythm section, because they are working as a *unit* now (Liebman 1973).

Along with his leadership and organization within the band, Davis's concepts in composition were well thought out. Davis had other outside inspirations such as European classical composition styles that were incorporated into the music. While working with composer Paul Buckmaster during the *On the Corner* sessions, Davis apparently became interested in J.S. Bach. Davis compared his use of unconventional melodic organization with the compositional style of Bach:

> The melody can be in the bass, or a drum sound, or just a sound. I may write something around a bass line. I may write something around a rhythm. . . . I always place the rhythm so it can be played three or four different ways. It's always three rhythms within one, and you can get some other ones in there too. It's almost like Bach. You know how Bach wrote (Chambers 1985, 244).

When Roy was looking back at the session he recalled having mixed reactions towards the outcome:

> I remember when it came out. I didn't even play it for two days. It just didn't hit me. I thought it was a cluttered sound. Honestly, after all these years, I feel *On the Corner* is a great CD. The fact that I can differentiate [the instruments]

> has given me so much pleasure. Everybody's playing so beautifully (Roy 1999).

Even in recent times, *On The Corner* has been given another listening. Like Roy, people have been discovering some of the many facets that make up the record. Columbia/Legacy rereleased the album under their "Columbia Jazz Masterpieces" collection in 1993 and released another edition in 2000.

For many, the album still remains a mystery. Again, the purpose of this study is not necessarily to justify the music, but to give the listener a perspective from the musicians who had worked on the inside. Solving some of these mysteries and presenting a firsthand account could perhaps allow many listeners to come to terms with the album on their own.

Davis's music from this period was very complex and challenging. Much of his work contained innovative and contemporary ideas that provoked controversy and confusion. However, both the *In a Silent Way* and *On the Corner* sessions present concepts familiar from Davis's previous recordings: that is, before *In a Silent Way* was recorded, we can find precursors of his ideas.

As mentioned, Davis had been experimenting with more open-formed harmonic structures since the late 1950s. He started with the use of modes (*Milestones*, *Kind of Blue*), which eventually led to the one-chord vamps in the late 1960s and early 1970s. Open forms allowed the band to become more focused on tone color and rhythm.

The rhythm section began to grow, and its role in the ensemble became more emphasized throughout the 1960s. Slower moving and more open themes in compositions such as Shorter's "Dolores" (1966) and "Nefertiti" (1967) allowed a more flexible role in accompaniment. The melodies are more fragmented, and there is plenty of space to allow the background to come forward.

Davis's quintet in the mid-1960s began to enlarge on April 12, 1967, with the addition of guitarist Joe Beck. This session, which produced "Circle in the Round," also featured various percussion instruments such as chimes and bells. The following year, Davis went into the studio with six other musicians including three keyboardists to record "Splash" (November 25), "Directions I and II," and "Ascent" (November 27).

Rather than striking out in a completely new direction, Davis was engaging in business as usual. He was constantly moving ahead. As Chick Corea recalled, ". . . like any musician who's moving on, it's always in a period of transition" (Grime 1979, 84). With diverse insights from new band members and other influences, Davis's music continued to expand.

REFERENCES

Belden, Bob. 1997. Liner notes from *The Complete Studio Recordings of the Miles Davis Quintet, 1965–June 1968.* Columbia/Legacy 67397.

———. 1998. Liner notes from *The Complete Bitches Brew Sessions.* Columbia/Legacy 65570.

———. 2000. Liner notes from *On the Corner* (CD). Columbia/Legacy 53579.

Chambers, Jack. 1985. *Milestones II: The Music and Times of Miles Davis Since 1960.* Toronto: University of Toronto Press.

Cole, Bill. 1974. *Miles Davis: A Musical Biography.* New York: William Morrow. 165.

Crouch, Stanley. 1996. On the Corner: The Sellout of Miles Davis. In *Reading Jazz,* edited by Robert Gottlieb. New York: Pantheon.

Davis, Miles. 1974. Interview by John Runcie. *Melody Maker.* September 7, 22.

Davis, Miles, and Quincy Troupe. 1989. *Miles: The Autobiography.* New York: Touchstone.

Getz, Stan. 1973. Blindfold test. *Downbeat* 40, no. 9 (May 10), 31.

Grime, Kitty. 1979. *Jazz at Ronnie Scott's.* London: Robert Hale.

Liebman, David. 1973. Interview by Larry Hicock. *Downbeat* 40, no. 16 (October 11): 16–17.

———. 1999. Telephone interview by the author, December 22.

Macero, Teo. Original session sheets and memorandums. Teo Macero Collection. New York Public Library (Library of the Performing Arts at Lincoln Center).

Milkowski, Bill. 1993. Liner notes from *On the Corner* (CD). Columbia/Legacy.

Morgenstern, Dan. 1973. At Last: Correct *On the Corner* Personnel. *Downbeat* 40, no. 8 (April 26): 9.

Roy, Badal. 1999. Interview by the author, December 14, East Brunswick, New Jersey.

———. 2000. Telephone interview by the author, April 10.

Zawinul, Josef. 1971. Liner notes from *Zawinul.* Atlantic.

A PHOTO GALLERY: PHOTOGRAPHS BY TAD HERSHORN

Tad Hershorn, archivist at the Institute of Jazz Studies since 1999, began taking photographs in his hometown of Dallas, Texas, in 1969. His work as appeared in such publications as *JazzTimes* and *Swing Journal*, and on record covers of such jazz figures as Ella Fitzgerald, Count Basie, and Dizzy Gillespie. He is currently completing his biography of jazz impresario, record producer, and civil rights activist Norman Granz.

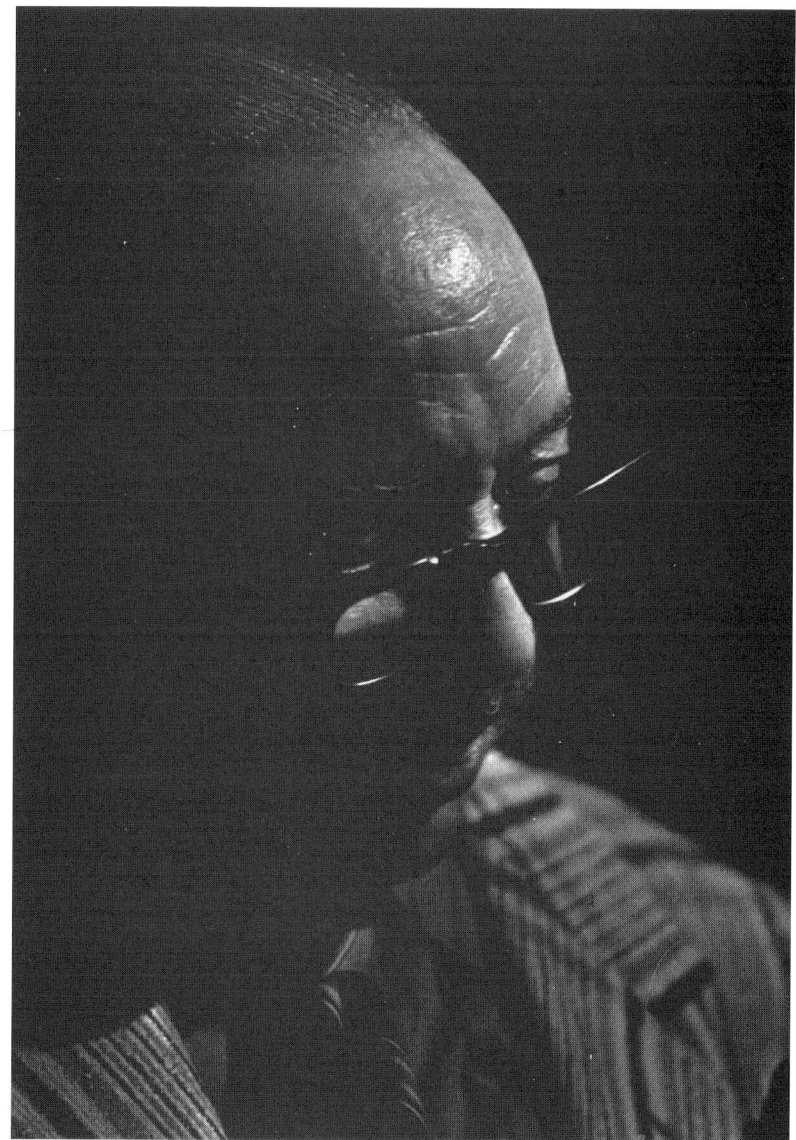

Red Garland, Dallas, Texas, 1979

Top: Miles Davis, Houston, 1990
Bottom left: Milt Jackson, Galveston, Texas, 1989
Bottom right: Jimmy Rowles, Los Angeles, 1986

Top: Ella Fitzgerald and Joe Pass, Houston, 1983
Bottom: Peggy Lee, Dallas, 1971

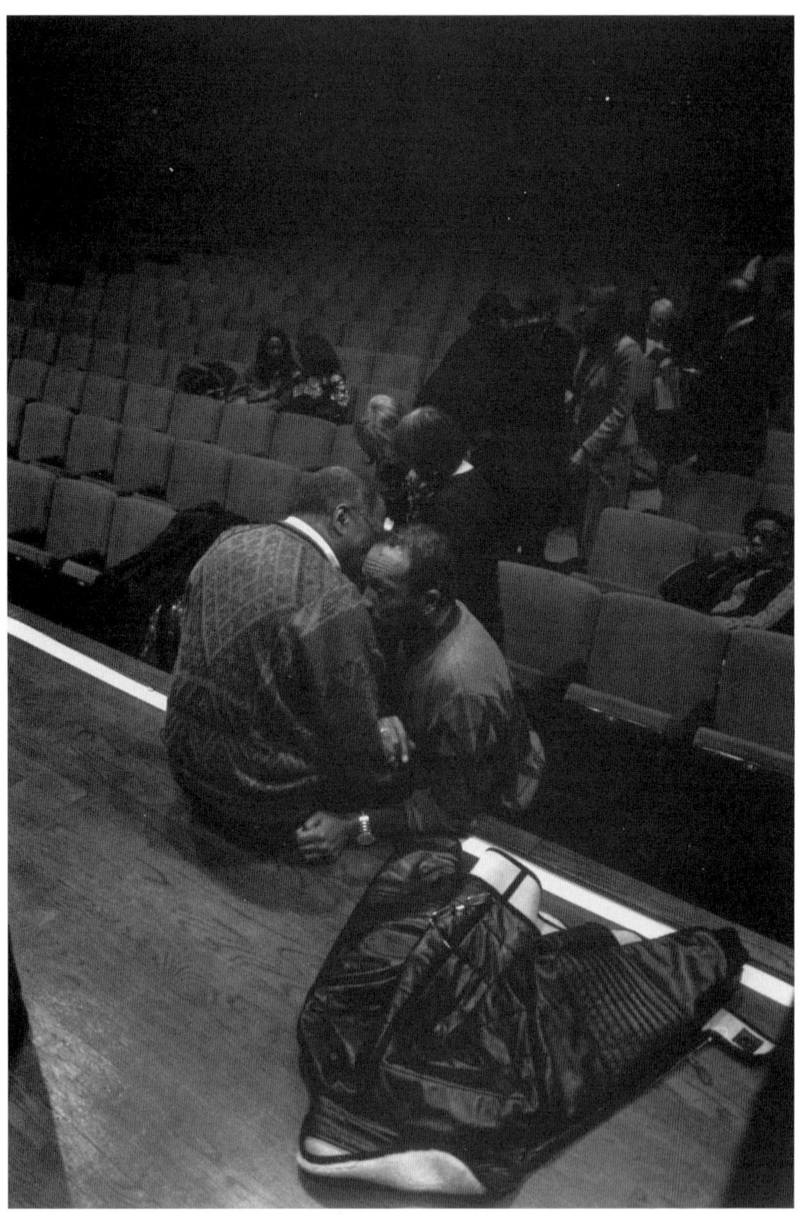

Clark Terry and Quincy Jones, New York, 1990

Upper left: Mel Tormé, Fort Worth, Texas, 1989
Upper right: Gato Barbieri, New York, 1990
Bottom: Gerald Wilson, The Hague, 1990

Top: Art Blakey, Stamford, Connecticut, 1989
Bottom: Norman Granz and Ella Fitzgerald, Dallas, 1980

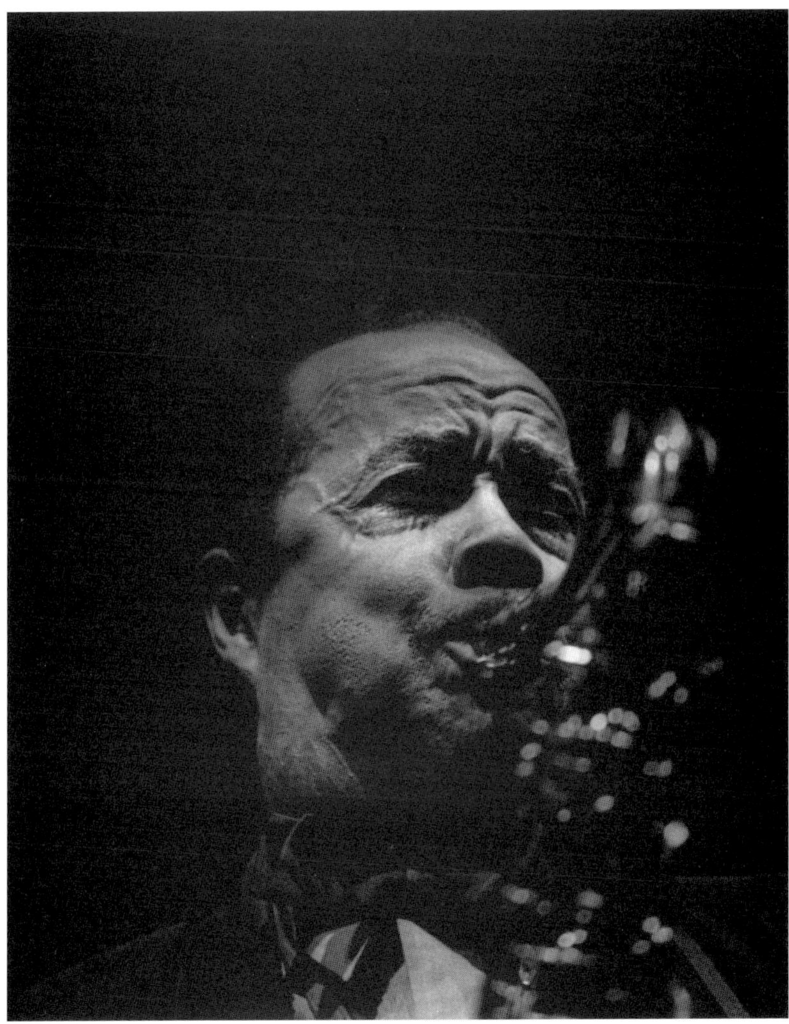

Buddy Tate, Sherman, Texas, 1979

Ray Charles, The Hague, 1990

Top: Count Basie, Dallas, 1980
Bottom: Stephane Grappelli, Houston, 1989

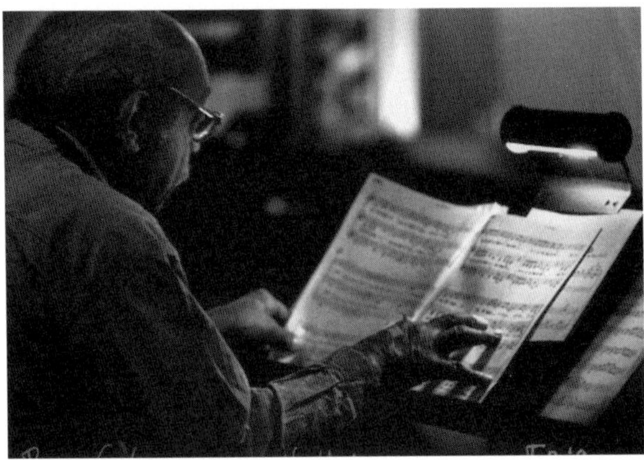

Top: Buster Smith and Jay McShann, Sherman, Texas, 1979
Bottom: Benny Carter, New York, 1990

Clark Terry, New Orleans, 1990

Top: Cab Calloway and Melissa Manchester, New York, 1990
Bottom left: Benny Goodman, Dallas, 1980
Bottom right: Wynton Marsalis and Doc Cheatham, New York, 1990

Top: Modern Jazz Quartet (l-r): John Lewis, Connie Kay, Milt Jackson, Percy Heath, Houston, 1988
Bottom: Sarah Vaughan, San Antonio, Texas, 1988

Top: Jim Hall, New York, 1990
Bottom: Dave McKenna, New York, 2000

Top left: Tommy Flanagan, New York, 1989
Top right: Dizzy Gillespie, Houston, 1991
Bottom right: James Moody, New York, 1990

Danny Barker, New Orleans, 1990

JAZZ FICTION: AN ANNOTATED BIBLIOGRAPHY

David Rife, with Ellen Caswell

Although the scholarship on jazz fiction lacks a work as comprehensive and authoritative as Sascha Feinstein's *A Bibliographic Guide to Jazz Poetry* (Westport, CT: Greenwood Press, 1998), two commendable annotated bibliographies provide a productive point of departure for both aficionados and scholars of the genre. Marcella Breton's "An Annotated Bibliography of Selected Jazz Short Stories" (*African American Review* 26: 299–306 [Summer 1992]) contains plot descriptions of 51 stories. Still more valuable are Richard N. Albert's fiction annotations (269 stories and 93 novels, as well as numerous dramatic pieces, anthologies, and criticisms) in his book-length study, *An Annotated Bibliography of Jazz Fiction and Jazz Fiction Criticism* (Westport, CT: Greenwood Press, 1996). The objectives of the present undertaking are to fill in some of the gaps in the earlier works, broaden their scope somewhat, and bring them up to date; readers will quickly note, for example, that much notable jazz fiction has appeared since Albert's 1996 study.

One brief cautionary note: for reasons too numerous (and tedious) to explain, the length of the entries that follow does not necessarily indicate their relative significance. In general—though not by any means always—we felt that the rarer or more obscure the jazz fiction, the more we should say about it, so that readers might determine whether trying to locate and possibly purchase the annotated item would be worthwhile.

We wish to acknowledge persons and institutions who have contributed to this study, from offering leads to often obscure jazz fiction to actually lending such works from their personal libraries; and from tracking down and borrowing items on interlibrary loan to providing funding for research. Thanks to all of the following for their many kindnesses:

Richard N. Albert, Robert Bomboy, Andrew Brown, David Cayer, John Clement, Sascha Feinstein, William Ford, Bill Moody, Luis Manuel, Dan Morgenstern, Arthur L. Newman, the Professional Development Grant Committee at Lycoming College, Thomas Simek, the Snowden Library staff at Lycoming College (especially Marlene Neece and Janet Hurlbert), and Sheran Swank.

JAZZ IN FICTION

Adams, Alice. *Listening to Billie*. New York: Knopf, 1978.

The protagonist, a young unmarried pregnant woman at first, is in a New York nightclub to hear Billie Holiday. The physical presence—and the music—of the great singer makes an indelible impression on the young woman and sets the tone (of sadness, loss, contingency) that characterizes the novel. The theme concerning the growth of a self is nicely realized here, and that alone goes far to negate and perhaps even triumph over the heavy losses the protagonist suffers in the course of a vividly experienced life that is still in mid-career at the end of the book. As in some of Billie Holiday's greatest songs, strength can flow from suffering and loss.

Albert, Richard N., ed. *From Blues to Bop*. Baton Rouge: Louisiana State University Press, 1990.

A sterling collection of short jazz fiction with an informative introduction. A reader with a deep interest in the subject could not do better than this and Breton's (q.v.) anthologies.

Allen, Steve. *Bop Fables*. New York: Simon and Schuster, 1955.

Four fairy tales "as they might be told by a 'progressive' musician." Allen wrote these, apparently, to edify adults so that they might understand what their jive-talking children were saying, and also because he found himself "amused by jazz language for its own sake." The retold fables are "Goldilocks and the Three Cool Bears," "Three Mixed-up Little Pigs," "Crazy Red Riding Hood," and "Jack and the Real Flip Beanstalk." To use the language of the fables, this book is "like the end, ya know?"

Anderson, Alston. "Dance of the Infidels." In *Lover Man*, 150–67. Garden City, NY: Doubleday, 1959; London: Cassell, 1959.

When the young black speaker encounters a man with his ear up to the juke box in a café, he knows he's found a soul brother—someone who loves the music as much as he. But when they get together to listen to their beloved jazz, the speaker discovers that Ronald is not only a piano player but also a dope addict. When they reunite in New York City sometime later (the story starts in the South), the speaker discovers the depth of and infers some of the reasons for Ronald's addiction. The story is named after a Clifford Brown composition. Other stories in this collection make passing reference to classic jazz artists, like Ellington and Earl "Fatha" Hines.

Angelou, Maya. "The Reunion." In *Confirmation: An Anthology of African American Women*, edited by Amiri Baraka and Amina Baraka, 54–58. New York: Morrow, 1983.

An often funny story in which black jazz pianist Philomena Jenkins encounters a white girl from her past, Beth Ann Baker, in a South Side Chicago club—in the company of a handsome black man no less! Beth Ann's family, it turns out, had employed Philomena's family down home in Georgia. Now Beth Ann wants to know how to handle her dilemma of wanting to marry a black man; when she says to Philomena, "He's mine. He belongs to me," Philomena tells her to go to hell and returns to the deep satisfaction of her status-free music.

Arrhenius, Peter. *The Penguin Quartet*. Minneapolis: Carolrhoda Books, 1998. [First published as *Pingvinkvartten*. Stockholm, Sweden: Bok Forlaget Natur och Kultur, 1996.]

An illustrated book for young children. Bored with watching over their soon-to-be-hatched eggs in the South Pole, four father penguins, all named after jazz greats (Herbie, Charlie, Miles, and Max), decide to form a jazz quartet and play the cool jazz clubs in New York City. They do just that, become a rapidfire success, but then rush home, happy to have undertaken their adventure but even happier to be back with their families.

Asher, Don. "The Barrier." In *Angel on My Shoulder: Stories*, 46–67. Santa Barbara, CA: Capra, 1985.

A white piano player catches the bebop bug in the 1950s and takes himself into the black worlds of New York and Boston in order to learn to swing—in short, to see if he can adopt the black qualities that will make him a first-rate jazz musician. After several years and setbacks, he is accepted by the hip blacks he plays with. He never makes it all the way to jazz distinction, but he gets close enough for self-respect. A well- and hiply told story with powerful musical content and provocative racial overtones. Asher is a professional jazz musician.

———. *The Electric Cotillion*. Garden City, NY: Doubleday, 1970.

Dedicated to Hampton Hawes and Jacki Byard with an epigraph quoting Dizzy Gillespie to Benny Carter, this novel limns the scruffy existence of Miles Davey[!], a lapsed Jew who wants to continue playing jazz in a world that has turned to rock 'n' roll. Reduced to playing in a band-for-hire, Davey humiliates himself by performing for events like a gay costume ball. He soon falls into a relationship with a teenager from Utah (he's 40) whose rock 'n' roll sensibility clashes with his serious jazz perspective. A breezy-flaky novel set in San Francisco in the late 1960s. Art Tatum makes a cameo appearance. Much booze and drugs.

Atkins, Ace. *Crossroad Blues: A Nick Travers Mystery.* New York: St. Martin's, 1998.

Former New Orleans Saint and current blues historian at Tulane University, Nick Travers becomes involved in a case related to the mysterious death of the legendary blues musician Robert Johnson and to the whereabouts of a rumored stash of Johnson's hitherto unheard recordings. The narrative shuttles among Memphis, Clarksdale (MS), and New Orleans—always with an emphasis on the blues and its history—as the past is called upon to unriddle the mystery in the present.

———. *Leavin' Trunk Blues: A Nick Travers Mystery*. New York: Thomas Dunne Books, 2000.

The second in the series of mysteries featuring Nick Travers, the New Orleans blues historian. In this case, Nick travels north to Chicago during the frigid Christmas season in an effort to get to the bottom of the mystery surrounding the murder of blues producer Billy Lyons that sent his lover and accused killer (one of the greatest blues singers in the history of a great blues town) to prison forty years earlier. A very gritty, atmospheric novel steeped in the blues and saturated with violence. If this series is any indication, you have not only to be persistent but tough as nails to be a blues historian.

Austin, Alex. "Dancers." In *Jazz Parody (Anthology of Jazz Fiction)*, edited by Charles Harvey, 21–26. London: Spearman Publishers, 1948.

An end-of-the-world fantasy in which a "she" ends up dancing with a "he." Although the musical references are to jazz and blues, they could as easily have been to the polka and minuet.

Austin, William A. *Commit the Sins*. Chicago: Newsstand Library, 1961.

In this "Adult Reading" paperback original, tall, "slim hipped and flat chested" taxi driver Patricia Warren is frustratingly conflicted over her own sexuality. Although she is seriously attracted to one of her female passengers, she soon becomes equally attracted to Champ, a jazz trumpeter who "looks like people want jazz men to look . . . and acts like they want them to act . . ." The tension (if a pulp novel like this can be said to have tension) is generated by Pat's sexual quandary, which does have an unusual resolution. Despite the fact that much of the action takes place in Detroit jazz clubs in the late 1950s with jazz musicians as characters, the musical dimension of this story does not exude authenticity.

Avery, Robert. *Murder on the Downbeat*. New York: Mystery House, 1943.

A mystery that tries, sometimes successfully, to be breezy, after the fashion of Dashiell Hammett's Thin Man series. Recording company scout and jazz columnist, Malachy Bliss, presses himself into service as an amateur detective when first one and then another ranking jazz musician is murdered, and his girlfriend is jailed as a suspect. The milieu is the swing clubs in mid-town Manhattan and the after-hour joints in Harlem where musicians, both black and white, can go after work "to play honest, uninhibited jazz with the best musicians in the world." Good musical description toward the beginning.

Baird, Jack. *Hot, Sweet, and Blue*. New York: Gold Medal, 1956.

Growing up in Pittsburgh on the wrong side of the tracks with a drunken musician father, Johnny Burke yearns to play jazz; after acquiring a cornet at a pawn shop, Johnny takes lessons and eventually becomes the leader of the best jazz band in town. He falls in love with a black singer, Lily, and the two of them make beautiful music together, literally and metaphorically, but their love is not strong enough to overcome racial barriers. All the stereotypical trappings of the jazz life are here: booze, sex, violence, etc.

Baker, Dorothy. "The Jazz Sonata." *Coronet*, April 1, 1937, 27–32.

Hilda Means had been famous in Montana as an interpreter of Liszt and as a music teacher, but the stakes are higher here in New York as she prepares to give a Beethoven recital and the pressure is getting to her. Enter Archie Grove, jazz pianist, who comforts her in unexpected ways, while demonstrating that music is music, whether by Jelly Roll Morton or Mozart.

———. "Keeley Street Blues." In *O.Henry Memorial Award: Prize Stories of 1939*, 65–76. New York: Doubleday, Doran, 1939.

Geraldine Evans has a plan to get out of the delinquent's home where she was sent by mistake. She will win the twenty-five dollar prize at the Bijou Theater's amateur night for singing "I've Got a Right to Sing the Blues." Then she will surely get an audition with her idol, Duke Ellington, who will hire her on the spot. The trouble is, the audience proclaims an off-key blonde the winner, leaving Geraldine doubting that her dream will ever come true.

———. "They Called It Swing." In *My Favorite Stories*, edited by Maureen Daly, 119–35. New York: Dodd, Mead, 1948.

In this section from *Young Man With a Horn* (q.v.), Rick Martin has begun to make a name for himself and is about to have the opportunity to make the big time.

———. *Young Man with a Horn*. New York: Houghton Mifflin, 1938.

The author claims that this novel was inspired by the music—but not the life—of Bix Beiderbecke. It is yet another bildungsroman, this time a portrait of the Artist as a Young Man Who Didn't Live Very Long at All. Rick Martin is an outsider; he has no family to speak of and no education but a real feel for music and improvisation. In fact, a central conflict involves his powerful desire to improvise while being restricted to the big band charts. Rick is the prototype of the self-destructive jazz hero of the kind who achieves apotheosis a few years later in the life and legend of Charlie Parker. Although this was the first "important" jazz novel and remains the most famous in the genre, its fame derives as much from a movie adaptation as its literary distinction.

Baldwin, James. *Another Country*. New York: Dial, 1962; London: Corgi, 1962.

A long, prosy novel that attempts to explore the issues of sex, gender, race, and identity. Apart from the fact that a central character, Rufus (who commits suicide early on), was once a promising jazz musician and his sister, Ida, is a fledgling singer, the book contains surprisingly little jazz content.

———. *If Beale Street Could Talk*. New York: Dial, 1974; London: Michael Joseph, 1974.

If Beale Street *could* talk, it would—astonishingly—have nothing to say about jazz!

———. "Sonny's Blues." *Partisan Review* 24: 327–58 (1957).

The most widely anthologized jazz story and still one of the best. Two brothers, separated by age and outlook, are poignantly brought together through the medium of the blues. Through music, the older, schoolteacher brother comes to understand Sonny's suffering and through that, the suffering of the black race. The description of the music in the transcendent moment when this occurs could not be better.

Ballenger, Walter. "Strand." *Chicago Review* 11 (2) (Summer 1957): 19–35.

Pork Chops plays his trombone wherever he can. He has no other life, no other name, no past, and certainly no future. When a young drummer acquaintance is beaten to death by a white man, Pork Chops goes to the viewing hoping to get some much-needed grub. While there, Pork Chops is accused by the deceased's mother of not having come to her son's aid—even though Pork Chops had not been present when her son was attacked. At story's end, Pork Chops is still hungry.

———. "When the Saints Go Marching In." *Chicago Review* 10 (4) (Winter 1957): 25–39.

Because his parents were social climbers and he was enthralled by Dixieland jazz, Park Cudahy ran away from home when he was eleven and never looked back. Now about fifty and living hand-to-mouth, he is astonished to discover that his parents had died, leaving him a mansion and $50,000. So Park leaves his Chicago gig and, in the company of musician friends, returns to his parental home in Ohio, where he and his fellow revelers threaten to throw the staid community into chaos with their loud music and socially unacceptable behavior. In the end, Park and company lead the town in a riotous march (to the strains of "The Saints") to the train station, where they prepare to return to Chicago, Park having covertly donated what was left of his fortune to the local college.

Bambara, Toni Cade. "Medley." In *The Sea Birds Are Still Alive: Collected Stories*, 103–24. New York: Random House, 1977.

A very funny, tartly told tale concerning the break-up between the speaker, Sweet Pea, and her live-in lover, Larry, a mediocre jazz musician but a fun lover. Their cavorting in the shower together evokes the making of music—specifically a jazz medley. Many jazz references, especially to bassists and singers.

———. "Mississippi Ham Rider." *The Massachusetts Review* (Summer 1964): 621–30.

Two representatives (one black, one white) for a New York recording company go south to try to coax old-time bluesman Ham Rider to come north with them to make some recordings. Badly in need of money, he agrees—but only on his own terms; a case of the exploiters getting a taste of their own medicine.

Bankier, William. "The Dog Who Hated Jazz." In *Ellery Queen's Prime Crimes*, edited by Eleanor Sullivan, 38–47. New York: Dial, 1983.

When blind pianist Joe Benson lands a gig at a piano bar, his jazz-hating dog has to be sequestered in the manager's office, whence he is instrumental in solving a mystery. When Joe is asked if he was conflicted by playing "Flying Home" on a Saturday night and "Harvest Home" on Sunday morning, he replies: "If God had meant us to create music only in church . . . he wouldn't have given us Art Tatum and Oscar Peterson."

Baraka, Amiri [LeRoi Jones]. "A Monk Story." *Brilliant Corners* 2 (Summer 1997): 57–60.

Months after attending Thelonious Monk's funeral, the speaker runs into the dead pianist on the streets of Newark.

———. "The Screamers." *Genesis West* 2 (5) (1963): 81–86.

When a group of jazz musicians follow their honking saxophonist leader outside the club where they are playing, the patrons follow them into the street creating, for a brief moment, the spirit of revolution. Many references to honking tenor saxophonists like Illinois Jacquet, all of whom are portrayed in mythic terms.

Barnes, Harper. *Blue Monday*. St. Louis: Patrice, 1991.

A young idealistic reporter with a love of jazz suspects that Bennie Moten's death during a tonsillectomy was really murder. He plays detective and solves the questions surrounding Moten's death. Set in Kansas City in 1935, the novel contains much about the interrelationships among the jazz scene, the Pendergast political machine, and racial issues. In addition to Moten, Lester Young, Ben Webster, and Count Basie (among others) make brief appearances. And, yes, there's a nice love affair too.

Barthelme, Donald. "The King of Jazz." *New Yorker*, February 7, 1977, 31–32.

An absurdist parody of a cutting contest between Hideo Yamaguchi, "The top trombone man in all of Japan," and the American king of jazz, Hokie Mokie, whose music generates "the real epiphanic glow." When Hideo wins, it seems like Hokie will lay down his horn for good, but then he enters into another contest with Hideo and wins back his crown—no King Emeritus for him, thank you!

Beardmore, Paul. *The Jazz Elephants*. London: Abacus, 1993.

Not seen.

Beaumont, Charles. "Black Country." *Playboy*, 1954. In *The Hunger and Other Stories*, 213–34. New York: Putnam, 1957.

Energetic story about legendary black trumpeter Spoof Collins and young white saxophonist Sonny Holmes, who takes over the band when Spoof dies and seems to *become* Spook, in his playing at least. Drummer Hushup Paige relates the story in appropriately rhythmic—i.e., jazzy—language. At the climax, as Sonny's horn speaks for Spoof, "The melody got lost, first off. Everything got lost, then, while the horn flew. It wasn't only jazz; it was the heart of jazz, and the insides, pulled out with the roots and held up for everybody to see; it was the blues that told the story of all the lonely cats and all the ugly whores who ever lived, blues that spoke-up for the loser lamping sunshine out of iron-gray bars and every hophead hooked and gone, for the bindlestiffs and the city slickers; for the country boys in Georgia shacks and the High Yellow hipsters in Chicago slums and the bootblacks on the corners and the fruits in New Orleans, a blues that spoke for all the lonely, sad and anxious downers who could never speak for themselves . . ."

———. "Night Ride." *Playboy*, 1957. In *The Howling Man*, edited by Roger Anker, 417–38. New York: Tom Doherty Associates (TOR), 1988.

A young pianist joins a band and plays with a depth of feeling seldom seen, making the octet (the Band of Angels) an outstanding group. Davey Green's remarkable ability is connected to the death of his young wife; he translates his grief into music. He meets another young woman, falls in love, gets engaged—and then the leader of the band ruins the relationship by claiming to have slept with Davey's fiancée, causing Davey to commit suicide, which creates a sense of loss among the other band members.

Biggie, Patrick. "St. Louis Blues." In *B Flat, Bebop, Scat*, edited by Chris Parker, 176–84. London: Quartet, 1986.

Through a chance encounter on a golf course in Cuba, a foreign service agent discovers that he and his wife occupy the former home of Thomas Lincoln McAndrews, a businessman and jazz connoisseur who had been forced to leave Cuba pretty much with his shirt on his back. While sorting through the household goods the McAndrewses had left behind, the new occupants of the house hear, mysteriously, the sad strains of Sidney Bechet's "St. Louis Blues" emanating from the house, leading the narrator to bend his diplomatic status to send McAndrews in Florida a couple of items, including McAndrews' treasured recording of "St. Louis Blues."

Bird, Brandon [George Evans and Kay Evans]. *Downbeat for a Dirge*. New York: Dodd, Mead, 1952.

Murder and mystery within the dance band milieu. Good descriptions of the mechanics of a band at work and of the travails of life on the road. The band sticks to the charts, playing some Stan Kenton kinds of things but leaving "goatee jazz to other bands."

Blaine, Laurence. *Sweet Street Blues*. Los Angeles: Holloway House, 1978.

After serving seven years in prison, Milton "Jazz" McGhee returns to the violent, drug-infested world of Detroit where he hopes to discover who had set him up and then to seek revenge. He is also hoping to come to terms with the phantoms from his past: his lost daughter, his lost sweetheart, his lost (and unknown) mother, and his lost dreams of becoming a ranking jazz musician. "Jazz" had been a hot musician who played sax and flute and also composed. There are inevitably some references to jazz and its "spiritual spontaneity," but the novel is marred by excessive violence, an unfocused narrative, and melodramatic coincidence. At the end, we learn that "Jazz" has been telling his story from a psychiatric hospital, where he has undergone seven years of counseling and rehabilitation. Not unlike a Donald Goines crime novel.

Blakemore, Charles. *The Subjective Truth*. Nashville: Winston-Derek, 1993.

Two boys, one black the other white, become best friends through their mutual love of jazz. The black pianist is an exceptional musician, and the white drummer is no slouch either. They form a band, move from Chicago to New York, and achieve considerable success; meanwhile, their lives start to spiral downward because of booze and drugs. The black, Jimmy, moves to Europe while his white buddy, Joe, returns to the Midwest where he embraces a very middle-class existence. At Jimmy's funeral, Joe has an epiphany concerning the roots of Jimmy's music—its subjective truth. Many jazz references to and cameo appearances by such musicians as Eric Dolphy, Thelonious Monk, Charlie Mingus, Duke Ellington, and Illinois Jacquet. Nevertheless . . . a very weak novel.

Blankfort, Michael. *Take the A Train*. New York: Dutton, 1978.

Almost all of the music in this book is contained in the title. The story involves the bonding relationship between a young Jewish man and an older black underworld figure from Harlem, where much of the narrative takes place right after World War II. There is some jazz in the background, but you have to use an ear trumpet to hear it.

Bloch, Robert. "Dig That Crazy Horse!" In *Ellery Queen's Awards: 12th Series*, edited by Ellery Queen, 81–98. New York: Simon and Schuster, 1957.

When he discovers that the drummer JoJo Jones and his band are coming to town, Professor Talmadge (who is secretly writing a book on jazz) excitedly calls his girlfriend Dorothy. They go to the club together. Later, Talmadge discovers that Dorothy has been hanging out at the club, has become friendly with Jones, and is talking like a jazz musician. Dorothy seems to have become addicted to Jones, and likely to heroin as well, for she mysteriously dies. Talmadge confronts Jones, with fatal results. Jones and his men are described in vampire-like terms in this tale of horror. Significant jazz content.

Bonnie, Fred. "Take a Seat, Not a Solo." In *Wide Load*, 65–86. Ontario, Canada: Oberon Press, 1987.

A Milquetoast harmonica player, Howard Metts, believes he can do great things with his harp, but is hampered by agoraphobia. But one night, in the company of friends and with the help of much beer, he sits in at the Blues Basin with Big Fredda and is a hit. During the second set, he is asked to do an encore; he attempts to do so, despite being drunk and in desperate need of the gentleman's room. Confusion—chaos—follows, he ends up in jail overnight, and plays his harp for the cops next morning.

Bontemps, Anna. *Lonesome Boy*. Boston: Houghton Mifflin, 1955.

A very short illustrated children's book about a young black boy who wants to become a musician.

Borneman, Ernest. *Tremolo*. New York and London: Harper, 1948.

The epigraph quotes Jelly Roll Morton on the relationship between tremolo and suspense. One of the first northern whites to catch on to

New Orleans-style jazz, Mike Sommerville gave up the jazz life to design and manufacture jazz instruments and settle down in an idyllic house with his picture-perfect family. But mysterious things begin to disrupt the household order, leading Mike and his wife Marge at first to suspect that their house is haunted and then that one or both of them are psychologically disturbed. Just as things reach breaking point, Mike solves the mystery, removes its source—his own mother!—and succeeds in restoring his world to its Edenic state. Solid jazz content with descriptions of musical sessions, many references to Dixieland notables, and a dog named Buddy Bolden.

Bourjaily, Vance. *The Great Fake Book*. New York: Weidenfeld and Nicolson, 1986.

A hodgepodge of literary techniques comprising letters, memos, calendar notations, journals, diaries, and a novel-within-a-novel, this book details Charles Mizzourin's quest to discover who his father really was. The father died thirty years earlier when the son was an infant, so Charles has to rely on those artifacts from the past that have survived. One of these is the "Great Fake Book," his father's lost diary that contains a contraband collection of musical phrases from which a jazz musician performs. It is in these sections of the novel that we find the fairly considerable jazz content.

Braly, Malcolm. *Shake Him Till He Rattles*. New York: Belmont, 1963.

A noir novel set in San Francisco. Bass sax player Lee Cabiness is stalked by a member of the narcotics squad whose obsession with Cabiness, we discover late in the novel, derives from his own addiction. The beatnik scene is well rendered, and there is a wonderful description of a cutting contest in which three saxophonists try to outdo each other. Frequent references to such jazz musicians as Cannonball Adderley, Charlie Parker, and Erroll Garner. Jazz musicians are referred to as "the original carriers of the Beat infection." The novel also touches on the persistent theme in jazz fiction of the artist-musician in pursuit of some indefinable aesthetic, possibly spiritual, goal.

Brand, Pat. "Headlines! Headlines!" In *Jazz Parody (Anthology of Jazz Fiction)*, edited by Charles Harvey, 5–20. London: Spearman Publishers, 1948.

One of the legends of early jazz, pianist Lonnie da Silva disappeared from the music scene twenty-five years ago, right after World War II, but has now been reported to be alive and well in South Wales, where he's been playing in a pub. A concert in London is arranged, but when Lonnie shows up to perform before 3,000 screaming jazz buffs, the result is unexpected.

Branham, R.V. "Chango Chingamadre, Dutchman, & Me." In *Full Spectrum 3*, edited by Lou Aronica, Amy Stout, and Betsy Mitchell, 380–92. New York: Foundation/Doubleday, 1991.

Bassist Mervyn Eichmann (M. E.—the "Me" of the title) relates this drug-drenched story about his attempt to save his buddy Chango, a bop drummer who was determined to sit in with the house band that night and play "secret music"—music in which no sound emanates from the instruments. The soundless music, beatnik ambiance, and fantasy mode of this story invite comparison to Thomas Pynchon's "Entropy" (q.v.). Several references to jazz musicians: Louis Armstrong, Charlie Parker, Miles Davis, and Dave Brubeck, to name a few.

Breton, Marcela, ed. *Hot and Cool: Jazz Short Stories*. New York: Plume, 1990.

An excellent, varied collection of many of the best jazz short stories with an informed introduction.

Brickman, Marshall. "What, Another Legend?" *New Yorker*, May 19, 1973: 32–33.

Purporting to be liner notes for an album in a Giants of Jazz series, this story spoofs the efforts of jazz historians who tirelessly exhume long forgotten "great" musicians. The "greatness" of this story's subject, 112-year-old Pootie Le Fleur, can be inferred from the deadpan statement that after Le Fleur played for James P. Johnson, Johnson "urged him to go to New York or any other city a thousand miles away."

Brossard, Chandler. *Who Walk in Darkness*. New York: New Directions, 1952; London: Lehman, 1952.

Set in New York's Greenwich Village not long after World War II, this novel focuses on several rootless and often jobless young acquaintances who seek to fill the void of their lives by hanging out in Harlem dance halls, participating in dope parties, and attending prize fights. The book employs considerable bop terminology and makes some references to jazz and jazz musicians, but generally speaking music is used as background accompaniment to the actions of the self-absorbed characters.

Brown, Beth. "Jazzman's Last Day." *The North American Review* 268 (1): 16–17 (1983).

An inventory of the banal facts of Jimmy "The Truth" Jackson's last day. Inspired by Lee Morgan, whose mistress shot him while he was performing on stage.

Brown, Carlton. *Brainstorm*. New York and Toronto: Farrar and Rinehart, 1944.

An almost clinical account of one man's mental deterioration with sporadic references to jazz.

Brown, Carter. *The Ever-Loving Blues*. New York: Signet, 1961. [First published as *Death of a Doll*.]

Hardboiled, wise-cracking private eye Danny Boyd is in Hollywood to find a missing woman who was last seen in the company of jazz folks. The jazz trumpet player is a boozer and is also on the needle and talks hep-cat talk; in short, he's a stereotype. Jazz in this mystery is pretty much window dressing; its function is to provide exotic appeal.

Brown, Frank London. "McDougal." *Phoenix Magazine*, Fall 1961, 32–33.

Trumpeter McDougal is the only white in a jazz combo. But because he's been beaten down by life and has a pregnant black wife and three brown children, he can play as soulfully as the rest.

———. "Singing Dinah's Song." In *Soon One Morning: New Writing by American Negroes, 1940–1962*, edited by Herbert Hill, 349–54. New York: Knopf, 1963.

A punch press operator, Daddy-O, deals with the assaultive noise and more generally his wretched life by singing amid the racket of the workplace. When the narrator asks Daddy-O what he is doing, Daddy-O says, "Baby, I'm singing Dinah's songs. Ain't that broad mellow?" After Daddy-O cracks up and is taken away, the speaker sings Dinah Washington songs in rhythm with his machine.

———. "A Way of Life." In *Music '59: Downbeat Fourth Annual Yearbook*, 66–67. Chicago: Maher, 1959.

The speaker and his dying friend, Charlie, are waiting for an ambulance while the guy in the next room plays Sonny Stitt's recording of "Old Folks" over and over. Although Charlie hated music, he didn't want to go to the hospital because Stitt "played so goddamned pretty."

Bunyan, Pat. *I Peddle Jazz*. Fresno: Saber, 1960. [First published as *The Big Blues*. Newsstand Library, 1958.]

Paul Parto, the trumpet-playing band leader and narrator of this rare novel, has a problem: how to manage a life that includes a wife and daughter; a common-law wife who has two children, a mother, and later a husband too; a day job as a journalist; a nocturnal career as a leader of a jazz combo; and a serious case of satyriasis which requires him (at 5'7", 145 pounds clearly the sexiest man on earth) to bed down every dame he encounters (usually several times per evening)—all of this while smoking and drinking incessantly. For most men this side of James Bond and Indiana Jones, such a life would be a stretch—but not for Priapic Paul, for whom—obviously—time expands to meet the need. What would probably have been called soft porn in its day would simply be called shlock today, as witness this typical passage: "I put my arms around her and we kissed. I felt her soft, sweaty flesh start to quiver as I became an octopus. Her breath got heavy. I pushed her up, turned out the light and pulled her over to the bed. I turned her towards me and crushed her in a passionate embrace, kissing, kissing, both of us making like savages. I pulled away and started to unzip her dress, my fingers impatient as hell, half-ripping, half-tearing it off. She unhooked her bra, and threw herself at me." And so on. Say what you will, they just don't write 'em like that anymore. Although the novel has a jazz focus and Paul claims to play from his soul, the music is overwhelmed by a surfeit of sex, violence, and decadence; in short, the book promotes many of the ugly stereotypes associated, from the beginning, with jazz.

Burnap, Campbell. "A Bit of a Scrape." In *B Flat, Bebop, Scat*, edited by Chris Parker, 72–92. London: Quartet, 1986.

Charlie Dunnicliff and three of his schoolmates become enamored of jazz and form an unofficial jazz society, sitting around and listening attentively to classical jazz 78s and discussing them and other matters related to the music. When they form a band of their own and are asked to play for the school dance, they are sure they are going to be ridiculed but then give a dazzling performance with Charlie outdoing himself on the washboard and winning the affection of his dream girl.

Cabbell, Edward J. "The Soul's Sting." *Phylon* 30 (4) (Winter 1969): 413–19 .

A saxophonist in a dance band in Harlem tells of a chance encounter with a young man who has recently come from the South, like the narrator himself four years earlier. The cycle will continue.

Carter, Charlotte. *Coq au Vin*. New York: Mysterious Press, 1999.

Nanette Hayes, the sassy heroine of this novel, plays sax on the streets of New York. In this second installment of a series, Nan returns to her beloved Paris to search for a missing relative. While there, she soon teams up with expatriate Andre, who plays jazz violin and is passionate about jazz history, especially as it relates to black American expatriates in Paris. Nan facetiously claims to be Django Reinhardt's illegitimate gypsy granddaughter. Many references to black musicians who sought refuge from racism in Paris.

——. *Drumsticks*. New York: Mysterious Press, 2000.

Sassy, sexy, saxophone-playing Nanette Hayes is back home in New York after a disastrous sojourn in Paris (see *Coq au Vin*) and her life is seriously on the skids until she buys a mojo doll from Harlem folk artist Ida Williams, which seems to turn her life around. When Nan lands a gig to play her sax in a trio, she comps Ida to opening night—but halfway through the first act, Ida is shot and killed, sending Nan on a case that is improbably (but enjoyably) complicated as it stretches across Manhattan (with a brief segue into Brooklyn) and involves a strikingly disparate cast of characters. As always in this series, jazz is prominent. For instance, this novel titles its chapters after jazz tunes, refers to Charlie Rouse in the first sentence, and is dedicated "To the Bennys: Carter, Golson, and Green. . . ."

———. "A Flower Is a Lovesome Thing." In *Blue Lightning*, edited by John Harvey, 7–20. London: Slow Dancer Press, 1998; Chester Springs, PA: Dufour Editions, 1999.

Four years ago Big Martha Little had made it big rather late in her professional life as second lead in an all-black Broadway revue; now she is scraping along as a nightclub singer specializing in Bessie Smith covers and Duke Ellington compositions. On the night of the story, we are in Martha's mind most of the time as she reflects on her broken-down life.

———. *Rhode Island Red*. London and New York: Serpent's Tail, 1997.

Amateur sleuth Nanette is doing OK playing her saxophone on the streets of New York, but her life changes radically when an undercover cop dies in her apartment. She enters into a passionate relationship with a mysterious man who wants Nan to teach him the essence of Charlie Parker, one of whose saxophones plays a major role in this breezy series mystery. Many references to jazz musicians; chapters are titled after tunes associated with Thelonious Monk: "I Mean You," "Nutty," "Rhythm-a-ning," and so forth. In fact, early on Nan says: "When it comes to the piano . . . it's Monk whom I have accepted as my personal savior. All that quirky, absent-minded professor, mad as a hatter, turn-everything-on-its head brand of genius. Oh, do I love that man."

Cartiér, Xam Wilson. *Be-Bop, Re-Bop*. New York: Ballantine, 1987.

The narrator is a black woman who recounts her life as a child growing up in St. Louis and later as a single mother on the West Coast. Her father had schooled her in jazz. The novel contains many references to jazz and blues notables and to the cultural significance of the music for blacks. Like *Muse-Echo Blues* (q.v.), it employs rhythmic, alliterative language, as if in an effort to emulate certain musical properties.

———. *Muse-Echo Blues*. New York: Harmony, 1991.

The narrator is a black female composer suffering composer-block, causing her to shuttle back and forth in time in search of her own identity. The story is dense with references to jazz artists.

Casey, Scott. *One More Time!* New York: Tower, 1965.

Dedicated to "George Probert, whose music inspired this book," this novel gets off to a rousing start as Cal Lewis (22-year-old white soprano saxophonist in an otherwise all-black combo led by his surrogate father Sully) first meets a femme fatale and then, after hours, gigs with Louis Armstrong. Cal's painfully complicated existence is made more so as he relinquishes his beloved Dixieland jazz to earn big bucks playing in a Lawrence Welk-like big band. Although the novel is centrally concerned with jazz, it devotes considerable time to sex, booze, dope, and race. One important character, Page Jackson, seems to be based on Charlie Parker.

Catling, Patrick Skene. *Jazz Jazz Jazz*. London: Blond and Briggs, 1980; New York: St. Martin's, 1981.

Thirteen-year-old Alan Poindexter, son of a prominent cotton-broker in the New Orleans of 1913, is introduced to jazz by his friend Moses, the descendant of slaves, and becomes entranced by this powerful new music. This novel dramatizes the relationship between these two young men and their travels at the same time that it chronicles the evolution of jazz history from its beginnings through bop.

Chappell, Fred. "Blue Drive." *Moments of Light*, 1982. In *Stories of the Modern South*, edited by Ben Forkner and Patrick Samway, S.J., 77–100. New York: Penguin, 1986.

When old-time bluesman Stovebolt Johnson reaches the place where he thinks he has a gig, he finds that its new owner has no time for an aged black guitarist. Nevertheless, he hangs out at the saloon, whose guests greatly enjoy "the best music in the world" (according to Stovepipe). Scattered references to blues musicians like B. B. King and John Lee Hooker.

Charters, Samuel. *Jelly Roll Morton's Last Night at the Jungle Inn: An Imaginary Memoir by Samuel Charters*. New York: Marion Boyars, 1984.

A researched story that mixes fact and fiction as it details certain highlights from the life of the egotistical Jelly Roll Morton, who here credits himself with having invented jazz.

Cliff, Michelle. "A Woman Who Plays Trumpet Is Deported." In *Bodies of Water*, 53–60. New York: Dutton, 1990.

Inspired by and dedicated to Valaida Snow, who escaped from a concentration camp, this story dramatizes the plight of an American black woman trumpeter in the 1930s who is forced (because of her color and instrument) to flee to Paris to practice her craft. When the club where she has a gig closes in 1940, she moves to Copenhagen before she is arrested and incarcerated by the army of occupation. The second paragraph effectively encapsulates the situation of the story: "A woman. A black woman. A black woman musician. A black woman musician who plays trumpet. A bitch who blows. A lady trumpet-player. A woman with chops."

Coggins, Mark. *The Immortal Game.* Berkeley: Poltroon Press, 1999.

After being hired to investigate a case involving advanced chess software theft, private eye August Riordan takes the reader on a wisecracking, action-packed ramble through San Francisco's kinky sex milieux, including S/M and bondage emporia. Riordan is very much the jazz buff: he prides himself on his collection of straightahead jazz recordings from the 1930s through the 1950s and even more on his hi-fi system made of components manufactured and sold before 1980, "before the introduction of digital recordings on CD ROM, and before stereo manufacturers started caring more about glitzy consoles with small footprints than they did about the quality of the sound." A purist, in other words. Riordan is also a semipro jazz bassist who lugs his cherished string bass wherever he can fill in on a gig. Chapter 10 ("in the key of g") contains solid descriptions of a jazz combo in action, in one of the very few clubs in the area that still cares about the music.

Cohen, Elaine. "Blevins' Blues." In *B Flat, Bebop, Scat*, edited by Chris Parker, 150–74. London: Quartet, 1986.

Dipsomaniacal trumpeter J. A. Blevins had apparently entered into a compact with the devil years ago: his soul in exchange for musical expertise. Now in his final hours, Blevins has a phantasmagorical experience, beginning with an encounter with a mouse in his seedy New York hotel room, moving to a bar where he encounters a senator from his past and a whore from his present, and ending with a conflagration and his mouse in flight. Not much music.

Cohen, Octavus. "Music Hath Charms." In *Dark Days and Black Knights*, 1–44. New York: Dodd, Mead, 1923.

A humorous story hinging on the comeuppance of a con man who claims to blow a mean horn when in fact he can neither read nor play a note.

Cohn, David L. "Black Troubador." In *A Caravan of Music Stories*, edited by Noah D. Fabricant and Heinz Werner, 247–53. New York: Frederick Fell, 1947.

Joe Moss is a three-harp black man who, "when he bears down hard on his two-bit harmonica . . . can make trouble leave your weary mind, set your tired feet to stomping, bring sweet Jesus to your back-sliding soul." And, according to him, his playing also causes men to shut their doors and send their women to the kitchen till Joe passes by.

Coleman, Wanda. "Jazz at Twelve." *Brilliant Corners* 5: 33–41 (Summer 2001).

Moonlighting songwriter Babe and her husband Kevin are out on the town to see the hot James Ditzi Quintet. The story comprises Babe's reflections on her personal life, on jazz, and on the music industry in general. The technique of the story is both unusual and effective as it recapitulates future events while recording action in the present. Much reference to narcotics.

Collier, James Lincoln. *The Jazz Kid*. New York: Henry Holt, 1994.

Intended for a juvenile audience, this novel dramatizes the story of teenager Paulie Horvath, who breaks from his blue collar parents in order to become a jazz musician in the Chicago of the 1920s. Many references to gangsters and jazz musicians of the time.

Conroy, Frank. *Body and Soul*. New York: Houghton Mifflin, 1993.

Yet another bildungsroman dramatizing the rise from obscurity to fame of Claude Rawlings, child prodigy of the piano growing up in Manhattan in the 1940s. Although the musical content generally focuses on the developments occurring in the new classical music of the times, it also contains a few resonant passages relating to jazz, especially to the music of Art Tatum and Charlie Parker. For instance, in one scene, as Claude and his mentor listen to a Parker recording, "The sharp sound of Parker's alto saxophone cut the air with a twisting, syncopated blues line, repeated after twelve bars. At the twenty-fifth bar two things happened: . . . the pianist . . . began to play the cycle of fifths based on Parker's bebop changes . . . and second, Claude began to play the twelve-tone composition he'd been working on all night." Claude's teacher soon realizes that "the two fit together harmonically, as if the bebop were accompaniment for the twelve-tone, or vice versa." And then, in Chapter 20 of this long novel, there is a scene in which Claude plays a jazz duet with another pianist in London, and the two experience an epiphanic moment as they spontaneously create an entirely new harmonic base while escaping tonality. Devotees of jazz fiction might welcome the recommendation to read this chapter and skip the rest.

Cook, Bruce. "Just a Gig." *Michigan's Voices.* Winter 1962: 13–23.

Family man Kelly receives a call from old friend Benny, who desperately needs Kelly to play trumpet that night. Kelly has been out of music for several years; first he was in detox, then he got married and had a child. Nevertheless, jazz is in his blood, so he joins Benny's group, performs well, has a terrifying experience, and returns to the bosom of his family, telling his wife that "It was just a gig."

Cortázar, Julio. *Hopscotch*. Translated by Gregory Rabassa. New York: Pantheon, 1966. [First published as *Rayuela*. Editorial Sudamericana Sociedad Anónima, 1963.]

A postmodernist novel recounting the astonishing adventures of Horacio Oliveira (an Argentinian writer living in Paris), his mistress, and their circle of bohemian friends. For the first nineteen chapters, this reads like the jazz novel to end all jazz novels, with constant reference to and provocative discussions of jazz and its musicians; after that, however, as the plot mechanics kick in, the musical content becomes sporadic.

———. "El Perseguidor." In *Las Armas Secretas*, 99–183. Buenos Aires: Sudamericana, 1959. Translated by Paul Blackburn as "The Pursuers." In *End of the Game and Other Stories*, 182–247. New York: Pantheon, 1967.

Dedicated to "Ch. P.," this novella dramatizes certain key events in Charlie Parker's last days. Many references to sex, dope, and booze. Much of the story's dramatic tension derives from discussions between Johnny Carter (the Parker figure) and Bruno, the narrator, a jazz critic who has recently published a biography of Carter; particularly at issue is the unbreachable disparity between what the artist tries to accomplish through his music and how this is (mis)interpreted by the critic. Johnny is the pursuer of the title, a quester after the ineffable, but so is the narrator a parasitic pursuer of Johnny and reflected glory. In short the pursuer is also the pursued—and vice versa.

Cotterell, Roger. "Blues for Night People." *Jazz & Blues* 2 (7) (October 1972): 14–15.

Thanks to a popular album, pianist Lou was moving up in the music world. Now, he thought, he'd be able to play some "real" jazz—some music from the soul. But he soon discovers that if he wants to continue to land gigs, he will have to provide his audiences with the popular music he had become famous for, leaving his truly creative stuff for . . . another time.

Coxhead, Nona. *Big-Time Baby*. London: Magnum, 1981.

Not seen.

Creech, J.R. *Music and Crime*. New York: Putnam, 1989.

Living on the nether fringes of the music world in Los Angeles and New York, Ray the Face is an accomplished saxophonist and composer who simply can't make a career in music, so with his bassist partner Lonnie, he takes to street crime. Along the way, he discovers what he'd rather not have known about the grim reality of the cutthroat music industry. Much of this novel's sadness derives from our witnessing artists whose lives are made wretched by the music that might have liberated them, had circumstances been different.

Cresswell, Jasmine. *Contract: Paternity*. Toronto and New York: Harlequin, 1997.

Although this romance is set in New Orleans and its heroine is a jazz singer and nightclub owner, it contains precious little jazz content, apart from glancing references to such musicians as Ernestine Anderson, Duke Ellington, and Billie Holiday. Rather, it concerns Antoinette "Toni" Delacroix's desire to have a baby—a plan she puts on hold in order to help disentangle her lawyer brother from a blackmail scheme.

Crouch, Stanley. *Don't the Moon Look Lonesome: A Novel in Blues and Swing*. New York: Pantheon, 2000.

A very long foray into the culture of the U.S. at the end of the twentieth century as filtered through the consciousness of a callipygous white female jazz singer from South Dakota (in other words, a white woman in a black woman's body or at least a woman embodying qualities and characteristics of both races) whose long-term relationship with a more successful black saxophonist is at risk. Set in Manhattan and Houston and almost totally lacking in dramatic action or conventional plot, this book resembles works of urban anthropology in its explorations of such matters as race, jazz, family, homosexuality, drugs, and city life in general. Crouch dedicates the novel to his "mentors," Albert Murray, Ralph Ellison, and Saul Bellow, and in fact it often reads as if the latter two giants had collaborated to produce an early draft of a novel provisionally titled *Invisible Man Meets Mr. Sammler's Planet*. Although the book contains powerful passages and ideas worth dramatizing, the reader who finds the protagonist, Carla Hamsun, less than thoroughly engrossing will tire of the novel long before the midway point.

Crow, Bill. "Andy's Ashes." *Brilliant Corners* 5:42–45 (Summer 2001).

A macabrely humorous story concerning the disposition of trumpeter Andy's final remains. The setting is a midtown Manhattan tavern to which all the jazz musicians eventually gravitate. Author Crow is a professional jazz bassist and widely published jazz writer.

Culver, Monty. "Black Water Blues." *Atlantic Monthly*, May 1950: 34–38.

As the only white musician in an otherwise all-black band, pianist "Lion" Rohrs lives with the tension of an outsider. When trouble breaks out, he knows that the band leader, Bump Roxy, will be quick to use him as a scapegoat.

Cundiff, Lucy. "Trumpet Man." *Saturday Evening Post,* June 19, 1954, 31+.

Trumpet man Dan Daly lost his lip years ago and his nightclub gig is in serious jeopardy until one night when a leading orchestra leader joins the audience, inspiring Dan to recover his musical mastery (for the moment). As a result, the song Dan wrote for his wife becomes a longtime hit, allowing Dan and Molly to open the little club of their dreams. Embarrassingly romantic.

Curran, Dale. *Dupree Blues*. New York: Knopf, 1948.

A refugee from a middle class existence in Duluth, the title figure, Dupree, plays in a New Orleans-style jazz band not far from Memphis. A gambler and boozer with a sharp pain in his gut, Dupree falls in love with the beautiful but marginally talented singer in the band. When he gets in over his head financially, his life crumbles and then comes apart. The novel intends Dupree to represent the kind of little-guy folk hero that inspires the blues. Frequent and considerable descriptions of gambling and music-making.

———. *Piano in the Band*. New York: Reynal & Hitchcock, 1940.

Toward the end of the Depression, George Baker plays piano in a dance-hall jazz band. Much attention is given to the on-the-road existence of such a group: the frustrations of rehearsals and constant travel and the tensions that inevitably grow out of these. These tensions peak when the bandleader hires a beautiful blonde singer, affecting the group dynamics of the all-male band. Another conflict—and a common one in jazz fiction—arises because some of the musicians want to create "real" music rather than follow the strict routines of the bandleader, who plays it safe to ensure financial success. Finally, circumstances make it possible for George to consider joining a largely black band where he'll be free to create—and, presumably, where he will be able to help loosen the rigid color line. Some booze and dope and much musical description.

Cuthbert, Clifton. *The Robbed Heart*. New York: L. B. Fischer, 1945.

The only son of a well-to-do New York family, Denis Sloane is a music critic who takes jazz and jazz bands very seriously. His devotion to this music takes him frequently to Harlem where he meets the beautiful, intelligent, light-skinned Judy Foster, daughter of a prominent Harlem businessman. The novel dramatizes the complexities of a love affair between people from different races. Some references to musicians of the time and to the dispiriting compromises musicians must make in order to ply their trade for money; one of Sloane's black friends, Bert, feels forced to give up his trumpet and deal dope in order to survive.

Davis, Clive. "I Could Write a Book." In *B Flat, Bebop, Scat*, edited by Chris Parker, 122–33. London: Quartet, 1986.

Insurance salesman and weekend jazz man, Scott dreams that his hero Miles Davis asks him to fill in for him while he drives to the airport to pick up a girl. Years later, Scott prepares to go to a Miles Davis concert in London to see Miles in his fusion mode and again fantasizes that Davis asks him to participate in the music-making.

Davis, David. *Jazz Cats*. Gretna, LA: Pelican, 2001.

A juvenile book—a story in rhyme—involving (according to the Library of Congress summary) "Cool cats entertain[ing] crowds with their music in the French Quarter of New Orleans." Not seen.

Dawson, Fielding. "The Blue in the Sky." In *Will She Understand?*, 27–32. Santa Rosa, CA: Black Sparrow, 1988.

The narrator remembers the time when he and two of his young chums went to East St. Louis to hear Charlie Barnett and his orchestra. June Christy and Jo Jones triggered powerful emotions in the speaker who, after making eye contact with Jones, wonders what effect the experience might have had on the drummer. This and the following entries by Dawson should probably be classified as fantasies.

——. "Full Circle." In *Will She Understand?*, 53–54. Santa Rosa, CA: Black Sparrow, 1988.

"The Poet" returns to the bar featured in "The Reason" (q.v.) and reports that the Miles Davis Quintet was "getting better and better and better." Always standing—never sitting while absorbing music—the young poet "knew how to listen to music, and he was listening to this music in that way of hearing new work that the opening outward of the inner ear does something to balance. In suspense hearing nothing but music, there was nothing but music, anywhere, he was up in a world and the world was music." In short, a description of the Miles Davis group in action.

——. "Miles." In *Will She Understand?*, 55–59. Santa Rosa, CA: Black Sparrow, 1988.

The poet remembers encountering Miles Davis and giving him a booklet of his poems and telling him of Robert Creeley's remark that Creeley's "poetic line follows your [Davis'] melodic line, on 'But Not For Me.'" When the poet and Davis meet again years later, Davis not only recognizes the poet but tells him he still has the book.

——. "The Planets." In *Will She Understand?*, 49–51. Santa Rosa, CA: Black Sparrow, 1988.

Three young buddies in 1953 go to Le Downbeat to hear some music. When they get there they find Stan Getz, Bob Brookmeyer, Roy Haynes,

Tommy Potter, and Al Haig jamming to an empty house. Miles Davis drops by and sits in with the group, playing a transcendent "The Way You Look Tonight."

———. "The Reason." In *Will She Understand?*, 13–14. Santa Rosa, CA: Black Sparrow, 1988.

In 1957, a "fair-skinned lad with a powdered wig and big ears" listens to the Miles Davis Quintet at Café Bohemia and then, to Davis's astonishment, transcribes, note for note, the music the quintet had just played.

———. "September in the Rain." In *Will She Understand?*, 47–48. Santa Rosa, CA: Black Sparrow, 1988.

The speaker ("the poet") has an epiphany while listening to Red Garland play "They Didn't Believe Me" in a nightclub.

Deaver, Jeffery Wilds. *Mistress of Justice*. New York: Doubleday, 1992.

Paralegal at a preëminent Wall Street law firm by day, jazz pianist by night (whenever she can land a gig), Taylor Lockwood becomes involved in crime in high places. Despite a mini-subplot concerning Lockwood's dream of landing a recording contract and thereby becoming rich and famous, this blockbuster novel contains disappointingly little jazz content apart from infrequent references to such musicians as Billy Taylor, Cal Tjader, Paul Desmond, Dave Brubeck, and Miles Davis.

Deelder, J. A. *Verhalen en Gedichten.* Amsterdam: De Bezige Bij, 1992.

Apparently a collection, in Dutch, of stories and poems related to jazz. Not seen.

Denver, Paul. *Send Me No Lillies*. London: Consul Books, 1965.

At first Benny Carlton is just another young trumpet player in the sticks of England, happy to be playing weekend gigs and longing to get married, settle down, and lead an ordinary life. Marry he soon does, but at the same time his combo turns pro and soon establishes a reputation that makes it in demand in London and the Continent. Because Benny's very ordinary wife can neither understand jazz nor tolerate her status as jazz widow, their marriage soon dissolves. In the last scene, as Benny solos, a friend remarks to Benny's ex-wife: "I don't reckon to know much about the kind of thing Benny plays, but it's his life, isn't it? . . . It sounds like everything that means life to him is in his playing."

Deutsch, Hermann. "Louis Armstrong." *Esquire*, October 1935, 70+.

An early example in fiction (of any kind) of a work that blurs the distinction between fact and fiction; the author—or editor—in fact calls it "semi-fiction." The story is a vernacular account of Armstrong's rise from street kid to renowned musician. The writer's knowledge of black dialect would seem to derive from minstrel shows.

De Veaux, Alexis. *Don't Explain: A Song of Billie Holiday*. New York: Harper and Row, 1980.

A biographical novel—or novelistic biography—in the form of a prose poem, this ultimately uncategorizable book (unless "Mistake" is a category) is organized chronologically around certain events of Billie Holiday's life. Although sadness suffuses the book (as clearly it did the life), the legendary singer's strength and courage win out—as one can only wish they had in life.

DeVries, Peter. "Jam Today." *New Yorker*, February 4, 1950: 34–35.

When the speaker takes a swing record to a platter party, he is embarrassed to discover that the host and the other party-goers are devotees of the new bebop and so he futilely tries to conceal his squareness. A humorous satire of jazz pretentiousness.

Diniz, Tailor. *O Assassino Usava Batom. [The Killer Wore Lipstick.]* Porto Alegre, Brazil: Mercado Aberto, 1997.

Based on the jacket copy and a skim-through, this is a crime novel set in Brazil (and in Portuguese) involving a murder investigated by detective Walter Jacquet. There are many references to jazz, especially to singers and Bill Coleman's recording of "Satin Doll"; in fact, the resolution of the crime relates to the music on the CDs the victim had been listening to when he died.

Dobrin, Arnold. *Scat!* New York: Four Winds, 1971.

Eight-year-old Scat's dad plays jazz trumpet, and Scat wants to play an instrument too, despite the disapproval of his churchly grandmother. When she dies, however, he follows her advice to follow his heart and teaches himself the harmonica. For young readers.

Douglass, Archie. "'Mrs. Hopkins Pays a Call.'" In *Jazz Parody (Anthology of Jazz Fiction)*, edited by Charles Harvey, 86–91. London: Spearman Publishers, 1948.

A breezy first-person narrative in which the speaker, a jazz trumpeter, sticks his nose where it doesn't belong and gets involved in a scheme relying on a female impersonator to play Cupid.

Downs, Hunton. *Murder in the Mood*. London: Wright, 1998.

A sweeping, researched thriller involving Nazis, Neo-Nazis, drug cartels, the Mafia, the new billionaires, and—most importantly—speculation concerning what really happened to Glenn Miller during Hitler's reign of terror. The plot turns on the discovery in the present of a "Secret Broadcast" disc Miller recorded in 1944; solid Miller background.

Duke, Osborn. "Oh Jazz, Oh Jazz." In *Eddie Condon's Treasury of Jazz*, edited by Eddie Condon and Richard Gehman, 461–88. New York: Dial, 1956.

The travails of a group of musicians shortly after World War II who want to make serious music and earn a living doing it. But there is no escaping a host of problems: living on a bus for days at a time, wildly erratic hours making any kind of normal life impossible, fiscal difficulties of every sort, and the omnipresent pressure of giving the audience what they want: popjazz.

——. *Sideman*. New York: Criterion, 1956.

A very long, windy novel—a kind of panoramic survey of the lives, professional and personal, of several members of a large, post-Korean War dance band. The protagonist is sideman Bernie Bell, who leaves college in Texas to join the band in Southern California. Although Bernie plays his trombone for money, he moonlights by composing "serious" music; in short, another Portrait of the Artist as a Young Man. Much music talk and good descriptions of the improvisational process. Several references to such jazz men as Stan Kenton, Bill Harris, and Dizzy Gillespie—and some focus on race and marijuana. One character has a dog named Bijou after the Bill Harris recording.

Dumas, Henry. "Will the Circle Be Unbroken?" *Negro Digest*, November 1966, 76–80.

Three young whites are reluctantly admitted to the all-black Sound Barrier Club in Harlem. They have come to hear Probe, who has recently returned from exile. But when Probe plays his "new-sound" jazz on his mystical instrument (one of only three afro-horns in existence), the vibrations and volume overwhelm and kill the interlopers.

Duncan, Alice Faye. *Willie Jerome.* New York: Macmillan Books for Young Readers, 1995.

When summer comes, Willie Jerome plays jazz from the rooftop all day. His little sister Judy "feels" the music—the "sizzlin' red hot bebop" Willie plays on his trumpet. But everyone else regards Willie's music as noise until, one day, Judy persuades her mother to "Just close your eyes. Rest your mind, and let the music speak to your spirit." Mom does as instructed and apologizes for having criticized Willie's playing. For young readers.

Duncan, Neal Holland. *Baby Soniat: A Tale From the Jazz Jungle*. Memphis: St. Luke's, 1989.

Although this novel is set in New Orleans and carries a subtitle implying significant jazz content, its only reference to the music is a jazz funeral; in short, yet another misleading title.

Dyer, Geoff. *But Beautiful: A Book about Jazz.* London: Jonathan Cape, 1991; New York: North Point, 1996.

The author defines this work as "imaginative criticism," explaining that he took many scenes from legendary episodes in the lives of jazz musicians and created his own versions of them—improvising, as it were, in keeping with the subject matter. Dyer devotes a chapter to each artist: Lester Young, Thelonious Monk, Bud Powell, Ben Webster, Charles Mingus, Chet Baker, and Art Pepper. This book is a wondrously evocative combination of re-creation and reflection. But some readers "in the know" will be offended by the emphasis on the pain, sadness, and neurosis of the jazz life; some of these readers will put down the book in anger, knowing for instance that Dyer's Ben Webster barely resembles the original. If only Dyer had given fictitious names to his musicians . . .

Edwards, Grace F. *If I Should Die*. New York: Doubleday, 1997.

Although Mali Anderson, the series heroine, lives in Harlem, patronizes jazz clubs, makes frequent references to jazz musicians, and has a jazz musician father, this and the following two mysteries contain much less jazz content than one might hope for.

——. *No Time to Die*. New York: Doubleday, 1999.

——. *A Toast before Dying*. New York: Doubleday, 1998.

Ellis, Walter. *Prince of Darkness: A Jazz Fiction Inspired by the Music of Miles Davis*. London: 20/20, 1998.

A more accurate subtitle would substitute "life" for "music" because this book, unfortunately, is much more concerned with Davis's life than his art. Employing facile psychology, this novel attributes Davis's lifelong anguish to racism and a drunken mother while failing to make a convincing case for his being "the prince of darkness." Although the book has an interesting structure, it falls far short of its colossal subject.

Ellison, Ralph. *Invisible Man*. New York: Random House, 1952.

In this landmark novel, an unnamed (hence "invisible") young southern black man moves north with "great expectations." A panoramic novel of American culture toward the mid-point of the twentieth century, *Invisible Man* is not, strictly speaking, a jazz novel, though jazz and blues do play a significant role in the way they give body to key thematic moments (as in references to Louis Armstrong's "What Did I Do to Be so Black and Blue") and also to the way they inform the technique and style, as in this passage where the narrator, after hearing a moving speech, recalls his own addresses to fellow students: ". . . I too had stridden and debated, a student leader directing my voice at the highest beams and farthest rafters, ringing them, the accents staccato upon the ridgepole and echoing back with a tinkling, like words hurled to the trees of a wilderness, or into a well of slate-gray water; more sound than sense, a play upon the resonances of buildings, an assault upon the temples of the ear. . . ." [Eat your heart out, Jack Kerouac.] Those who are interested in pursuing the relationship between Ellison's ideas about jazz and fiction will find much to ponder in the introduction to his essays, *Shadow and Act* (New York: Random House, 1964), and in the collection of letters he exchanged with his friend Albert Murray, *Trading Twelves: The Selected Letters of Ralph Ellison and Albert Murray*. Edited by Albert Murray and John F. Callahan. New York: Random House, 2000.

Ellroy, James. *White Jazz*. New York: Knopf, 1992; London: Century, 1992.

An ultraviolent crime novel set in the Los Angeles of the 1950s. Apart from some broken jazz records that provide a significant clue in a vicious crime and a few references to such jazz figures as Stan Kenton and Art Pepper, there is very little jazz content. The "jazz" in the title is apparently intended to torque up the already dense noir atmosphere.

English, Richard. *"Strictly Ding-Dong" and Other Swing Stories*. Garden City, NY: Doubleday, Doran, 1941.

A dozen stories linked by their connection to swing and the occasional reappearance of Ding-Dong Williams, "the king of swing" and the hottest clarinetist in the land. In the title story Ding-Dong has been contracted by Hollywood to provide the swing finale for a movie in production. The complication occurs when Ding-Dong reveals that he can neither read nor write music; but not to fret: where slapstick comedy is concerned, this turns out to be no problem at all. The humor of these stories is of the kind best encountered in Saturday morning movies on TV, as when Ding-Dong, announcing he is a "rug cutter," elicits this response from one of the studio people: "That's all right. . . . One of our best producers used to be a tailor." Ding-Dong's definition of swing goes far to characterize the language and tenor of these stories: "You can't explain swing. . . . You gotta be gut-bucket at heart to understand it. I've always been a gate, and gates swing wide. If you're a sender, you get to rug cutting when you're grooving a wax, what with the suitcase man being hot on the skin, and because you're not a paper man, you gotta lick it high and wild to be happy. Swingaroos are born with a lotta jive, and they just hafta play go-instruments, not icky or straight ones, and a union card riding a go-toy gets that old Dixie Land fever, and he's stomping it out before he knows it. The cats get to crying then, and when they twitch you know you've got 'em. That's swing."

Eskew, Robert. "Time of the Blue Guitar." *Coastlines,* Spring-Summer 1958. *Music '59: Downbeat Fourth Annual Yearbook*, 77–80. Chicago: Maher, 1959.

Told in jazz idiom, this story concerns the difficulties a combo has with its leader, Zabe, a fast-talking hustler who finally talks himself out of the combo by alienating his players.

Estleman, Loren D. *Lady Yesterday.* Boston: Houghton Mifflin, 1987.

A hardboiled mystery in which detective Amos Walker goes in search of a jazz musician who dropped out of sight twenty years earlier. Although Walker's investigation leads him into Detroit's rich jazz heritage, including the few remaining clubs where the music is still performed, the novel has only superficial jazz content.

Evans, Robert. "The Jazz Age." In *Jazz Parody (Anthology of Jazz Fiction)*, edited by Charles Harvey, 27–31. London: Spearman Publishers, 1948.

Hardly a story at all, but rather a species of free writing designed (apparently) to suggest the conventional idea that jazz originates in *real* experience, in pain and suffering and deprivation. A few interesting verbal riffs describing jazz in the making.

——. "There's a Great Day Coming . . ." In *Jazz Parody (Anthology of Jazz Fiction)*, edited by Charles Harvey, 77–85. London: Spearman Publishers, 1948.

In this continuation of or companion-piece to the author's "The Jazz Age" (q.v.), the writer tries to penetrate to the heart of jazz—its origins, meanings, and implications. Very much about jazz but very little a "story" or parody.

Ewing, Annemarie. *Little Gate*. New York and Toronto: Rinehart, 1947.

Joe "Little Gate" Geddes is obsessed with jazz and is accepted as a young man both by blacks and other musicians. He leaves his small Iowa town for Chicago where he lands a long-running gig in a speakeasy frequented by mobsters. He moves to New York after prohibition and plays his sax in a band that does mostly novelty music, causing Joe to flee to Harlem after hours for the music he loves. Joe eventually forms his own band, goes on the road (all the way to Los Angeles and back), makes a hit record, becomes a celebrity, and discovers that he and his music have become commodities over which he has no control. Meanwhile, Joe's love life becomes seriously complicated.

Fairweather, Digby. "The Killers of '59." In *B Flat, Bebop, Scat*, edited by Chris Parker, 96–107. London: Quartet, 1986.

After auditioning for and winning a place in a British dance band around 1960, "the trumpeter" encounters several stark realities of big band life, including the competitiveness of musicians, the technical challenges of producing live music night after night, and the treachery of booze.

Fales, Dean. "Solo on the Cornet." *Story*, 1941. In *A Caravan of Music Stories*, edited by Noah D. Fabricant and Heinz Werner, 30–48. New York: Frederick Fell, 1947.

After hearing Joel Pulmacher play the cornet, the religious young narrator resolves to master the instrument at whatever cost. Years later, when he jazzes up his rendition of "Nearer My God to Thee," a fierce thunderstorm strikes, and he wonders if God is punishing him for sacrilege. Slight jazz content.

Farr, John. *The Deadly Combo: The Sour Note of Blackmail*. New York: Ace Double Novel Books, 1958.

A hardedged mystery, very much of its time—a good example of pulp noir. Plainclothes detective and jazz devotee Mac Stewart determines to track down the killer of one-time great trumpet player, Dandy, who has long since resided in the gutter. Mac believes that Dandy may have brought on his own death by bragging to some stranger about the solid gold trumpet he had once received from the jazz community in tribute to his playing—without mentioning that the instrument had been pawned years earlier. The novel takes place in Los Angeles's Jazz Row; comprises considerable clipped, staccato dialogue, much of which seems borrowed from B-movies ("What do you want, you big gorilla?"); and is riddled with jazz references. When Dandy is finally buried, all of the jazz notables (including representatives from *Downbeat* and *Metronome*) show up to give him a proper send-off.

Feather, Leonard. "Bass Is Basic Basis of Basie." *Metronome*, 26 (April 1944).

Under the pseudonym of Snotty McSiegal, the jazz man-of-all-works Leonard Feather published a series of jazz parodies in *Metronome* and other places. McSiegel is a pompous ass who is ready to explicate, in overbearingly obvious terms, anything related to jazz in its many forms and to take credit for any success surrounding the music. The titles of this and the following McSiegel entries provide adequate annotation for the stories.

———. "Be-bop? I Was Pre-bop!" *Metronome*, 24 (December 1948). See "Bass Is Basic . . ." (above).

———. "Hi-Fi Fable I: The Class Treatment." In *Laughter From the Hip*, edited by Leonard Feather and Jack Tracy, 87–92. New York: Horizon, 1963.

A band leader's scheme to allow his black soloist to perform in the segregated South backfires.

———. "Hi-Fi Fable II: Double Jeopardy." In *Laughter From the Hip*, edited by Leonard Feather and Jack Tracy, 115–19. New York: Horizon, 1963.

The speaker thinks he has beaten the system by using technology (a tape recorder in this case) to land a job with a big band, but his scheme backfires.

Feather, Leonard. "I Invented Bossa Nova!" In *Laughter From the Hip*, edited by Leonard Feather and Jack Tracy, 163–67. New York: Horizon, 1963.

———. "I Invented Jazz Concerts." In *Laughter From the Hip*, edited by Leonard Feather and Jack Tracy, 101–7. New York: Horizon, 1963.

———. "Le Jazz Hep." *Metronome*, 15 (June 1943); 17 (July 1943); 15 (August 1943); 18 (September 1943); 19 (November 1943); 19 (December 1943); 30 (January 1944); 20 (February 1944); 24 (March 1944); 26 (April 1944).

Professor McSiegel's fatuous history of jazz and taxonomy of its instruments.

———. "McSiegel Blind at Christmas: *Metronome*'s Hindmost Authority Returns to Take Special St. Nicksiegel-land-Type Test." *Metronome*, 20–21 (January 1951).

———. "McSiegel's Method." *Metronome*, 11 (June 1945).

———. "Professor McSiegel Tells About Sax!" *Metronome*, 44–45 (October 1943).

———. "Slide, Snotty, Slide." *Metronome*, 19 (December 1943). See "Bass Is Basic . . ." (above).

———. "You Gotta Get Lucky." In *Music '59: Downbeat Fourth Annual Yearbook*, 73–75. Chicago: Maher, 1959.

A light piece in which Joe, the trumpet-playing narrator, tries to pull a fast one on Frankie Wood, the band leader, by running away with the band's vocalist. But Frankie is too fast for Joe: when last heard from, Frankie was on the road with Helene and headed for a honeymoon, leaving Joe to reflect that some guys have all the luck.

Federman, Raymond. "Remembering Charlie Parker or How to Get It Out of Your System." In *Take It or Leave It: An Exaggerated Second-hand Tale to be Read Aloud Either Standing or Sitting*. New York: Fiction Collective, 1976. Unpaginated.

This story eulogizes Parker and promotes the notion that blackness is essential to the making of jazz, all of this around a concert performance by Parker of "Lover Man."

Finn, Julio. "The Blue Bayou." In *B Flat, Bebop, Scat*, edited by Chris Parker, 137–45. London: Quartet, 1986.

Early in the twentieth century a hobo with a guitar enters the bayou country of Louisiana in search of the hoodoo doctor who can put him in touch with the devil. Although the guitarist hopes to gain supremacy over music, he learns that in order to accomplish this, he must first get in touch with his own origins, especially those relating to the slavery of his progenitors.

Fisher, Rudolf. "Common Meter." Parts 1, 2. *Baltimore Afro-American* February 8, 15, 1930, 11, 11.

A humorous piece involving a battle-of-the-bands in late 1920s Harlem told in a lively, "jazzy" style with much tart dialogue and realistic descriptions of musical performance. As usual, a woman is the cause of the battle between the bands, and because "They can't use knives and they can't use knucks . . . they got to fight it out with jazz."

Flender, Harold. *Paris Blues*. New York: Ballantine, 1957.

Saxophonist Eddie Cook has been an expatriate in Paris for twelve years and would probably have been content to live out his days there playing jazz and leading a bachelor existence had he not fallen in love with a vacationing school teacher who, like him, is African American. The primary tension in their relationship derives from his generally negative memories of the racial prejudice he had encountered in his hometown of Kansas City and her much more positive view of the racial situation in the U.S. Connie's argument combines with Eddie's love for her to lead him to think that maybe he should give his natal home another try. This novel comprises much discussion of jazz and contains several scenes set in the jazz club where Eddie and his combo have an ongoing gig.

Flowers, Arthur. *Another Good Loving Blues*. New York: Viking, 1993; London: Secker and Warburg, 1993.

A love story involving bluesman Lucas Bodeen and conjure woman Melvira Dupree and the forces that threaten their relationship. The story takes place largely in Memphis on famed Beale St. in the second decade of the twentieth century. Much reference to Delta blues and scattered references to the new music, jazz, which was still in its infancy.

Foote, Shelby. "Ride Out." In *Jordan County: A Landscape in Narrative*, 1–52. New York: Dial, 1954. [First published in slightly different form as "Tell Them Goodbye." *Saturday Evening Post*, February 15, 1947.]

After Duff Conway is executed for killing a man, the county physician at the execution cobbles together, from accounts of Duff's friends and acquaintances, a biography of the man who had been a remarkable cornetist. Born in the Deep South, Duff formed an ineradicable attachment to music at a young age; learned to master his horn, sometimes while behind bars; went north to Harlem where he expanded his musical horizon; and then returned south to recuperate from tuberculosis. There he killed a man who had stolen his woman.

Fox, Charles. "'Got the World in a Jug, Lawd!'" In *Jazz Parody (Anthology of Jazz Fiction)*, edited by Charles Harvey, 99–110. London: Spearman Publishers, 1948.

After young, enthusiastic cornetist Joe Dumaine is hired to play on a Mississippi riverboat, he believes he has "the world in a jug." Refreshingly, this story dramatizes the positive qualities of the jazz life.

Fox, F. G. *Funky Butt Blues*. New Orleans: St. Expedite, 1994.

A free-lance librarian in New Orleans is interviewed by an eccentric old-line citizen to catalog the books of his estate. Early jazz records are found among the books; one of these is suspected of being the only recording of the first jazzman, Buddy Bolden. Much on early jazz and Bolden, more on New Orleans, and most on the mechanics of librarianship. Several holes in the plot and incredible events conspire to rob this mystery of its interest.

Frankel, Haskel. *Big Band*. Garden City, NY: Doubleday, 1965.

High schooler Bob Allen plays a mean trumpet and is encouraged by early success to drop out of school and pursue a career as a musician. He makes a deal with his dad: if Bob can successfully arrange a summer band tour, then he can quit school to devote himself full-time to music. Bob of course jumps at the opportunity, assembles a band with some of his buddies, and takes to the road—with predictable results: flat tires, miscommunications, and shady managers. Bob and Dad achieve a lovely—if predictable—rapprochement.

Freeman, Don. "Big City Blues." *PM Magazine* 14: 1–4; 15: 1–4 (May 1943). Not seen.

Fuller, Jack. *The Best of Jackson Payne*. New York: Knopf, 2000.

White, middle-aged musicologist Charles Quinlan has devoted much of his life to the study of jazz and is now embarked on writing a biography of the titular Jackson Payne, a black tenor saxophonist and "the last towering colossus of jazz. Listening to his late works is like being in touch with an element as pure and reactive as free oxygen." In attempting to fathom the truth of Payne's rise and fall, of his tortured existence, of his increasingly—and dauntingly—complex musical ideas, and of his quest for TRUTH through music, Quinlan is compelled to wrestle with the often ambiguous complexities of his own life. This rich novel is notable for the number and variety of voices it employs as Quinlan interviews the folks who had known Payne and for the multi-faceted portrait it paints of its protagonist, who is a composite of every agonized artist in the history of modern jazz. It is also notable for the clarity of its dramatization of questions relating to race, sex, drug addiction, the process of creativity, and the search for total originality and, through that, transcendence and spiritual deliverance. The epigraph from James Baldwin is particularly apt: "What one's imagination makes of other people is dictated, of course, by the laws of one's own personality, and it is one of the ironies of black-white relations that, by means of what the white man imagines the black man to be, the black man is enabled to know who the white man is."

Garceau, Phil. "The Price of Swing." In *Jazz Parody (Anthology of Jazz Fiction)*, edited by Charles Harvey, 69–76. London: Spearman Publishers, 1948.

When great swing band leader Denny Fletcher falls in love, he compromises his music by becoming commercial in order to win over his sweetheart: "If you bought him a drink, he might tell you how he strived to interpret the sincere music of his race. How a woman persuaded him to play for the public. How she walked out on him . . . How he thought he could revert to his beloved swing and still remain in the top spot. How he flopped."

Gardner, Martin. "The Devil and the Trombone." *The Record Changer* 7:10 (May 1948).

An allegorical fantasy in which the speaker walks into a chapel where an angel is playing sonorous chords on the organ; soon the angel is joined by the devil playing jazzy trombone. Through this collaboration, the speaker (a college professor) achieves an epiphany regarding the seemingly contradictory nature of jazz. (The popularity of this piece led *The Record Changer* to open its pages to fiction.)

———. "The Trouble with Trombones." *The Record Changer* 7: 10 (October 1948).

A humorous story in which the narrator begins by reflecting on the clownishness of trombone players; then, one night while trying to impress a pretty girl in the audience by manipulating the slide with his toes, he injures himself. So she sits in, taking his place, and impresses everyone with her superior skills—and then disappears. The narrator tracks her down, finds her playing oboe in a symphony orchestra, sits in for her, and then replaces her as she in turn takes to the trombone. Both succeed in their new milieux, they marry, and are destined to live happily ever after.

Gibney, Shannon. "How I Remade Coltrane." *Brilliant Corners* 5: 30–52 (Winter 2000).

A coming-of-age story about a Coltrane-obsessed young mulatto who discovers—and accepts—her lesbianism as she prepares to go away to college and a new life.

Gilbert, Edwin. *The Hot and the Cool*. Garden City, NY: Doubleday, 1953.

Music is very much at the center of this novel as it dramatizes the hectic career of a sextet that is coming to terms with the "new" jazz that appeared after World War II. When the band members are not performing, they are discussing the music or going to the city—Manhattan—just across the way from their gig in New Jersey to listen to it. As happens so often in jazz stories, just as the group achieves balance, a female singer materializes, changing the group dynamics and creating a negative impact on the music. Kip, the beloved pianist, falls in love with the vocalist beyond logic and his own considerable resistance (cf. Jake Barnes in Ernest Hemingway's *The Sun Also Rises*). The novel is chock full of references to jazz musicians, clubs, and—of course—the music itself. And, furthermore, it demonstrates the time-honored idea that art has the capacity to heal all.

Glaser, Elton. "Blue Cat Club." *Louisiana Literature* 3 (1986): 22–27.

A new white boy in town, nine-year-old Luther Thibodeaux, is attracted, as if by a magnet, to the all-black Blue Cat Club and the sound of the jazz saxophone that emanates from it. Luther becomes the subject of a police raid occasioned by the violation of the segregation law but is not found. Instead, he becomes privy to a lovers' quarrel and witnesses a shooting that wounds a musician.

Gould, Philip. *Kitty Collins*. Chapel Hill, NC: Algonquin, 1986.

A long, wooden novel centering on the life of Kitty Collins who becomes a jazz pianist. The book attempts to evoke the excitement of the New York jazz scene in the 1940s but succeeds primarily in cataloguing the names of clubs and musicians.

Green, Benny. *Fifty-Eight Minutes to London*. London: MacGibbon and Kee, 1969.

An insider's view of struggling young musicians in the Brighton dance-hall scene of the 1950s.

Greenlee, Sam. "Blues for Little Prez." *Black World*, August 1973. In *NOMMO: A Literary Legacy of Black Chicago (1967–1987)*, edited by Carole A. Parks, 141–47. Chicago: OBAhouse, 1987.

Nicknamed after Lester Young, "Little Prez" "couldn' do nothin' else 'cep rap an' he could rap like the real Prez blew, an' when Little Prez got big everybody knew he was gonna blow tenor too." Trouble is, "Little Prez" can't blow a lick so squanders his life by shooting up, listening to jazz records, and dying young. Told in urban black vernacular, this story raises provocative questions about race, drugs, and jazz. Frequent references to jazz notables, especially Count Basie's men.

Grennard, Elliott. "Sparrow's Last Jump." *Harper's*, May 1947, 419–26.

Based on Charlie Parker's notorious "Lover Man" recording session which the author (himself a professional musician) had attended, this story underscores the Parker figure's (Sparrow's) disintegration from drugs and mental incapacity.

Grime, Kitty. "Seeing Her Off." In *B Flat, Bebop, Scat*, edited by Chris Parker, 22–30. London: Quartet, 1986.

Obnoxious vocalist Gennie succeeds in the unfeeling, male-dominated world of jazz—but her success doesn't last long. The story is structured around telephone conversations and answering machine messages.

Guralnick, Peter. *Nighthawk Blues*. New York: Seaview, 1980.

A young white music promoter in the Northeast tracks down a legendary old bluesman, Screamin' Nighthawk (real name: Theodore Roosevelt Jefferson) in (surprise!) Mississippi and tries to turn him into a national star, even though he is old and feeble. Readers interested in the recrudescence of the Delta blues in the 1960s will find much of interest here.

Gwinn, William. *Jazz Bum*. New York: Lion, 1954.

A very pulpy story featuring Vic Ravenna, son of immigrants living in New York's Lower East Side. As a teenager, Vic becomes seriously interested in mastering jazz clarinet; at the same time he develops an interest in reefer, booze, and Zora, who becomes an obsession with him. Vic spends a year in reformatory, where he hones his musical skills. When he gets out he starts playing professionally, eventually abandoning swing for progressive jazz, at which he becomes the "crown prince." Meanwhile, Zora has become a chanteuse (and a slut to boot). For over 15 years Vic has not been able to get Zora out of his head—but when he encounters her, he sees through her for the first time, allowing him to transcend his obsession and declare his love to his nice-Nelly sweetheart. The last lines of the book are spectacular in their badness: "'What? Wh-what d-did you say?' There was a loveable little catch in that pretty voice when she was breathless. 'I want to say it real andante, so you'll hear it.' 'Say it! Please say it, Vicky, before I faint!' 'I love you, apple,' Vic said."

Hanley, Jack. *Hot Lips*. New York: Designs Publishing, 1952.

An extremely rare pulp novel that proclaims itself to be much, much more lurid than it actually is. The cover depicts one woman playing torrid sax and another dancing sexily, while a man, tie akimbo, sits transfixed. The cast of characters includes bandleader Solly Royall, "Midwife to the music of a collection of drunks, tarts, hoydens, tea-hounds, and 'nice girls.'" In addition, many readers of this "Intimate Novel #18" must have been disappointed to discover that the title refers only to the playing of musical instruments. The story is unsurprisingly simple: when the lead saxophonist of the all-girl band is hospitalized with delirium tremens, a replacement materializes almost immediately, the beautiful and talented 19-year-old Althea Allen. She is desperate to escape her evil stepfather who, in concert with the musical motif, "wanted to fiddle" (with Althea, of course). Band manager Pete Dwyer falls instantly in love with Althea, but so does fellow band member Mona Storm, whose second husband has stolen her clothes to enter a drag contest. The vagabond (i.e., travelling) band prospers, Althea becomes a star, and she and Pete are destined to live happily-ever-after. Descriptions of the band's rehearsing and performing are approximately as convincing as the plot.

Hannah, Barry. "Testimony of Pilot." In *Airships*, 17–44. New York: Knopf, 1978.

A coming-of-age account of two boys who play together in the high school band and later, in college, put together a group called "Bop Friends." The piano-playing narrator, William, becomes deaf but makes it through college anyway, while his saxophone-playing chum becomes a pilot and goes to Vietnam. Slight jazz content apart from scattered references to jazz artists of the day (Kenton, Desmond, Joe Morello, et al).

Harvey, John, ed. *Blue Lightning*. London: Slow Dancer Press, 1998; Chester Springs, PA: Dufour Editions, 1999.

An apparently commissioned collection of "eighteen brand new stories," each of which revolves around music of some kind. The following writers contribute jazz- and blues-related stories: Charlotte Carter, John Harvey, Bill Moody, Walter Mosley, Peter Robinson, James Sallis, and Brian Thompson (qq.v.).

———. "Cool Blues." In *Blue Lightning*, edited by John Harvey, 127–44. London: Slow Dancer Press, 1998; Chester Springs, PA: Dufour Editions, 1999.

Jazz-loving detective Charlie Resnick is called in on a case involving a handsome con man who has been fleecing the women he so expertly picks up. Resnick recognizes the con man's aliases as little known brass men from Duke Ellington's orchestras and is thus able to solve the case.

———. *Cold Light*. New York: Henry Holt, 1994; London: Heinemann, 1994.

A pretty conventional plot revolving around a psychopathic killer. Jazz lover Charlie Resnick presides over this gritty procedural. In his leisure time, he tends his four cats, all named after bebop musicians (Dizzy, Miles,

Bud, and Pepper), listens to jazz, and reads *The Penguin Guide to Jazz.*

——. *Easy Meat.* New York: Henry Holt, 1996; London: Heinemann, 1996.

British cop Charley Resnick is a jazz aficionado whose primary form of unwinding is reading about and listening to jazz, primarily straightahead bebop, like Lester Young, Howard McGhee, Monk, and Prez. The music goes far to characterize Resnick as a deeply caring person whose ability to sympathize with others derives from his own suffering. The characters in this violent police procedural do truly dreadful things to each other.

——. *Last Rites.* London: William Heinemann, 1998; New York: Henry Holt, 1999.

In this, the tenth and last novel in the series, Charlie Resnick once again takes comfort from jazz, especially from Thelonious Monk, as the world of Nottingham, England, seems about to crumble under the pressure of violent drug wars. In a postscript (called "Coda"), Harvey writes: "The odd sandwich aside, I think it was jazz that kept Charlie sane, that provided him with both release and inspiration. Me, too. In the writing of these books I have relied, again and again, on the music of Duke Ellington, Billie Holiday, Thelonious Monk, Spike Robinson, Ben Webster with Art Tatum, and Lester Young. Let it live on." Incidentally, Harvey's newsletter is called *In a Mellotone.*

——. *Still Waters.* New York: Henry Holt, 1997.

In this, the ninth Charlie Resnick procedural, jazz-loving Resnick goes in search of a serial killer, tracking him down against a background of Duke Ellington music.

Hassler, Jon. *Rookery Blues.* New York: Ballantine, 1995.

A long campus novel that takes place in the turbulent 1960s. Rookery State College in Rookery, Minnesota, is an academic backwater in a place that's about as far north as you can get and still be in the United States. Five faculty members, all yearning for some sort of community, miraculously discover the kind of companionship that brings deep satisfaction to their lives; they accomplish this through the jazz combo they form one frigid winter afternoon, The Icejam Quintet. But when the first labor union in the school's history comes disruptively into town, the musicians must struggle with their various allegiances.

Hentoff, Nat. *Does This School Have Capital Punishment?* New York: Delacorte, 1981.

In school, trouble seems to follow Sam Davidson around, so when he enrolls in New York's prestigious Burr Academy everyone wonders how long he will last. At first, Sam seems to be making a comfortable adjustment; he even becomes absorbed by an oral history assignment that brings him into close contact with a legendary jazz trumpeter, Major Kelley. When Sam is wrongfully accused by a teacher of possessing marijuana, his school career is jeopardized. But Major Kelley comes to the rescue—a black man saving a privileged white kid's skin. This young adult novel contains significant jazz content, from references to jazz musicians to the history of the genre.

——. *Jazz Country*. New York: Harper, 1965.

Intended for a juvenile audience, this is the story of a white boy who is influenced by black musicians to become a jazz trumpeter. As in many "Young Adult" works, the protagonist is faced with the dilemma of whether to go on to college after graduation or try to make it as a musician. The novel is at least as much interested in civil rights as it is in jazz.

Herzhaft, Gerard. *Long Blues in A Minor*. Translated by John Duval. Fayetteville, AR: University of Arkansas Press, 1988.

During the French liberation, a teenage French boy is befriended by a black American soldier, Sugar, who gives the boy stacks of comics and records when he returns to the States. Much later, the boy (now a man) plays the records for the first time and discovers "the America of the blues." Then Champollion starts playing the guitar to the accompaniment of Sugar's records. He then takes to playing in the streets until he is roughed up several times by the gendarmes. So he gets a good job, makes a success of it, and then, to the amazement of all, quits to pursue his interest in the blues. After seeing an American blues singer in Paris, he determines to go to Chicago to follow his passion. There, he insinuates himself into the black community, where he attempts to locate the legendary Big Johnny White. When he finds his quarry, the two of them bus to Clarksdale, Mississippi, where the protagonist experiences segregated America for the first time. After his encounter with black America, "The blues stuck to my skin, not a music but a state of mind." In short, a novel with a sociological perspective and a message that you don't have to be black to experience the blues.

Hesse, Hermann. *Der Steppenwolf*. Berlin: Fischer, 1927. Translated by Basil Creighton as *Steppenwolf*. New York: Henry Holt, 1929.

A jazz saxophonist urges the introspective protagonist, Harry Haller, to abandon intellection and follow his instincts and emotions—a familiar twentieth century theme (see, e.g., Nikos Kazantzakis, *Zorba the Greek*. New York: Simon and Schuster, 1953).

Hewat, Alan V. *Lady's Time*. New York: Harper and Row, 1985.

The Lady of the title is Winslow, not Day, and she is an attractive woman of mixed blood passing for white in New England after fleeing an abusive life in turn-of-the-century New Orleans. She supports herself and her son by giving music lessons and playing ragtime piano at a local inn. When she dies mysteriously in 1919, some suspect murder, others mischance. The reader, knowing more than the characters, believes that Lady Winslow's death is her debt for having entered into a pact with voodoo spirits to save her son from premature death. The late William Matthews's jacket blurb is too lovely—and accurate—not to quote in part: "At the heart of *Lady's Time* is Alan Hewat's understanding of how ragtime and jazz both subverted and transcended the racially pained culture that nourished them. And of how that music, for the brave, came to be about freedom and the acceptance of death. . . ."

Hill, Richard. *Riding Solo with the Golden Horde*. Athens, GA: University of Georgia Press, 1994.

A coming-of-age novel involving a high school student, Vic Messenger, whose burning ambition is to become a jazz saxophone artist rather than just a talented performer. The novel (aimed at a teenage audience) takes place in St. Petersburg, Florida in the late 1950s and involves Messenger in the world of black jazz in a segregated time and place. Much reference to jazz and jazz musicians and to the burgeoning Civil Rights movement. The spirits of Billie Holiday and Charlie Parker hover over the novel, Louis Armstrong has a walk-on role, and Gene Quill plays a significant part. Drugs, booze, and sex are central factors in Messenger's growing maturation.

Holmes, John Clellon. *Go!* New York: Scribner's, 1952.

A jazz novel only to the extent that it refers frequently to jazz musicians and dramatizes the Beats' attraction to the music.

———. *The Horn*. New York: Random House, 1958.

As Edgar "the Horn" Pool tries to regain his stature as ranking saxophonist, his skills, as well as his psychological condition, rapidly deteriorate. Pool is likely a composite of Charlie Parker and Lester Young, and other characters also derive from actual jazz figures: the model for Junius Priest, as the name implies, is Thelonious Monk, and another character closely resembles Billie Holiday. A bible of the Beat generation, this jazz-soaked novel frequently relates jazz artists to nineteenth century American romantic writers.

Hoobler, Dorothy, Thomas Hoobler, and Carey-Greenberg Associates. *Florence Robinson: The Story of a Jazz Age Girl*. Silver Burdett: Parsippany, NJ, 1997.

For juveniles. When Flo's father returns to Mississippi after serving in France in WWI, he can no longer tolerate the racism he had left behind, so he goes to Chicago in search of a better life for his family. Flo, who must be around 10, discovers what it means to live where she is not excluded because of her race; and, thanks to her father who has a gift for jazz piano, she is also introduced to jazz, whose "secret," she comes to realize, is "what it meant to be free."

Houston, James D. *Gig*. New York: Dial, 1969.

One night in the life of piano bar pianist Roy Ambrose, who would much rather to be able to support himself by composing and playing jazz. Unfortunately, the 1960s zeitgeist is not conducive to that kind of music. Ambrose gears the songs he plays to what he perceives to be the audience's needs: "Tea for Two" for dancers, "Embraceable You" for lovers, "Roll a Silver Dollar" for singalongers, and so on.

———. "Homage to the Count." In *The Men in My Life and Other More or Less True Recollections of Kinship*, 125–29. Berkeley: Creative Arts, 1987.

A fictionalized memoir of the writer's disappointment in seeing his hero, Count Basie, at 79 unable to employ "the famous Basie right hand."

Houston, Margaret Belle. "The Jazz Heart." *Collier's*, February 15, 1930, 14+.

Terry, a Yankee conventioneer in New Orleans, wrangles an introduction to the enchanting (and enchantingly named) Cydalise, who is engaged to marry her cousin—a marriage of convenience. As Terry tells Cydalise about life back home in Indiana, he mentions his hometown jazz band, leading her to exclaim, "Me . . . I have a jazz heart." Terry says he does too, they arrange to spend a jazz evening together, and . . . love prevails, leaving cousin Leon fuming.

Howard, Brett. *Memphis Blues*. Los Angeles: Holloway House, 1984.

A fact-based fiction involving Harold Green, a fair-skinned mulatto orphan who works his way up from the gutter to relative prominence during Beale Street's heyday. When a good-hearted whore is killed, Harold avenges her death by slitting the throat of her killer, becoming "a real, honest-to-God black man." Much emphasis is given to Beale Street as the vital center of black life and the blues that flows from that experience. Many of the epigraphs to individual chapters contain blues references, and jazz and blues musicians are frequently mentioned.

Howard, Clark. "Horn Man." *Ellery Queen's Mystery Magazine*, June 2, 1980: 54–65.

When trumpeter Dix returns to New Orleans after serving sixteen years in prison for a murder he didn't commit, he has only one thing in mind: to find the woman he took the rap for. Even though he is offered an old silver trumpet that had been the property of a legendary Vieux Carré horn man, Dix claims to have no interest in returning to music. But when he discovers that the woman he is seeking will be unavailable for quite a long while, he picks up the trumpet again and seems destined to once again make jazz the center of his existence.

Huddle, David. *Tenorman: A Novella*. San Francisco: Chronicle, 1995.

For tenorman-composer Eddie Carnes, jazz is his life. Seemingly at the end of the road, he is brought back to the United States from Sweden by a branch of the National Endowment for the Arts and supplied with all the necessities of life on the condition that he allow every aspect of his daily life to be studied and recorded. Through the process of this experiment, the lives of the researchers are changed in positive ways: Eddie's commitment to his art has brought to their lives newfound depth and intensity, making them more fully human. Much jazz reference to such figures as Joe Henderson, Stan Getz, Johnny Griffin, Sonny Stitt, and David Murray—and a surprise cameo appearance by Branford and Wynton Marsalis.

Hughes, Langston. "The Blues I'm Playing." *Scribner's*, May 1934, 345–51.

Oceola Jones and Mrs. Dora Ellsworth come from different worlds: Jones is a young black pianist with southern roots and Ellsworth is an elderly white blue-blood patron of the arts in New York City. Mrs. Ellsworth wants Oceola to sacrifice everything—including her medical school boyfriend and her racial identity—to become an artist in the classical tradition, but Oceola cannot relinquish her love for the jazz-blues-gospel music of her heritage or her desire to live a balanced life. A story rich in implication, including the questions of the struggling black artist and the wealthy white patron; would Bessie Smith have ended up sounding like Kate Smith if she had had the "proper" patronage?

——. "Bop." In *The Best of Simple*, 117–19. New York: Hill and Wang, 1961.

Hughes's series character, Simple, a lover of bebop, explains to the dubious narrator that the music is more than just nonsense syllables, that in fact its name derives from the sound made when cops hit blacks on the head with their billy clubs, thus creating an authentic "colored boys" music.

——. "Guitar." *Not Without Laughter*. New York: Knopf, 1930. In *A Caravan of Music Stories*, edited by Noah D. Fabricant and Heinz Werner, 71–79. New York: Frederick Fell, 1947.

A story about a loving man, Jimboy, who plays guitar and sings, mostly the blues, and in so doing brings people together. The story is interspersed with the lyrics to the songs Jimboy sings.

——. "Jazz, Jive, and Jam." In *Simple Stakes a Claim*, 186–91. New York: Holt, Rinehart and Winston, 1957.

This story presents a conciliatory picture of the racial issue as Simple argues to his woman, who has been dragging him to talks on integration, that jazz would be far more effective in promoting racial harmony than any number of seminars on the topic because, since everyone loves jazz, blacks and whites would dance together to the music, and racial differences would dissipate.

——. *Not Without Laughter*. New York: Knopf, 1930.

Although not a jazz novel per se, Chapter 8, "Dance," shadows forth the importance of jazz in black culture and celebrates the individuality that characterizes the music.

Hunter, Evan. *Second Ending*. New York: Simon and Schuster, 1956; London: Constable, 1956. [Also published as *Quartet in "H."* New York: Pocket Books, 1957.]

When young jazz trumpeter Andy Silvera imposes himself on his erstwhile friend, Bud Donato, he brings havoc along with him. Bud needs to cram for exams, and Andy has become deeply involved in narcotics and consequently requires constant attention, forcing Bud into the role of nursemaid. The sections on music-making, especially in Book I, ring true; there are also frequent references to Kenton and Gillespie, among others.

——. *Streets of Gold*. New York: Harper and Row, 1974.

Yet another dramatization of the corrosive power of the American Dream. The birthblind speaker, Dwight Jamison, is a second-generation Italian American who abandons his study of classical piano after listening to Art Tatum recordings. After paying his dues for several years, Jamison becomes very successful, thanks largely to a fluke hit recording. At the height of his success, however, he falls victim to the corruption surrounding the music industry as well as to rock 'n' roll, which is making bebop obsolete. Jamison comes to realize that the streets paved with gold that his grandfather spoke of on his deathbed referred less to the fame and fortune connoted by the jazz musicians' street of gold, 52nd Street, than to hard-earned moral values. Although this novel concerns the melting-pot experience of an immigrant family, the second half contains much of interest for readers of jazz fiction: namely, solid discussions focusing on the mechanics of the music, several descriptions of jazz performances, and frequent references to such musicians as Dizzy Gillespie, Oscar Peterson, and George Shearing.

Isadora, Rachel. *Ben's Trumpet*. New York: Greenwillow, 1979.

A nicely illustrated juvenile book about young Ben who loves jazz and plays an imaginary trumpet until the trumpeter from a neighborhood jazz club fixes him up with a real instrument.

Islas, Arturo. *La Mollie and the King of Tears*. Edited by Paul Skenazy. Albuquerque: University of New Mexico Press, 1996.

Jazz saxophonist Louie Mendoza is in the emergency ward of a San Francisco hospital telling the story of his day—and, really, his life—to a stranger with a tape recorder. This unfinished novel elaborates the complexity of the chicano condition in spicy vernacular language. Surprisingly, though Mendoza is a jazz musician, he has little to say about music.

Jackson, Jon A. *Man with an Axe*. New York: Atlantic Monthly, 1998.

A mystery featuring detective "Fang" Mulheisen of the Detroit PD. In this number in the series, Mulheisen goes in search of a collection of notebooks left behind by a late colleague; this in turn involves Mulheisen in a quest to discover what really happened to Jimmy Hoffa one long-ago weekend at an isolated African American resort community on the Great Lakes. Mulheisen is a jazz buff and the book contains many references to bop and free jazz and to the jazz musicians who matriculated in the "old" Detroit. One important character had played sax in Phil Woods's band, while another turns out, in a neat novelistic twist, to be the daughter of Albert Ayler. A rambling yet always interesting narrative, especially for lovers of jazz fiction.

James, Stuart. *Too Late Blues*. New York: Lancer Books, 1962.

Pianist Ghost Wakefield and his quintet aren't exactly getting rich or famous playing their special brand of jazz around Southern California, but they are pretty much sustained by performing the music they love with musicians they enjoy and respect. Enter a beautiful woman, an agent or two, and a recording contract and things soon spin out of control, leaving everyone at odds with Ghost and destroying the combo. Many references to jazz musicians and several scenes set in jazz clubs and the recording studio. The fact that this book came out almost simultaneously with the movie of the same title, is a paperback original, and is copyrighted by the director/producer of the movie, John Cassavetes, and one John Smith leads one to suspect that it is what is sometimes called a novelization.

Jeffers, H. Paul. *Rubout at the Onyx*. New Haven and New York: Ticknor and Fields, 1981.

A mystery set in the 1930s in Manhattan. Jazz buff private eye Harry MacNeil (the "Mick Dick") undertakes to get to the bottom of a mob hit that occurred at the Onyx Club—"the best jazz joint on Fifty-second Street"—on New Year's Eve when Art Tatum was playing piano. Tatum, Paul "Pops" Whiteman, and George Gershwin have limited roles. In an "Author's Note," the writer glosses the lives of some of the real people who appear in the novel and claims that if it achieves any authenticity of mood, this is largely because of the 1930s jazz records he played while writing.

Jesmer, Elaine. *Number One with a Bullet*. New York: Farrar, Straus and Giroux, 1974; London: Weidenfeld and Nicolson, 1974.

A novel by a former Motown secretary about the monstrous greed and corruption that infests the music industry. Although the record firm at the book's center is black-owned, it nevertheless exploits its black artists as it strives to produce a "bullet," a hit record that promises to go on generating income. Sex, profanity; negligible jazz content.

Jessup, Richard. *Low Down*. London: Secker and Warburg, 1956; New York: Dell, 1958.

Not seen.

Johns, Veronica Parker. "Mr. Hyde-de-Ho." In *Ellery Queen's Awards: 11th Series*, edited by Ellery Queen, 106–51. New York: Simon and Schuster, 1956.

When the speaker finds out that a jazz musician has apparently fallen in love with her very rich, obese friend, she is first incredulous and then frightened. The women soon find themselves entangled in mysteriously frightening circumstances—a variation on the single-woman-in-distress theme. In explaining the predictably bad behavior of jazz musicians, the narrator says, "All the talent, the fire that makes them great, burns with a bright alcoholic flame." The speaker is a receptionist at a recording company that specializes in jazz and "the better bop"; in addition, the story contains many references to the 1950s jazz scene, recording sessions, and jazz clubs.

Johnson, Clifford Vincent. "Old Blues Singers Never Die." In *The Best Short Stories by Negro Writers*, edited by Langston Hughes, 414–27. Boston: Little, Brown, 1967.

In Paris one day, a black American serviceman encounters legendary blues singer River Bottom, who was "sporting a big fat diamond ring" and clothes to match. This leads to reflections on race (France versus the U.S., for instance) and the majesty of the blues.

Johnson, James Weldon. *The Autobiography of an Ex-Coloured Man*. Boston: Sherman, French and Company, 1912.

A light-skinned boy of mixed parentage discovers a talent for music, masters classical piano, and turns classical music into ragtime, achieving success in the process. He later determines to turn ragtime into classical music—in other words, to give voice to the African American experience through the structures and techniques of classical music. He masquerades successfully as a white, takes a white wife (blonde and blue-eyed), and leads a comfortable life, uneasily believing that he had betrayed his race, sold his "birthright for a mess of pottage." An early, important book about the trauma of confused racial identity and of the potential that music has to promote the welfare of the black artist and, by implication, the race itself. The first "pre-jazz" novel?

Jones, Gayl. *Corregidora*. New York: Random House, 1975.

Although the first-person protagonist is a blues singer, neither she nor the novel has much to say about music (beyond the obligatory I-sing-cause-I-gotta-sing). Scattered references to blues and jazz artists. At one point, when asked what the blues does for her, the speaker reflects, "It helps me to explain what I can't explain." Much more about the legacy of slavery and black feminism than music.

Jones, James. "The King." *Playboy*, 1955. In *Eddie Condon's Treasury of Jazz*, edited by Eddie Condon and Richard Gehman, 337–49. New York: Dial, 1956.

Probably based on the return of Bunk Johnson, this story concerns Willy "King" Jefferson, a legendary trumpeter who played an important role in the development of jazz. When King makes a comeback, he fails to generate much interest—because, frankly, he isn't playing very well and also because interest in his old-timey New Orleans brand of jazz has passed.

Joseph, Oscar. "Suite for Queen." In *NOMMO: A Literary Legacy of Black Chicago (1967–1987)*, edited by Carole A. Parks, 192–98. Chicago: OBAhouse, 1987.

Steve Anderson reminisces about his past while standing alone on a Harlem street playing "Suite for a Queen" on his saxophone in homage to his mother and happier days. At one point Anderson compares his solitary playing to Sonny Rollins's dropping out of music for years and practicing his horn on the Williamsburg Bridge. Much of the story attempts to approximate the bebop sounds Steve creates on his horn.

Kaminsky, Wallace. "The Sound-Machine." *The University Review* 31 (3): 163–74 (March 1965).

After being introduced to jazz by his black army buddy, Buster, Nick (the speaker) resolves to become the best saxophonist on earth; in addition,

Nick feels the compelling need to be accepted by black musicians. Nick gets his chance to perform with ranking musicians and more than holds his own but loses his dear friend Buster in the process.

Kanin, Garson. *Blow Up a Storm*. New York: Random House, 1959.

The first-person narrator is a playwright and saxophonist; he tells the story of an old buddy from the past, Woody Woodruff, whose trumpet playing was in a class with Louis Armstrong's and Bunny Berigan's. The novel—which takes place on either side of WWII—contains many references to jazz artists and some excellent descriptions of music in the making, including a very effective scene in which seven band members blend their very different talents, personalities, and backgrounds, supporting a central theme: ". . . if we could all learn to play together . . . why is it we couldn't learn to live together?" Much emphasis on race and booze. One character, Slug (a drummer), seems to be modeled after Charlie Parker.

———. *The Rat Race*. New York: Pocket Books, 1960.

Lee Konitz had once told the hayseed protagonist, Pete Hammer, that he liked Hammer's tone, so Pete goes to New York hoping to make it big on the saxophone. When Pete is forced by circumstances to share a small apartment with a gal who'd been knocked around, they fall in love and face the harsh realities of big city life together. This book is a novelization of Kanin's screenplay for the 1960 movie of the same name, and the movie was an adaptation of Kanin's and Ruth Gordon's play (1949, 1950), also of the same title.

Kay, Jackie. *Trumpet*. London: Picador, 1998; New York: Pantheon, 1998.

A first novel from the self-described "Black Scottish poet," Jackie Kay, *Trumpet* dramatizes the life and, more significantly, the death of jazz trumpeter, Joss Moody, who is revealed to have been a woman—despite having been married for many years to Millie, with whom he raised their adopted son Colman. Told in flashbacks through multiple points of view, this intriguing work raises resonant questions about the indefinability of gender and identity and how these can be deeply complicated through music, as in this passage where we see Joss reflecting on his relationship to the music he produces: "The music is his blood. His cells. But the odd bit is that down at the bottom, the blood doesn't matter after all. None of the particulars count for much. True, they are instrumental in getting him down there in the first place, but after that they become incidental. All his self collapses—his idiosyncrasies, his personality, his ego, his sexuality, even, finally, his memory. All of it falls away like layers of skin unwrapping. He unwraps himself with his trumpet. Down at the bottom, face to face with the fact that he is nobody. The more he can be nobody the more he can play that horn. Playing the horn is not about being somebody coming from something. It is about being nobody coming from nothing. The horn ruthlessly strips him bare till he ends up with no body, no past, nothing." Whether or not this novel was inspired by the 1992 movie, *The Crying Game*, or the even more recent revelations about real-life jazz man Billy Tipton who turned out to have been a woman (see Diane Wood Middlebrook, *Suits Me: The Double Life of Billy Tipton*. Boston and New York: Houghton Mifflin, 1998), it adds a fascinating new dimension to such works.

Kelley, William Melvin. "Cry for Me." In *Dancers on the Shore*, 180–201. Garden City, NY: Doubleday, 1964.

The young narrator's Uncle Wallace comes up to New York City from the South. One night in Greenwich Village Uncle Wallace becomes outraged when he happens upon a blues/folk performer singing a song *he* had written and mangling it in the process. Uncle Wallace takes over the stage, becomes a big hit, and ends up at Carnegie Hall where he brings together the members of the audience, black and white, in a joyous dance. This is what Simple in Langston Hughes's "Jazz, Jive, and Jam" (q.v.) advocates.

——. *A Different Drummer*. New York: Doubleday, 1959, 1962.

With a black writer who wrote a significant jazz novel and a title that implies a musical instrument, you'd expect this book to contain considerable musical reference. Alas, there is none; rather it is a densely political novel of the Civil Rights movement.

——. *A Drop of Patience*. New York: Doubleday, 1965.

An affecting fable about a blind-from-birth horn player who leaves the South for New York and Chicago where he is finally recognized for his seminal role in shaping the new music—undoubtedly bebop. Ludlow Washington may be a genius but his blindness, his blackness, and his total devotion to his music do not allow him to fit in anywhere. Washington cracks up after being exploited and betrayed by commercialism and racism, recovers, rejects the belated recognition he is receiving, and sets out to find a church—anywhere—in need of a good musician.

Kelly, Rod. *Just for the Bread.* London: Robert Hale, 1976.

After filling in with a rock band at a large society ball in London—"just for the bread"—struggling jazz trumpeter Cornelius Lefroy is seduced by the sensation-seeking hostess, Lady Gabrielle Damian. Unfortunately, their liaison is secretly filmed and Lady Gabrielle is blackmailed. When she opens her checkbook to Lefroy to resolve the matter, he accepts for two compelling reasons: he needs the money and he is booked for a week at Ronnie Scott's famous jazz club to play opposite Freddie Hubbard, "who would blow him into the ground every night." Apart from this, however, there are only a few references to the different styles of Dizzy Gillespie and Don Cherry. In short, although this a rare novel, it is not worth seeking out for its jazz content.

Kennett, Frances. *Lady Jazz*. London: Victor Gollancz, 1989.

A long novel chronicling the struggles of Ida Garland to succeed as a singer in the London of the 1930s. Ida was born into a show business family and is determined to carry on the tradition of her grandfather, an African American who came to London in the 1890s. But just as her career begins to flourish, WWII breaks out, and she leaves the stage—until love reënters her life. Given its length and subject matter, this novel contains disappointingly little jazz content.

Kerouac, Jack. *Desolation Angels*. New York: Coward-McCann, 1965.

As usual, Kerouac's persona (or alter ego), Jack Duluoz, is in search of Truth ("God or Tathagata") and in praise of America. Passing references to such musicians as Sarah Vaughan, Breu [sic] Moore, and Dizzy Gillespie and a scene or two involving musical performance.

———. *Maggie Cassidy*. New York: Avon, 1959.

Much reference to the big bands Kerouac listened to in the late 1930s.

———. *On the Road*. New York: Viking, 1957.

Like all of Kerouac's novels, this is not, strictly speaking, a jazz fiction, though it is shot through with references to jazz musicians and contains a few scenes of music in performance. More importantly, the prose style of this novel attempts to emulate the spontaneity of the music.

———. *The Subterraneans*. New York: Grove, 1958.

A confessional narrative depicting the protagonist's love affair with a black girl. Occasional references to Charlie Parker underscore the novel's hallucinatory mode.

———. *The Town and the City*. New York: Harcourt Brace, 1950.

Hipsters and bop musicians with their dark glasses and berets are mentioned.

———. *Visions of Cody*. New York: McGraw-Hill, 1972.

A companion piece to *On the Road* with the members of the Beat generation (before it was so named) frantically exploring the America—and the Mexico—of the late 1940s and early 1950s. Jack Duluoz, Kerouac's persona, narrates this diaristic novel that focuses on Cody Pomeray, whose endless thirst for experience coupled with boundless energy make him the new American hero. At one point, Duluoz follows Lee Konitz down the streets of New York, not knowing why. The book contains many other references to jazz and its artists, Charlie Parker and Coleman Hawkins among others.

Kirkwood, Valerie. *Torch Song*. New York: Kensington, 1996.

A time-travel romance with only a few scattered jazz references to such artists as Benny Goodman, Louis Armstrong, and Bessie Smith.

Kitt, Sandra. *Serenade*. New York: Pinnacle/Windsor, 1994.

Alexander Morrow has devoted her existence to music but isn't making much headway until Parker Harrison reënters her life. Equally adroit at classical music and jazz, Parker had stolen—and broken—Alex's heart years ago and now sets about to repair the earlier damage. The story is set in Washington, D.C.; significant scenes take place in the famous jazz club, Blues Alley; all of the characters are African Americans with ties to the music world; and the jacket copy claims that "Alexander Morrow has struggled long and hard to make it in the red-hot electric world of jazz." Despite all of this, the jazz content is less than negligible. In short, a "Pinnacle Romance."

Klavan, Andrew. *Hunting Down Amanda*. New York: William Morrow, 1999; London: Little, Brown, 1999.

A mid-tech, melodramatic thriller involving a heartbroken black sax player who becomes involved in a truly incredible plot, which includes, among other things, the search for a young girl with miraculous healing powers. The jazz content is limited to a solid chapter or two on the jazz man—Lonnie Blake—at work, scattered references to musicians like James Carter, and occasional chapter titles taken from such jazz standards as " 'Round Midnight" and "Stardust." At one point, having been bested by Lonnie, the evil antagonist says, "I should never have sent you guys up against a jazz musician. Those guys are dangerous."

Knight, Damon. "Coming Back to Dixieland." *Orbit 18,* 1976. In *The Planet on the Table*, edited by Kim Stanley Robinson, 168–97. New York: Tom Doherty/TOR, 1986.

A science fiction story in which several miners on Titania must overcome serious obstacles in order to compete in a musical competition fifteen million miles away. The Hot Six is a Dixieland combo that plays "old Earth-type music," but their tuba player is missing. Miraculously, they find a replacement at the last minute—a musician no one has ever heard of and who had learned his instrument on Mars. After a stunning (and well-described) performance, the boys are awarded a grant: a four-year tour of the Solar System. Music is very much at the heart of this story; ample reference to Louis Armstrong.

Knight, Phyllis. *Shattered Rhythms*. New York: St. Martin's, 1994.

Lesbian PI Lil Ritchie follows around a great Franco-American jazz guitarist, Andre Ledoux, using his music as an anodyne for her psychic wounds. When he disappears, she is hired to find him, allowing her to go to the great Montreal Jazz Festival. The book contains a few pretty good descriptions of music but as a whole it's generally a far-fetched, cliché-ridden, tensionless mystery with minimal jazz interest.

Kotzwinkle, William. *The Hot Jazz Trio*. Boston: Houghton Mifflin/Seymour Lawrence, 1989.

Although the titles of the three stories in this triptych—"Django Reinhardt Played the Blues," "Blues on the Nile," and "Boxcar Blues"—imply solid musical content, there is very little. In the first story, Django Reinhardt and his Hot Jazz Trio (which becomes the Duo and a Half when Reinhardt is halved!) are performing in Paris in the 1920s; other characters in this fantasy include Cocteau, Picasso, and Sartre. In one of the chief incidents, a box falls in love with a disappearing woman. There's no musical content in the second and third stories.

Lamb, David. *The Trumpet Is Blown*. New York: I Write What I Like, 1997.

Yet another coming-of-age narrative. Two seemingly inseparable young friends from the projects grow apart as they struggle to come to terms with their environment, the crack-and-violence-dominated world of Bedford-Stuyvesant. One of the boys, Shawn, embraces the world of drugs, while the other, Chris (later Jibril), dedicates himself to the trumpet and his adopted religion, Islam. Jibril has the good luck to be guided by Hassan, a jazz trumpet legend who teaches music with lessons drawn from basketball and religion. Many jazz references to such performers as Dizzy Gillespie, Miles Davis, John Coltrane, Art Blakey, and David Sanchez.

Lange, Art, and Nathaniel Mackey, eds. *Moment's Notice: Jazz in Poetry and Prose*. Minneapolis: Coffee House, 1993.

The editors claim that this is the first anthology to bring together both jazz-related poetry and prose. While it inevitably duplicates some entries from earlier collections (Richard N. Albert's *From Blues to Bebop: A Collection of Jazz Fiction*, Marcela Breton's *Hot and Cool: Jazz Short Stories*, and Sascha Feinstein and Yusef Komunyakaa's *The Jazz Poetry Anthology*), it also includes works that have not been previously collected; full-page photographs are interspersed throughout the text.

Lardner, Ring. "Rhythm." In *The Love Nest and Other Stories*, 163–83. New York: Scribner's, 1926.

At the heart of this story is the question of whether it is morally reprehensible—or acceptable behavior—for jazz composers to "borrow" from classical sources for their ideas. The implication is that such borrowing is integral to the composition of jazz.

Lea, George. *Somewhere There's Music*. Philadelphia: Lippincott, 1958.

A post-Korean War novel featuring that jazz stereotype, the self-destructive musician. Saxophonist Mike Logan simply drifts through life without goal or direction, consuming drugs and alcohol as if they were his raison d'être.

Lee, George Washington. "Beale Street Anyhow." In *Beale Street Sundown*, 13–35. New York: House of Field, 1942.

Matt Johnson, the Master of Revels for the annual carnival celebration in Memphis, hatches a plan to insure that the name of Beale Street not be changed to Beale Avenue. Although street music is clearly part of the Beale Street experience, it is not given much emphasis in this story.

———. "The Beale Street Blues I'm Singing." In *Beale Street Sundown*, 156–76. New York: House of Field, 1942.

After getting his best suit and good glass eye out of hock, Mushmouth Henry returns to Beale Street where he is disappointed to discover the prevalence of the blues, which he feels has a negative impact on the street. Mushmouth does his best to uproot the blues but, ironically, becomes a blues singer himself.

———. "The First Blues Singer." In *Beale Street Sundown*, 70–86. New York: House of Field, 1942.

When daughter of Beale Street, young Alberta, takes voice lessons and demonstrates excellent potential, she is discouraged from singing the blues she loves. Alberta becomes famous and travels all over but cannot resist singing her beloved blues; as the narrator says after hearing her sing: ". . . I thought I heard in her voice the rhythm of the Mississippi River when it laps at the foot of Beale Street and then rolls away gently to the sea."

———. "It Happened at an Amateur Show." In *Beale Street Sundown*, 36–47. New York: House of Field, 1942.

The speaker had never enjoyed amateur nights but when he overhears a mulatto woman encouraging her dark young friend to enter a contest that night, he decides to attend. The young girl is a great hit but gets into trouble after dedicating "The Ethiopian Blues" to her white employers, who consider the song too nasty for polite (i.e. white) society.

Lively, Adam. *Blue Fruit*. London: Simon and Schuster, 1988; New York: Simon and Schuster, 1989.

A time-travel novel in which a young ship's surgeon on a whaling vessel in the eighteenth century, John Field, is put ashore in twentieth century Harlem, where he is taken in by a black family. Field is befriended by Tommy, a talented, innovative saxophonist who guides Field through the jazz dives of Harlem. Several vivid descriptions of improvisational jazz in the making.

Lombreglia, Ralph. "Jazzers." *Iowa Review* 4 (1) (Winter 1984): 51–63.

The speaker meets his old buddy Bobby in a newly yuppified Baltimore bar where the sounds of jazz on the stereo system distract them from the question at hand: Bobby's woman problem. Many drinks and hours later, the two guys (who had had a jazz combo some years earlier) get involved in a lively jam session, ultimately turning their thoughts to the possibility of getting a band together and returning to music. As the title implies, the story is dominated by jazz.

London, Jonathan. *Hip Cat.* San Francisco: Chronicle, 1993.

Miles Davis and John Coltrane are among the dedicatees of this rhythmic story for young readers about a saxophone-playing hip cat (feline variety) who goes to the big city in search of fame and fortune only to discover that all the really cool clubs are owned by powerful dogs.

Loustal-Paringaux, Jacques de. *Barney and the Blue Note*. Translated by Frieda Leia Jacobowitz. Netherlands: Rijperman, 1988.

A graphic (i.e., illustrated) novel about a sax player, Barney, who had briefly been the talk of the jazz world in the 1950s. But the more famous he became, the more he retreated from the world. After a gig with Art Blakey and the Messengers, Barney starts shooting heroin, loses his talent, retreats into a life of cigarettes, booze, hotel rooms, sex, and existential remoteness. Despite the fact that Barney is clearly a lost soul, he is irresistible to one once-beautiful woman, whose love allows him to regain his chops. Because of his instability and his unpredictable behavior, record companies refuse to record him. After sitting in at the 5 Spot and being told by the black leader that he'd never heard a white man play like Barney (borrowing from an Art Pepper anecdote), Barney goes to California, disappears from the scene, kills a man over dope, spends several years in the slammer and mental institution, gets out, starts playing again, and then ODs. A *tres* noir book that exploits all of the worst jazz myths and stereotypes.

Lovin, Roger Robert. "Professor Latiolais' Last Stand." *Music and Sound Output*, September/October 1982.

Not seen.

Lowry, Malcolm. "The Forest Path to the Spring." In *Hear Us O Lord from Heaven Thy Dwelling Place*, 215–83. Philadelphia: Lippincott, 1961.

The narrator, a former jazz musician, decides to write a jazz symphony while trying to get his life together in the Pacific Northwest. Significant passages relating to the music and legendary performers of jazz.

Lutz, John. "The Right to Sing the Blues." *Alfred Hitchcock Mystery Magazine*, 1983. In *Murder to Music*, edited by Cynthia Manson and Kathleen Halligan, 203–33. New York: Carroll and Graf Publishers, 1997.

Jazz-loving private detective Nudger is summoned to New Orleans where legendary clarinetist Fat Jack McGee hires him to investigate the suspicious behavior of Willy Hollister, a club musician who "plays ultrafine piano." Nudger uncovers some disturbing coincidences in Hollister's past, and after relating these to his employer, Hollister mysteriously vanishes. Solid jazz content.

——. *The Right to Sing the Blues.* New York: St. Martin's, 1986. An expansion of the story by the same title (q.v.).

Mackey, Henry B. "The Phenomenal Resurgence of the Spasm Band." *Record Changer* 9: (December 1950).

A parody of the white critics' efforts to track down legendary musicians in order to discover the so-called truth behind the origins of jazz. When the critic-narrator finally locates the legendary 193-year-old kazoo wizard, Jug-Head Brown, in Africa, he asks such questions as, "When were legitimate instruments first used in jazz, Jug-Head?" The latter replies (in part): "That was a sad day, man. The real jazz, the true jazz, man, you can't play that on no legit' horn!"

Mackey, Nathaniel. *Bedouin Hornbook*. 1986. Los Angeles: Sun and Moon, 1997.

An epistolary fiction in which "N." addresses a series of letters to "Angel of Dust"; the letters are thick with jazz references and often contain lengthy meditations on various questions relating to mostly post-bop music. The following passage typifies the musical monologue at the heart of this plotless novel: "I've been listening a lot to Pharoah Sanders's solo on the version of 'My Favorite Things' on *Coltrane Live at the Village Vanguard Again!* The fellow who wrote the liner-notes quotes Trane as having said that he was 'trying to work out a kind of writing that will allow for more plasticity, more viability, more room for improvisation in the statement of the melody itself.' That may well be what I'm after as well. What gets me about Pharoah's solo is the way he treats the melody towards the end of it, coming on to it with a stuttering, jittery, tongue-tied articulation which appears to say that the simple amenities or naïve consolations of so innocuous a tune have long since broken down. He manages to be true to the eventual debris of every would-be composer. (Think about the movie the song is taken from.) It's as though he drank water from a rusted cup, the tenor's voice such an asthmatic ambush of itself as to trouble every claim to a 'composed' approach. To me it borders on prayer, though prayer would here have to be revised so as to implicate humility in some form of détente—an uneasy truce or eleventh-hour treaty—with hubris. Part prayer, part witch's brew."

——. *Djbot Baghostus's Run.* Los Angeles: Sun and Moon, 1993.

A continuation of *Bedoin Hornbook* (q.v.) and "volume two of *From a Broken Bottle Traces of Perfume Still Emanate,* an ongoing work." As in *Bedoin,* this unclassifiable fiction comprises a series of letters addressed to "Angel of Dust" that are punctuated with references to, and discussions of, music, especially jazz. The objectives of these experimental fictions by Mackey are obscure; any reader would welcome an explanatory note of some kind.

——. "From *Djbot Baghostus's Run.*" In *Breaking Ice: An Anthology of Contemporary African-American Fiction,* edited by Terry McMillan, 446–56. New York: Viking, 1990.

An excerpt from the novel of the same name (q.v.). This section contains substantial reference to Miles Davis's *Seven Steps to Heaven.*

Major, Clarence. *Dirty Bird Blues*. San Francisco: Mercury House, 1996.

In his mid-twenties, shortly after WWII, Manfred "Man" Banks strives to put his life back together. He lives for his wife and daughter and dreams of making music the center of his life: he "used the harmonica or the sax to say what he couldn't find words to say." But racism and booze in the form of Old Crow bourbon (the titular Dirty Bird) constantly threaten to turn his life into shambles. Man finally overcomes the obstacles that challenge his security and looks forward to a sanguine future. Man used to warm-up for Billie Holiday; the novel makes frequent reference to blues musicians and employs blues techniques in its narrative structure.

Malone, R. Pingank. "Sound Your 'A': The Story of Trumpeter Tom Stewart in Full-Length Novel Form." *Metronome* 58: 16–17 (September 1942); 58: 14–15 (October 1942); 58: 14–15 (November 1942); 58: 14–15 (December 1942); 59: 16–17 (February 1943).

A serialized novel focusing on a group of mostly young musicians with jazz aspirations who are reduced to playing in a pit band. One of the players, Tom Stewart, gets a chance to fill in with a name band that is unfortunately famous for its "tickety-tockety" style of music. The bandleader falls in love with Tom's corny playing, not realizing that Tom is making fun of the music. Tom switches bands, creates envy through his virtuoso playing, and gets in fights. Many references to such popular bands of the time as Woody Herman's and Charlie Barnet's.

Manus, Willard. *Connubial Bliss*. Los Angeles: Panjandrum Press, 1990.

A raucous, raunchily sexist farce featuring the improbable, often grotesque shenanigans of a not-so-young, not-so-nice Jewish boy from the Bronx, Lenny Samuels, who spews street Yiddish and the language of high culture with equal flippancy. The modest jazz connection involves Lenny's friend Sydney, whose Uncle Sol is a jazz musician who once played with Petronius Priest (obviously based on Thelonious Monk): "A singular figure in a derby and goatee, playing his crabbed single-line notes and crazy chords with wicked humor." Sydney also delights in showing off his record collection, which stretches from "Buddy Bolden to Ornette's *Enfante*, with a long loving stop en route for Charlie and Diz singing SALT PEANUTS, SALT PEANUTS and that Jackie McLean record with Donald Byrd on trumpet . . ."

———. "Hello Central, Give Me Doctor Jazz." *New Letters* 51 (2): 19–28 (Winter 1984–85).

In this section from *Connubial Bliss* (q.v.), Lenny is visiting jazzman Sol, who is taking the cure for drug addiction and doubting his ability to recover his musical talent.

Marsh, Ngaio. *A Wreath for Rivera*. London: 1943; Boston: Little, Brown, 1949.

A classic British mystery with eccentric characters, a baffling crime, and the redoubtable Scotland Yard detective, Inspector Alleyn. The jazz content is limited to the first third of the novel where Breezy Bellair and his boogie-woogie band prepare to unveil a novelty number involving mock killings of various band members; the mock of course, in an elaborate twist, becomes real.

Marsh, Willard. "Mending Wall." *Southern Review* n.s. 5: 1192–1204 (Autumn 1969).

In his native Mexico during a semester break, Miguel is more or less forced to provide hospitality to some of his fellow law students while they wait for a bus. The more Miguel's Anglo friends drink, the more contemptuous they become of Hispanic culture and even of the jazz they claim to love. In the case of this story, good fences *do* make good neighbors.

Marshall, Paule. *The Fisher King*. New York: Scribner, 2000.

Shortly after World War II, Sonny-Rett Payne fled New York to escape his family's disapproval of "the Sodom and Gomorrah" music he played and the racism that interfered with his art. Payne's legendary success as a jazz pianist in Europe and his subsequent death provide the background for this novel that explores the effect of his fame on the fragile dynamics of the family and community he left behind. Decades after his death, Payne's old Brooklyn neighborhood stages a memorial concert in his honor. It is in these pages (chapters 15–17) that the jazz focus is greatest.

Martin, Kenneth K. "The End of Jamie." *Negro Digest*, December 1964, 63–70.

Sullen teenager Jamie leaves Harlem to visit his uncle in the South. When he returns after a year, he has changed: not only is he much taller, but he has learned to play jazz on the harmonica; in fact, he has learned to externalize his dark moods through his music. But at one point, Jamie can no longer make his harmonica speak for him and so loses hope.

Martucci, Ida. *Jive Jungle*. New York: Vantage, 1956.

Basically a love story that incorporates jazz as background music. One character is a musician, and there are scattered references to such musicians as Barbara Carroll, Miles Davis, Howard McGhee, Kai Winding, Machito, and Stan Getz.

Matheson, Richard. "The Jazz Machine." *Magazine of Fantasy and Science Fiction,* 1963. In *The 9th Annual of the Year's Best SF,* edited by Judith Merril, 143–50. New York: Simon and Schuster, 1964.

The black musician telling this free verse narrative is approached by a white man ("Mr. Pink"), who tells the trumpeter that his music reveals that he has recently lost someone close to him. Then Mr. Pink shows the narrator a machine he had invented that changes the sounds of jazz into the feelings that created them. The narrator smashes the machine with his instrument, reflecting that, although whites may continue to exploit blacks in every way imaginable, they better not "come scuffling for our souls" (i.e., the feelings they play through their music).

McCarthy, Albert J. "My Home Is a Southern Town." In *Jazz Parody (Anthology of Jazz Fiction)*, edited by Charles Harvey, 57–61. London: Spearman Publishers, 1948.

Grant Farber, talented blues pianist, moves north where he achieves some grudging fame from the white society that patronizes him. He returns to the South, knowing that his destiny is to be killed by the racist society he couldn't escape.

McCluskey, John. *Look What They Done to My Song*. New York: Random House, 1974.

A first-person account of a young, down-and-out black jazz musician's search for racial identity during the 1960s. He says his sound has been described in many ways: "The Eldorado drive of Stanley Turrentine, the swift glad comedy of Sonny Rollins, the steady quest of John Coltrane." Yet he finds precious few opportunities to demonstrate these laudable qualities. At the end, he is in the process of incorporating into his musical compositions every variety of "blackness" he has encountered on his odyssey.

———. "Lush Life." *Callaloo* 13 (2) (Spring 1990): 201–12 .

Life on the road with "Earl Ferguson and America's Greatest Band." As Earl and his wonderful composer/arranger Billy Cox travel ahead of the band bus, they chat about what it's like to move from town to town trying to capture the interest of different audiences. After Billy tells an affecting story, Earl responds: "It's this music we play, Billy! It opens people up, makes them give up secrets. Better than whiskey or dope for that. It don't kill you, and you can't piss it away. You can whistle it the next day in new places. You can loan it to strangers, and they thank you for it. . . . It's what keeps us going all night." The story is also interesting for its dramatization of the creative process, as we see the two men struggle to put together a new song, wondering at the end if it will go over with their audiences.

McConduit, Denise Walter. *D.J. and the Jazz Fest*. Gretnor, LA: Pelican, 1997.

An illustrated book for juveniles "in commemoration of the 100th anniversary of jazz." When D.J.'s mom suggests to him that they go to the New Orleans jazz fest, D.J. thinks it's a boring idea. But when he gets there and sees Wynton Marsalis, B.B. King, and the Neville brothers and gets caught up in the excitement, he changes his mind. He is last seen, bright flag in hand, marching along with a band and, thanks to jazz, feeling special.

McKay, Claude. *Home to Harlem*. New York: Harper and Brothers, 1928.

Jazz is primarily used as background in this novel, but it is also dramatized (especially in chapter 4) as being central to black culture.

McMartin, Sean. "Music for One Hand Only." *Phylon 2* (Summer 1969): 197–202.

When Bernie McCafferty overhears an Ella Fitzgerald recording, he tracks down its owner, who, after claiming to be part black, offers to sell Bernie the record for an extortionate sum. In this futuristic story, plagues had decimated the black population of Africa, and now enormous numbers of British and American blacks have moved to Africa to repopulate the continent. It seems that what remains of black culture in the U.S. and the western world in general is at serious risk, threatening cultural impoverishment. Several references to black female jazz singers.

McNutt, William Slavens. "Jazz Justice." *Collier's* 5+, December 27, 1924.

Orphaned early and raised in the sticks by relatives, Shirley Horton moves to Manhattan where she becomes "a gold digger with a conscience," exploiting man after man until she meets her match in Ted Snowden: ". . . a slim, blond, modern troubadour. The generation of jazz shimmied to his tunes in Shanghai and hummed his lyrics in London. Wherever throughout the world were orchestras and dance floors, liquor and lights, men and women, love and laughter in combination, there was the sound of a Snowden tune, savagely gay, cynically sensuous, weirdly, intoxicatingly rhythmic, a mocking, insolent, yet hauntingly wistful expression in movement and melody of the syncopated soul of Now. As a reward for the songs that bubbled effortlessly out of him he received a yearly return greater than the annual salary of the President of the United States." Very much a tale of the jazz age with snappy dialogue, speedy roadsters, and high living in the big city.

McSiegel, Professor Snotty. See Feather, Leonard.

Merril, Judith. "Muted Hunger." *The Saint Mystery Magazine*, October 1963: 51–63. In *The Saint Magazine Reader,* edited by Leslie Charteris and Hans Santesson, 197–212. Garden City, NY: Doubleday, 1963.

The narrator is surprised when her detective-husband Pete (who is not a jazz fan) suggests they go to the Horn, a jazz club where a combo has been playing exciting music for a couple of months—or ever since a very hot blonde ("a bitch and a tease") started hanging out, causing competition among the musicians on the stand. Pete is right in thinking that his wife's deep knowledge of jazz will help him solve Cindi's brutal rape and beating. An unusual story of its kind because it gives as much attention to the music as to the mystery.

Millen, Gilmore. *Sweet Man*. New York: Viking, 1930; London: Cassell, 1930.

Dedicated to Carl Van Vechten and very much in the vogue of *Nigger Heaven*, this novel is the story of John Henry, a black plantation worker with a weakness for booze and women. After serving in France in WWI, John Henry enters into a relationship with a blonde woman, who keeps him—hence the title. Told largely in the southern black vernacular, this truly dreadful novel makes only passing references to the blues and jazz-blues. The name of John Henry is of course a familiar one in folklore and blues.

Miller, Fred. *Gutbucket and Gossamer: A Short Story*. Yonkers, NY: Alicat Bookshop, 1950.

A 27-page chapbook story recounting a boozy weekend in 1940 for two "temporary grass widowers." Their wives elsewhere, Teddy and

George get together to drink and listen to jazz; as so often happens under such circumstances, flirtations ensue. Many references to music and musicians: Mezz Mezzrow, Sidney Bechet, Clarence Williams, King Oliver, Muggsy Spanier, and Louis Armstrong, among others.

Miller, Warren. *The Cool World*. New York: Little, Brown, 1959.

A coming-of-age novel centering on gang life in Harlem. Perhaps because it has characters named Duke and Bebop and is told in jazzy language, this work has been cited in the scholarship regarding jazz fiction. But there are no musical scenes or jazz references. It was made into a movie with a soundtrack by Dizzy Gillespie.

Miller, William. *Rent Party Jazz.* New York: Lee and Low Books, 2001.

A juvenile book summarized thus by the Library of Congress: "When Sonny's mother loses her job in New Orleans during the Depression, Smilin' Jack, a jazz musician, tells him how to organize a rent party to raise money they need." Not seen.

Mitchell, Adrian. *If You See Me Comin'*. New York: Macmillan, 1962; London: J. Cape, 1962.

The events of a week are filtered through the hypersensitive consciousness of a British blues singer, Johnny Crane. Frequent references to American jazz artists and a couple of scenes depicting musical performance.

Moody, Bill. *Bird Lives!* New York: Walker, 1999.

Somebody's killing the Kenny G-like smooth-jazz musicians, and Evan Horne is called in—by the FBI no less—to help solve the serial murders. Horne's life is complicated by his attraction to one of the FBI agents assigned to the case (which strains his relationship with his longtime girlfriend) and by his commitment to a recording contract he has just signed with great anticipation. As usual in this series, there is ample reference to jazz and its musicians. Dave McKenna has a brief role.

———. *Death of a Tenor Man*. New York: Walker, 1995.

Second in a series featuring amateur detective Evan Horne. In this novel, Horne goes from his home-base in Los Angeles to Las Vegas to help an English professor friend at UNLV research the suspicious death of Wardell Gray, who died in Las Vegas in 1955. The jazz content is considerable and organic. The reader can make a transformative experience out of this series by playing the music that is mentioned while reading the novel. It works.

———. "Grace Notes." In *Blue Lightning*, edited by John Harvey, 171–82. London: Slow Dancer Press, 1998; Chester Springs, PA: Dufour Editions, 1999.

Ex-junkie saxophonist, Noel Coffey, is hoping for a comeback after two months in rehab. Years ago Noel had played with Miles [Davis] and had even recorded an album with him, but then his career got lost in the shuffle. Now he has landed a gig in Germany and wonders if he will be able to pull himself back together. The last sentence is a provocative shocker.

———. "The Resurrection of Bobo Jones." In *B Flat, Bebop, Scat*, edited by Chris Parker, 1–19. London: Quartet, 1986.

Brew Daniels is a talented tenor sax man whose outlandish pranks get him exiled to the nether fringes of the jazz world. When Brew's agent finally lands Brew a gig, it's at the musical equivalent of the last resort—the nicely named "The Final Bar"—where pianist Bobo Jones is trying to make a comeback after being institutionalized for mental incapacity. Anxious because of Bobo's reputation and also because he's the only white in an otherwise all-black combo, Brew nevertheless is able to help Bobo regain his musical genius. The story has a very satisfying denouement.

_______. *Solo Hand*. New York: Walker, 1994.

The first in a mystery series featuring Evan Horne, a jazz pianist who became an amateur sleuth after injuring his hand in an auto accident. Here he tries to disentangle two musicians from a blackmail scam that could ruin their careers. Characteristic of this series, the events shuttle between Los Angeles and Las Vegas and contain considerable jazz content. One of the musicians, Lonnie Cole, even named his dogs Miles and Bird, after the bebop greats, Miles Davis and Charlie Parker. An additional point of interest for music lovers is the discussion of the mechanics of the CD industry.

———. *The Sound of the Trumpet*. New York: Walker, 1997.

Jazz pianist Evan Horne turns detective while his hand, injured in an auto accident, undergoes rehabilitation. This novel—the third in an ongoing series—revolves around an audiotape that may be the last recording of the legendary trumpeter Clifford Brown, who died in a car accident when he was 25. References to jazz and jazz musicians, especially of the bop era, are ubiquitous. Moody incorporates a series of "Interludes" in which he imaginatively recreates the final days of Brown's life. Jazz fans will find much of interest in this novel, and so will obsessive collectors and mystery buffs. In a fascinating addendum on the life-imitating-art theme, an audio tape of one of Clifford Brown's last sessions (with Max Roach and Sonny Rollins) *was* unearthed after the publication of this novel and is expected to be produced by Blue Note.

Morgan, Max [pseud.]. *Aerobleu: Pilot's Journal*. San Francisco: Chronicle Books, 1997.

Printed in holograph font on "aged" newsprint and presented in an aluminum slipcase, this novel masquerades as the diary of World War II pilot, Max Morgan, who is at the center of the vibrant jazz scene in Paris in the late 1940s. Max first established his jazz credentials through his impressive collection of bop records and then by operating a jazz club, Aerobleu, which was frequented by all of the "names" of the era, from Josephine Baker to Jean Paul Sartre. There's jazz chat on practically every unnumbered page, and Dizzy Gillespie and Charlie Parker play significant roles. At one point, jazz critic Hugues Panassié denounces Morgan, along with Gillespie and Parker, for promoting rebop; later Panassié claims that Morgan "was a corrupting influence on jazz, and that . . . [Morgan's] Aerobleu sessions were leading French musicians astray . . ." Although *Aerobleu* comes in book form, it is no longer than the average short story.

Morrison, Toni. *Jazz*. New York: Knopf, 1992; London: Chatto and Windus, 1992.

An exploration of the lives of several African American characters who live in Harlem in 1926 but have their roots in the South. The triggering incident concerns Joe Trace, a married man in his 50s, and his lustful obsession with 18-year-old Dorcas, whom he kills when their affair goes awry. Joe's wife takes very unusual revenge by bursting into Dorcas's funeral and trying to slash the dead girl's face. The title of the book reflects its loose, improvisational structure more than its content, and comes from its association with sex, violence, and chaos: ". . . the music was getting worse and worse . . . songs that used to start in the head and fill the heart had dropped on down, down to places below the sash and buckled belts." The "Music made you do unwise disorderly things. Just hearing it was like violating the law." In short, for Toni Morrison in this novel jazz exerts a corrupting influence on the lives of the blacks.

Mosley, Walter. "Blue Lightning." In *Blue Lightning*, edited by John Harvey, 183–209. London: Slow Dancer Press, 1998; Chester Springs, PA: Dufour Editions, 1999.

A couple of days in the life of ex-con Socrates Fortlow, who is offered a promotion from his low-paying, menial job in Watts. Socrates' sleep is disturbed by a trumpet in the night; later he meets with the horn man, the two of them get drunk together, and the horn man rips off Socrates. Slight musical content.

———. *RL's Dream*. New York: W.W. Norton, 1995; London: Serpent's Tail, 1995.

Atwater "Soupspoon" Wise is an old, dying blues guitarist and singer from the Mississippi Delta living in New York. Seemingly at the bottom of his personal abyss, Soupspoon is befriended by Kiki, a young woman who is also from the South and who also experienced a painful past. Soupspoon's most haunting memories are of playing with the legendary bluesman Robert "RL" Johnson, whose music "would rip the skin right off yo' back" and "get down to a nerve most people don't even have no more." Thanks to Kiki, Soupspoon is able to record his memories on tape and in so doing lessen the pain of both of their lives.

Moss, Grant. "I Remember Bessie Smith." *Essence*, December 1978, 66+.

Whenever the speaker thinks of Bessie Smith or hears one of her recordings, he is immediately transported in his mind back to his younger days, growing up in the South, surrounded by friends and family. He thinks especially of Miss Lily Bonner, who townsfolk claimed "could beat Bessie singing the blues." When, much later, the narrator returns home to New Hill, he is saddened to discover that Miss Bonner no longer takes pleasure from the blues: "Nothing is ever the same as it once was" is his mature realization.

Muñoz Molina, Antonio. *El Invierno en Lisboa*. Barcelona: Seix Barral, 1987. Translated by Sonia Soto as *Winter in Lisbon*. London: Granta, 1999.

An atmospheric novel filled with smoky saloons, bibulous musicians, and the intertwining quests for love and meaning against the backdrop of international crime in San Sebastian and Lisbon, among other places. The main character, Biralbo, is a jazz pianist who lacks the gift of genius. Another major character is American trumpeter Billy Swann, who has—or had—that gift in abundance. These and other musicians play in clubs with names like Lady Bird and Satchmo, and their performances are nicely—and unobtrusively—described. It could be argued that the unfolding of the plot mimics the complex rhythms of jazz. In its obvious homage to jazz and film noir, this novel could accurately be described as jazz noir fiction. It contains several provocative meditations on music, such as: (a) ". . . musicians know the past doesn't exist. . . . Painters and writers accumulate the past on their shoulders, in their words and paintings, but a musician always operates in a void. His music ceases to exist the moment he stops playing. It's pure present." (b) "Music doesn't care about us. It doesn't care how much pain or passion we put into it when we play or listen. It uses us, like a woman with a lover she's indifferent to." (c) "The greatest perversion a musician can commit while playing is autobiography." The book won the Spanish National Prize for Literature and the Critics' Prize and has been translated into sixteen languages; in short, a work that deserves to be placed in the highest rank of jazz fiction.

Murphy, Dallas. *Don't Explain*. New York: Pocket Books, 1996.

A wacky mystery featuring Artie Deemer, his cash-cow dog, Jellyroll (who is famous for his TV commercial), and his lovely sweetheart, professional pool player Crystal Spivey. Despite the title from a Billie Holiday song, the dog named after a famous jazz musician, and Artie's love of listening to jazz (which he doesn't do in this novel), there is no jazz content in this book.

———. *Lover Man*. New York: Scribner's, 1987.

The first in a series, each edition of which (so far) takes its title from a jazz standard. In this novel, New Yorker Artie Deemer discovers that his old girlfriend has been murdered; after a period of inertia, he goes in search of her killer. Artie is accompanied by his dog, Jellyroll, who (like his master) loves listening to jazz, especially bebop. Artie's favorite activity is to kick back and listen to his beloved jazz heroes, many of whom are mentioned by name in this humorous mystery.

———. *Lush Life*. New York: Pocket Books, 1992.

Artie Deemer, amateur detective, loves to listen to jazz, especially such boppers as Thelonious Monk and Charlie Parker; and when he needs to think, he plays hard-driving, brain-blasting bebop. When he goes to bed with his new sweetheart for the first time, Johnnie Hartman provides the background music, no doubt enabling the lovers' simultaneous orgasm. The title of this series mystery comes from the famous Billy Strayhorn song.

Murray, Albert. *Seven League Boots*. New York: Pantheon, 1995.

In the final volume (to date) of an ongoing work, Scooter—now "Schoolboy"—first becomes a bassist and then leaves the band to write music for the movies, after which he joins the expatriate colony in France. In this and the previous two novels in the series, Murray appropriates, in syntax and structure, certain stylistic devices associated with Afro-American music while frequently referring to jazz and the blues and their performers.

———. *The Spyglass Tree*. New York: Pantheon, 1991.

In this, the second volume of a series, Scooter matures as he matriculates in college in the 1930s.

——. *Train Whistle Guitar*. New York: McGraw-Hill, 1974.

The first novel in a series involving the Scooter's coming-of-age. In this novel, Scooter is a young boy in Alabama in the 1920s who falls under the powerful influence of a couple of bluesmen.

Nash, Leslie Ann. *Martini Diaries,* discovered and introduced by Alston Chase. San Francisco: Chronicle, 1997.

This title appears because it is a companion-piece to Nash's *Observations from the Bar* and Max Morgan's *Aerobleu: Pilot's Journal* (qq.v.), both of which purport to document the goings-on at the Aerobleu Bar, the jazz center of Paris shortly after World War II. This brief book, on the other hand, compiles the martini recipes (with anecdotes concerning their origins) that supposedly were invented for such patrons as Miles Davis, Josephine Baker, and a friend of bandleader Meyer Davis's son. A fiction in the sense that the bar and the events are imaginary, but very little jazz content.

——. *Observations from the Bar*. San Francisco: Chronicle, 1997.

A companion-piece to Max Morgan, *Aerobleu: Pilot's Journal* (q.v.) and flaunting the same impressive gift box production values. This short novel covers much of the same ground as *Pilot's Journal* as it details, from Leslie Nash's point of view, the comings and goings at the Parisian Aerobleu jazz club of such figures as Charlie Parker and Dizzy Gillespie. The story also includes a diaristic account of Nash's falling in love with the mysterious Max Morgan, who is apparently involved in clandestine political activities. "Nash" and "Morgan" are obviously pseudonyms.

Neiderhiser, Ed. "Gone in the Air." In *B Flat, Bebop, Scat*, edited by Chris Parker, 113–19. London: Quartet, 1986.

The speaker, a lover of music and a jazz musician, philosophizes over the meaning of music, especially Eric Dolphy's comment that when the music is over "It's gone in the air" and can never be heard again. Although the speaker claims not to be a mystic, he describes one zen-like experience thus: "Seated at my piano, caressing the keys and shaping the sounds, I could integrate myself in the large scope of reality, the broader perspective. I joined the music in the air and became an intimate partner in the cosmos, not a separate entity fighting its flow. And I could participate in things visible and invisible according to their design, blending my consciousness with that of the creator."

Neil, Al. *Changes*. Toronto: Coach House, 1976.

A plotless first-person narrative containing the reflections and meditations of jazz pianist, Seamus Finn, as he details his drug addiction and jazz involvement in a hallucinatory or surrealistic style. The speaker's comments on music are substantive and generally of the sort (when they are not predictable) to be provocative to the fan—or student—of jazz fiction. Here is one short section on the necessity for jazz to break from the prison of the past: "It is one thing to be hip to Jelly Roll, Armstrong, Ellington, Pres and Bird but why accept what they did as valid for everyone. They most perfectly expressed their era sure enough, but that doesn't help us now does it? What we need is to free our minds of them, and move on, as Ornette is doing, unencumbered by tradition or anything else. Ornette just plays the emotion, it is pure expression, so don't try to fit him in yet, when he has only just started to free himself from Bird. Jazz can really open up now if we don't straight-jacket it too soon. Maybe there should be a moratorium on all critical articles, but then most jazz guys don't pay them any attention anyway."

Nemec, John. *Canary's Combo.* Hollywood: Tempo Publishing, 1964.

The cover of this rare "Nite-Time Original" paperback features an impressively voluptuous striptease artiste in mid-gyratic ecstasy. Behind her, a jazz combo is putting out some hot licks. We later learn that this group of Dixieland musicians are committed to the belief that they can achieve the ineffable through jazz but that "willing female flesh" interferes with their spiritual goal. "Jazz is a naked woman," we read, in a truly baffling metaphor. Clarinetist and saxophonist Joe Falcon is the leader of the band and the protagonist of the novel. He sleeps with Carmela Weims, the stripper on the cover, when he isn't sleeping with his wholesome, college-educated "canary" of the band, Ivy, or the black bombshell vocalist, Bess Diedlich, whose Cadillac becomes a bedroom at the touch of a button. The novel's first complication concerns Ivy's desire to make an honest man of Joe and settle into middle-class complacency. The second involves the brutal murder of Joe's good friend and fellow band member, Benny Sullivan. At this point, Joe appoints himself detective, vowing to avenge the death of his buddy, who turns out, to Joe's astonishment, to have been gay. While conducting his investigation, Joe is beaten, attacked by killer dogs, poisoned, and threatened with guns, razors, and switchblades. He is also embroiled in racial matters and accused of rape. When Ivy is then raped, forcing her—with obscure motivation—to relinquish her singing career as well as her dream of marriage, Joe must find a new "canary" for his band. In no time at all, an incredibly beautiful, talented, sexy career-oriented new singer materializes, reviving Joe's dream of achieving celestial heights through music. The final words of the novel, as Joe listens to the new vocalist, suggest that he may already be there: "Like *wow.*" Jazz purists may be challenged to understand how Joe and company can hope to achieve artistic nirvana with one distractingly provocative nude dancing before them while an equally sexy gal belts out "The Muskrat Ramble" behind them. The all-male audience on the cover do not *appear* to be jazz aficionados.

Newton, Suzanne. *I Will Call It Georgie's Blues*. New York: Viking, 1983.

In this novel for young readers, a Southern Baptist's 15-year-old son, Neal, feels compelled to hide his consuming passion for jazz because it doesn't conform to his family's rigid concept of social behavior. Neal listens to the great bebop pianists and tries to absorb their techniques without actually imitating the artists. Nevertheless, the music in this work is more plot device than topic exploration.

Odier, Daniel. *Cannibal Kiss*. Translated by Lanie Goodman. New York: Random House, 1989. [First published in France as *Le baiser cannibale* by èditions Fayard-Mazarine, 1987.]

With an epigraph from Archie Shepp, sprinkled references to classic bebop musicians, a cat called Lester Young, and a protagonist nicknamed Bird, this free-form novel (which traces the picaresque adventures of its 15-year-old heroine) apparently wants the reader to believe that it is the novelistic equivalent of an inspired Charlie Parker solo. One can only hope that the writer (who is more famous in America under the pseudonym Delacorta) will resist basing his next novel on the paintings of, say, Jackson Pollock.

Oglesby, W. M. Ellis. *Blow Happy, Blow Sad*. Edmonton, Canada: Commonwealth Publications, 1995.

An espionage novel of the resistance movement to the Nazi occupation of Denmark during WWII. Black American jazz man, Chops Danielson, risks his life in war-torn Denmark both by playing his cornet in underground jazz venues during which he sends coded military messages to England via his instrument (reminiscent of the French soldiers during the same war who used the numbers of Louis Armstrong records as code) and by trying to rescue his Danish classical violinist sweetheart from the clutches of the Nazis. There are too many crosses and double-crosses to keep track of in this long, melodramatic, espionage novel.

O'Hara, John. "The Flatted Saxophone." *New Yorker* 39: 28–29 (June 1, 1963).

The meager jazz content of this abbreviated story occurs in the beginning in a discourse on flatted tenor saxophones—that is, saxophones played out-of-doors, as at weddings—causing one character to respond that if he wants to listen to good saxophone playing, he will "find out where Bud Freeman's working." The rest of the story—all dialogue—concerns marriage.

———. "The Pioneer Hep-Cat." In *Assembly*, 103–16. New York: Random House, 1961.

A pleasantly discursive story in which an old newspaperman addresses a high school journalism club on the topic of the music from the 1920s that might be called prejazz. The speaker avows that he would much rather talk about someone from Pennsylvania's coal country who rose above his circumstances and made a great success of his life, but his young audiences always want to hear about the legendary singer, Red Watson, a jazz pioneer who drank himself into a shockingly early grave. The story is based on the legendary jazz singer from the Scranton area, Jack Gallagher, with whom (apparently) the author once sang a drunken duet of "Jazz Me." Considerable jazz reference to the Swing Era and the years immediately before and after.

Oliphant, Robert. *A Trumpet for Jackie*. Englewood Cliffs, NJ: Prentice-Hall, 1983.

The story of Jackie Hayes, a jazz trumpeter who gives up performing to become successful in other, nonmusical endeavors, all the time retaining his love for jazz.

Oliver, Chad. "Didn't He Ramble." *The Magazine of Fantasy and Science Fiction,* April 1957. In *The Best Science-Fiction Stories and Novels: Ninth Series*, edited by T.E. Dikty, no. 9, 85–96. Chicago: Advent, 1958.

When wealthy old Theodor Pearsall's wife nags him to throw a party, he manages to be transported back 200 years to Storyville, where he can be surrounded by his beloved music. When he dies, he's given a rousing jazz funeral parade: "Louis was there, and Bix, and Bunk. Ory's trombone and Teagarden's. Bechet and Dodds and Fazola on clarinets. Minor Hall, his drum muffled with a handkerchief."

Ondaatje, Michael. *Coming Through Slaughter*. Toronto: House of Anansi, 1976; New York: W.W. Norton, 1976.

A stunning novel in which the writer starts with the few known facts of one of jazz's "inventors," Buddy Bolden, and imaginatively recreates his disintegration. Taking us inside the head of the legendary cornetist, the author allows us to experience Bolden's schizophrenia, his obsession with women (love, sex?), and his relationship to the innovative music he creates. A serious novel that effectively employs modernistic techniques.

Ottley, Roi. *White Marble Lady*. New York: Farrar, Straus and Giroux, 1965.

The interracial marriage between African American Jeff Kirby (a failed composer but successful singer) and white blue blood Deborah Comstock seems doomed from the start and does indeed end tragically.

Although the novel takes place in a Harlem club where music is performed, numbers several jazzmen among the dramatis personae, and features a protagonist who is deeply involved in the music scene, it contains very little jazz content.

Painter, Pamela. "The Next Time I Meet Buddy Rich." *North American Review* 264: 30–34 (Spring 1979).

Living out of a suitcase for long stretches at a time has created tension between a young drummer and his girlfriend, Gretel. The conflict is resolved after Tony has had a chance meeting with his idol, Buddy Rich: Tony chooses the hard life of the itinerant musician rather than the more conventional alternative.

Parker, Chris, ed. *B Flat, Bebop, Scat*. London: Quartet, 1986.

A healthy collection of previously unpublished short stories and poems, many by not-so-famous writers. See entries for Patrick Biggie, Campbell Burnap, Elaine Cohen, Clive Davis, Digby Fairweather, Julio Finn, Kitty Grime, William J. Moody, Ed Neiderhiser, Alice Wooledge Salmon, Robert J. Tilley, and Zinovy Zinik.

Perlongo, Robert A. "Jollity on a Treadmill." In *Jazz 1959: The Metronome Yearbook, 1959*, edited by Bill Coss, 59–61. New York: Metronome Corporation, 1959.

Not seen.

Petry, Ann. "Solo on the Drums." In *The Magazine of the Year*, 105–10. New York: Associated Magazine, 1947.

Drummer extraordinaire Kid Jones has lost his wife to the piano player and deals with his grief in the best way he knows how: through his music and by identifying with that music as if "he were the drums and the drums were he."

Phillips, Freeman. "Little Nooley's Blues." *American Mercury,* March 1951: 281–92. *Negro Digest,* 9 June 1951, 78–86.

Little Nooley Jackson is so affected by the death of his buddy Buck Manos that he loses his ability to play the trumpet, until one day he returns to Buck's grave in the company of several other New Orleans–style musicians and joyously regains his touch: "And the way Nooley's horn kicked and Ray Bone lay down the beat on the guitar case, it seemed like even the trombones would have to get up and stomp around."

Phillips, Jane. *Mojo Hand*. New York: Trident, 1969.

Eunice Prideaux, the protagonist of this grim novel, is a mulatto whose skin color is such that she is rejected by both races. The story, much of which is told in southern black vernacular ("I axed you what you wants, girl") involves Eunice's fight to be accepted into the black community.

An important character is bluesman Blacksnake Brown, who is apparently modeled after Lightnin' Hopkins. The musical frame of reference is Deep South blues, and several chapters include music in performance.

Pines, Paul. *The Tin Angel*. New York: William Morrow, 1983.

An excellent, vividly atmospheric mystery set in New York's Lower East Side—the East Village—in the 1970s. Considerable jazz reference; indeed, a few folks associated with the jazz world, including Ted Curson and the Termini brothers, play small but significant roles. Dope is very much at the center of the book (in the ambience as well as the plot), but it is not romanticized. Author Pines actually owned a jazz club called "The Tin Angel" on the Bowery. Aficionados will find much of interest concerning the travails of operating a jazz venue.

Plater, Alan. *Misterioso*. London: Methuen, 1987.

A story involving a daughter's search for her father, in this case one whose life was enigmatically connected to Thelonious Monk's tune, "Misterioso."

——. *The Beiderbecke Affair.* London: Methuen, 1985.

References to jazz musicians, especially their recordings, abound in this lighthearted mystery involving reluctant—and unlikely—detectives jazz-lover Trevor Chaplin and his girlfriend Jill Swinburne. When a beautiful platinum blonde offers to sell Trevor some rare Bix Beiderbecke tapes at a very attractive price, he and his partner become entangled in an imbroglio between the local government of Leeds, UK, and white marketeers.

——. *The Beiderbecke Tapes.* London: Methuen, 1986.

A sequel to Plater's *The Beiderbecke Affair* (q.v.) and once again featuring amateur sleuths Trevor Chaplin and Jill Swinburne, who, this time, become involved in crime in high places. After striking a deal with the barman of the local pub for some Bix Beiderbecke tapes, Trevor and Jill find themselves in possession of quite a different kind of tape—one that has crucial significance to British nuclear policy and thus carries serious implications for all of Europe. Many references to jazz musicians.

Powers, J. F. "He Don't Plant Cotton." *Accent* 3: 106–13 (Winter 1943).

In Chicago (as, presumably, everywhere) a group of black jazz musicians is forced to compromise its musical integrity to cater to surly white audiences who "wanted . . . Mickey Mouse sound effects, singing strings, electric guitars, neon violins, even organs and accordians and harmonica teams" instead of the music they [the musicians] were born to, blue or fast, music that had no name." In this case, the musicians cannot deal with one more request by a group of drunken southern whites to play "Ol' Man River."

Pynchon, Thomas. "Entropy." *Kenyon Review* 22: 277–92 (1960).

This story qualifies as a jazz fiction because of its provocative (if zany) discussion concerning the relationship between jazz theory and the second law of thermodynamics. This is followed by a jam session in which the musicians *think out* the music they would produce if they had instruments; the second composition they "play" is a variation on Gerry Mulligan's root chords.

——. *Gravity's Rainbow*. New York: Viking, 1973.

Although this is not by any means a jazz novel, it does contain a significant reference to Charlie Parker, whose music contributes greatly to the "acoustic collage" that shapes the narrative. Note how the following passage—one long, breathless sentence—projects the writer's admiration for Parker's virtuosity even as it describes his music: " Down in New York, drive fast maybe get there for the last set—on 7th Ave., between 139th and 140th, tonight, 'Yardbird' Parker is finding out how he can use the notes at the higher ends of these very chords to break up the melody into *have* mercy what is it a fucking machine gun or something man he must be out of his *mind* 32nd notes demisemiquavers say it very (demisemiquaver) fast in a Munchkin voice if you can dig *that* coming out of Dan Wall's Chili House and down the street—shit, out in all kinds of streets (his affirmative solos honks already the idle, amused dum-de-dumming of old Mister fucking Death he self) out over the airwaves, into the society gigs, someday as far as what seeps out hidden speakers in the city elevators and in all the markets, his bird's singing, to gainsay the Man's lullabies, to subvert the groggy wash of the endlessly, gutlessly overdubbed strings."

——. *V*. Philadelphia: Lippincott, 1963.

As in most of Pynchon's works, jazz is more of a felt presence and an influence on style and texture than central to the narrative. Here, the character of McClintic Sphere seems to be based on Ornette Coleman; the novel also contains scattered references to Charlie Parker.

Rainer, Dachine. "The Party." In *New World Writing 12*, 174–206. New York: New American Library, 1957.

Love finally conquers all—even the chaos of jazz—as the speaker is asked to hostess a party in Greenwich Village in the 1950s. The band hired for the occasion plays jazz, mostly bop, which makes dancing difficult and leads to fighting. As the narrator says, "The music had been bebop, that weird, atonal, fundamentally antimusical conglomeration of sound, and to that dancing could arise only in complete indifference to the music . . ."

Ramsey, Frederic, Jr. "Deep Sea Rider." In *Jazz Parody (Anthology of Jazz Fiction)*, edited by Charles Harvey, 39–49. London: Spearman Publishers, 1948.

Playing trumpet in New York City after World War II, Nubs Wilkens reminisces over his long life in jazz, starting with his work with Buddy Bolden around the turn of the century. When a white jazz groupie creates disharmony among the band members, Nubs resolves to go home to New Orleans in time for Mardi Gras.

Raschka, Chris. *Charlie Parker Played Be Bop*. New York: Orchard Books, 1992.

A picture book for preschoolers with a text designed to help young readers *hear* Parker's music in their minds.

———. *Giant Steps.* New York: Atheneum Books for Young Readers, 2002.

According to the Library of Congress summary of this juvenile story, "John Coltrane's musical composition is performed by a box, a snowflake, some raindrops, and a kitten." Not seen.

Reed, Harlan. *The Swing Music Murder*. New York: Dutton, 1938.

A hardboiled mystery set in Seattle and containing the usual ingredients: nightclubs, booze, violence, snappy dialogue, and an idiosyncratic private eye, Dan Jordan. The murder at novel's center involves a popular purloined swing tune, "Poppy Seed Swing." Indeed, swing figures prominently toward the beginning, as Lance Grandy's Swing Swing Boys are seen in performance and in swing-music dialogue ("Man! What beautiful licks! Listen to him go out of key! Man!"). Despite the overwhelming popularity of this new music, Dan insists on requesting "Darktown Strutter's Ball" wherever he is.

Reed, Ishmael. *Mumbo Jumbo*. New York: Atheneum, 1972.

An unclassifiable, hyperkinetic text that parodies the overlapping histories of voodoo and jazz within the framework of a metaphysical mystery.

Reed, James. "The Shrimp Peel Gig." *Brilliant Corners* 2 (1): 23–37 (Winter 1997).

The speaker and his fellow musicians play wherever they can get work: small festivals, ball games, banquets, and so forth. On the night of the story, as he prepares to play Dixieland for an after-dinner crowd, he reflects on the life of small-town musicians like him. They have day jobs, of course, and play for the love of the music and camaraderie, poignantly aware that the clock is running out on dance bands. They are also keenly aware of the inevitable conflicts between their love for music and their familial responsibilities. A warm, nicely balanced story that gives a good sense of what it must be like to play in small-town, low-budget operations.

Richards-Slaughter, Shannon. "The Blossoms of Jazz: A Novel of Black Female Jazz Musicians in the 1930s." Ph.D. Diss., University of Michigan, 1990.

Not seen.

Richoux, Pat. *The Stardust Kid*. New York: Putnam, 1973.

The Stardust Kid is Mike Riley, a hot high school jazz trumpeter in Connor City, Nebraska, during World War II. Mike wants to become a great professional musician, but his mother opposes him, largely because she doesn't want him to follow in his musician father's footsteps. This coming-of-age novel provides a nostalgic look at small town America when the prospect of a one-night stand by Horace Heidt and His Musical Knights could raise goosebumps.

Rieman, Terry. *Vamp Till Ready*. New York: Harper, 1954.

In the middle (chapter 8) of this murder mystery set among the haute monde of the classical music set, there is, apropos of nothing, a discussion of the changing nature of jazz and an appearance by the Turk Murphy band, which "is belting out the most exciting music heard in the land since Louis Armstrong joined King Oliver."

Ritz, David. *Barbells and Saxophones*. New York: Donald I. Fine, 1989.

Twenty-seven-year-old Vince Viola lives for body-building, birds, sex, and his saxophone, and these often overlapping passions create the kind of conflicts that, along with a truly wacky family situation, lead Vince to the psychiatrist's couch. With an acknowledgement to "the many immortal saxists—Pres being the most prominent—who've brought me closer to God"—author Ritz has produced a free-wheeling, frequently raunchy novel that is saturated with references to jazz, especially the age-old theme regarding the conflict between art and commerce that causes jazz musicians to compromise their integrity.

——. *Blue Notes Under a Green Felt Hat*. New York: Donald I. Fine, 1989.

It's post-WWII New York, and 23-year-old Danny is obsessed with sex, hats, and jazz. In a jazz club on 52nd St., where bebop is gaining favor over swing, Danny meets a gifted but unknown black pianist-singer, Cliff Summer, and the two of them go on a series of adventures designed primarily to make Summer rich and famous. At the end Danny is selling hats and jazz records (hence the title) from his business in Harlem. A raunchy novel with many references to jazz and the jazz scene, including a writer for *Metronome*.

Robinson, Peter. "Memory Lane." In *Blue Lightning*, edited by John Harvey, 265–79. London: Slow Dancer Press, 1998; Chester Springs, PA: Dufour Editions, 1999.

A quintet (three expatriate Brits and two Canadians) have "another shitty gig" at a nursing home in Vancouver, B.C. While they are playing, the speaker reflects back on his WWII experiences, in love and war. When an inmate dies during a rousing number, the speaker-saxophonist experiences a shiver of memento mori. The spirit of WWII big band music hovers over this story.

Roelants, Maurice. "De Jazz-Speler." Amsterdam: Salm, 1938. Translated by Jo Mayo as "The Jazz Player." In *Harvest of the Lowlands: An Anthology in English Translation of Creative Writing in the Dutch Language*, edited by J. Greshoff, 357–75. New York: Querido, 1945.

The transformative experience of a boring businessman whose life is changed when he witnesses a black jazzman give an enraptured performance.

Roy, Lucinda. *Lady Moses*. New York: HarperFlamingo, 1998.

Nikki Giovanni's blurb reads: "I was not there when Charlie Parker started playing between the notes; I could not be there when Billie Holiday pondered the fruit of southern trees; I was unable to sit at a table when Miles Davis gave birth to the Cool but the musicians aren't the only ones who sing and I am here when Lucinda Roy makes her startling debut with Lady Moses." Given this puff and the protagonist's nickname, "Jazz," the most startling thing about this novel is that it contains not a single reference to jazz.

Rundell, Wyatt. *Jazz Band*. New York: Greenberg, 1935.

Although the protagonist is a 25-year-old banjo player and crooner in a popular dance band, the novel has much more to say about his soap opera love life than his career as a jazz musician. A misleading title.

Russell, Ross. *The Sound*. New York: Dutton, 1961.

A primer of the postwar hipster culture, this novel is a roman-à-clef inspired by Charlie Parker. The protagonist, white Jewish piano player Bernie Rich, is torn between going the big band college-circuit route with its financial security and the spontaneous, insecure Harlem scene where Red Travers, the Parker figure, is instrumental in transforming jazz from Benny Goodman to bop. Ross Russell's personal experience with Parker and the bebop scene gives this novel authenticity. There's much about race, a preponderance of sex and drugs, and occasional stereotyping, as when Red is described as being "fiercely possessive, with an overpowering virile odor and primitive genital force." Lots of good musical description.

Sachs, Ed. "Dogs Don't Always Eat Dogs." In *Music '59: Downbeat Fourth Annual Yearbook*, 69–71. Chicago: Maher, 1959.

Because of low attendance, the manager of a jazz club decides to incorporate a dog act into its jazz routine—with predictably humorous results.

Sadoff, Ira. "Black Man's Burden." *Brilliant Corners* 3: 15–25 (Summer 1999).

Thirty years afterward Erik remembers the summer of 1964 when he and a high school buddy, Rondel, shared an apartment in Manhattan's East Village. It was a summer of race riots, and civil rights and idealism were much in the air. When the two boys—one white, the other black—go to the Half-Note with their dates to hear John Coltrane, Erik comes to realize that bridging the gap between races is much more difficult than he had realized. Good description of Coltrane and company in action.

Salaverría, José. "The Negro of the Jazz Band." Translated by Dorothy R. Peterson. In *Ebony and Topaz: A Collectanea,* 63–66. Edited by Charles S. Johnson. New York: National Urban League, 1927; Freeport, NY: Books for Libraries, 1971.

The speaker, a writer, is intrigued by the black drummer in a mediocre jazz band playing at "The Charm of Russia Tea Room" along the far end of a European beach resort. When the protagonist later encounters the drummer, he is shocked to discover that he is actually white; the story provides an account of why (in the 1920s) an educated white American would masquerade as black. Slight musical content but interesting philosophical premise.

Salinger, J.D. "Blue Melody." *Cosmopolitan*, 50+ (September 1948).

A story based on the much mythicized death of Bessie Smith, and one of Salinger's lesser efforts.

Sallis, James. "Vocalities." In *Blue Lightning*, edited by John Harvey, 281–89. London: Slow Dancer Press, 1998; Chester Springs, PA: Dufour Editions, 1999.

A late night monologue by a disc jockey that begins with the pronouncement that there won't be any music tonight and ends with his changing his mind. In between, there are reflections on life, love, and music.

Salmon, Alice Wooledge. "Correspondence." In *B Flat, Bebop, Scat*, edited by Chris Parker, 42–55. London: Quartet, 1986.

Martha and Louis had been living for a long year in Los Angeles and are now on their way home to London. While restoring themselves on a Caribbean island, Louis, a conductor, is offered a temporary position he can't resist in Tokyo, leaving Martha to resume writing the book she had abandoned. One day she is invited by a jazz musician neighbor to listen to his group play that night. Martha is so moved by the jazz she hears on this and another night that she experiences a transfiguration.

Sand, Carter. *Two for the Money*. San Diego: Trojan Classic, 1973.

The only reason this title appears is because it shows up from time to time in references to "Fiction, jazz." It is a gay novel with no redeeming social or intellectual value whatsoever. The plot involves Phillip Denver meeting the giant stud of his dreams and falling in love with him. Things are complicated by the fact that Phillip's dreamboat is from Texas (the story begins in Manhattan) and has a wife and children; a further complication occurs when Phillip becomes involved with a handsome, older billionaire, who introduces Phillip into the world of very rough homosexual sex. Oh, Phillip is very vaguely a jazz pianist with a steady gig—to which he fails to show up in the course of the novel. This book may deserve a grand prix for smut but only a single upraised finger for jazz fiction.

Saroyan, William. "Jazz." *Hairenik Daily* [Boston]. In *My Name Is Saroyan*, 90–93. New York: Coward-McCann, 1983.

This story likens the melange of urban street sounds to the "nervous noise" called jazz that was sweeping the country.

Sayer, Mandy. *Mood Indigo.* Sydney, Australia: Allen and Unwin, 1990.

A vernacular novel-in-stories dramatizing ten or so years in the life of a young Australian girl, Rose, whose life and prospects are bleak. Rose loves her dad and the music he makes. Unfortunately, not many people are interested in listening to jazz piano; in fact, at one climactic moment when her dad starts to play "Mood Indigo," he's informed that it's happy hour at the bar and that his music should reflect that mood. Scattered references to jazz musicians, mostly pianists like Oscar Peterson, Count Basie, Nat King Cole, and Les McCann.

Schneider, Bart. *Blue Bossa*. New York: Viking, 1998.

Framed by the Patty Hearst kidnapping in 1970s San Francisco, this novel provides a rounded portrait of Ronnie Reboulet, a jazz trumpeter and singer who, like Chet Baker, had once been famous both for his music and his good looks. But at the height of his fame, he lost everything—his teeth, his looks, his lip—to drugs. Now in the company of a strong, loving woman, he is trying to resurrect his life and his career. The title is taken from a Kenny Dorham tune. Excellent descriptions of music-making and frequent references to bop era musicians; in fact, Charlie Parker has a cameo role. Among other things, this novel is about the complications of love and the never-ending search for a father. The dust jacket photo by William Claxton underscores the jazz connection.

Scott, Tony. "Destination K.C." In *The Jazz Word*, edited by Dom Ceruli, Burt Karall, and Mort Nasatir, 80–83. New York: Ballantine, 1960.

A short, ironic story told in hip jazz idiom disclosing the author's deep admiration for Charlie Parker as railroad workers load Parker's last remains on a train destined for Kansas City. The author, a jazz clarinetist, knew and played with Parker.

Shange, Ntozake. *Sassafrass, Cypress and Indigo*. New York: St. Martin's, 1982.

Dedicated to "all women in struggle," this is the story of three African American sisters and their mother in Charleston. One of the girls is a poet and weaver like her mother; another is a dancer. Both are involved with jazz musicians, one of whom is on the dope fringe, the other a serious artist and composer. Although there are pointed references to jazz musicians and the jazz scene, the musical content is slight.

Shaw, Artie. "Snow White in Harlem, 1930." In *The Best of Intentions and Other Stories*, 9–28. Santa Barbara: John Daniel, 1989.

When Al Snow drags his sax and clarinet uptown to Harlem late one night looking for a jam session to sit in on, he encounters a phenomenal piano player who lets Al (the only white in a black setting) show what he can do. Although the scene at the after-hours jazz club grows increasingly strange, Al thinks his dreams have come true.

Shirley, Peter. "Drink and Be Merry . . ." In *Jazz Parody (Anthology of Jazz Fiction)*, edited by Charles Harvey, 32–38. London: Spearman Publishers, 1948.

Pianist Babe Sheridan and his fellow band members are true jazz enthusiasts; music is their life. One night during a jam session, Babe can't help noticing a beautiful, mysterious blonde in the audience. When on a subsequent evening he meets her, she tells him she knows the whereabouts of his ex-wife. Unfortunately, Babe dies on the bandstand before he can elicit the information he desires.

———. "Sweet and Hot." In *Jazz Parody (Anthology of Jazz Fiction)*, edited by Charles Harvey, 92–98. London: Spearman Publishers, 1948.

A jazz accordianist frets over what has become of jazz: how it has become the exclusive province of the blacks and the darling of the intellectuals. He blames writers for creating this situation. At the end, he promises to give a writer-friend an exclusive story and does so in a shocking way.

Shurman, Ida. *Death Beats the Band*. New York: Phoenix, 1943.

First, despicable Andy Parker is killed just as he is getting into the groove singing his new hit, "Headlined in My Heart," and then another band member is killed and a third is assaulted with a trumpet as weapon. Since the orchestra and the patrons are marooned by a blizzard, the task of solving the several crimes falls to the band's new bassist. Considerable musical discussion and description, especially early on; in fact, there are several transcriptions of musical notation.

Sill, Harold D., Jr. *Misbehavin' with Fats: A Toby Bradley Adventure*. Reading, MA: Addison-Wesley, 1978.

Through the miracle of time travel, young New England white boy, Toby Bradley, is able to meet and hang out with his hero, Fats Waller, and to learn what it was like to grow up talented and black in segregated America. Frequent references to jazz musicians and several quotations from music associated with Waller.

Simmons, Herbert. *Man Walking on Eggshells*. Boston: Houghton Mifflin, 1962; London: Methuen, 1962.

Black trumpeter and football player Raymond "Splib" Douglas seems to be the hope of the future but relinquishes his wonderful potential to drugs. His mother opposed his jazz from the beginning, thinking it "a lot of sentimental bunk by a bunch of shiftless people who never had sense enough to grow up." Her brother, also a trumpeter, tells her that on the contrary, "that's your history coming out of them horns!" The story takes place in and around St. Louis and also Harlem during prohibition. Much talk of racial issues and of jazz, especially to "home boy," Miles Davis.

———. "One Night Stand." *Gamma #1*, 1963, 88–93.

Young Maury was the hottest trumpeter anyone had seen; he "made Louis, Diz and Miles sound like little boys playing with matches." But his fellow musicians worry that Maury has no interest in women—until one night he becomes infatuated with a woman in the audience and wins her over with his incredible playing.

Simon, George T. *Don Watson Starts His Band*. New York: Dodd, Mead, 1941.

Written for a juvenile audience and containing a foreword by Benny Goodman, this novel focuses on a young hayseed who determines to become a professional band leader.

Sinclair, Harold. *Music Out of Dixie*. New York and Toronto: Rinehart, 1952.

The story of Dade Tarrent in the first two decades of the twentieth century. Raised in the slums around New Orleans, Dade is moved by music early in his life, learns first to play the piano and then the clarinet, enjoys success and suffers defeat, becomes a composer and artist, and is headed for New York at the end. Jelly Roll Morton makes a small but important appearance. Dixieland, booze, dope, violence, race.

Sklar, George. *The Two Worlds of Johnny Truro*. Boston: Little, Brown, 1947.

A long novel about Johnny Truro, a large, artistically talented youth who undergoes the usual processes and experiences on his way to discovering himself. Frequent references to Bix Biederbecke, Kid Ory, Jelly Roll Morton, Count Basie, Wild Bill Davison, Coleman Hawkins and others; a scene in which Johnny explains to a buddy the difference between jazz and swing; and an explanation of how jazz provided catharsis and nirvana for Johnny and his chums—this is about the extent of the novel's jazz content.

Škvorecký, Josef. *Bassaxofon*. Toronto: Anson-Cartwright, 1977. Translated by Káca Poláckova-Henley as "The Bass Saxophone." In *The Bass Saxophone: Two Novellas*, 115–209. London: Chatto and Windus, 1978; New York: Knopf, 1979.

Although jazz is outlawed, a young jazz fan dreams of playing saxophone with an orchestra. Much emphasis on the protagonist's love of jazz and on the rarity of the instrument.

——. "The Bebop of Richard Kambala." Translated by Káca Poláckova-Henley. *Rampike* 3: 101–4 (1984–85).

After an exhilarating jam session, the title character commits suicide in a particularly grisly way.

——. *The Cowards*. Translated by Jeanne Nemcová. New York: Grove, 1970; London: Gollancz, 1970; New York: Ecco, 1980.

Danny Smiricky loves jazz and plays the sax with his friends at every opportunity. The story is set in Czechoslovakia after the fall of Nazi Germany as the Russians are moving in. The content is densely political, with very little specific jazz reference—though jazz does seem to serve as Danny's anodyne against the pain and confusion of his chaotic world.

——. "Eine Kleine Jazzmusik." Translated by Alice Denesová. *The Literary Review* 13: 47–61 (Fall 1969).

The speaker and his young chums are determined, in 1940 Czechoslovakia, to put on a jazz concert—much in violation of Aryan restrictions against various kinds of music and instruments. The Masked Rhythm Bandits (as the group comes to be known) cleverly succeed in their objective but with lamentable consequences. As in other works by Škvorecký, jazz is here associated with freedom and democracy; with everything opposed to totalitarianism.

——. *The Swell Season: A Text on the Most Important Things*. Translated by Paul Wilson. Toronto: L. and O. Dennys, 1982; New York: Ecco, 1986.

In these six interrelated stories, young Danny Smiricky (surely the author's alter ego) falls in love with practically every girl he encounters. He also loves jazz and his country, Czechoslovakia of the 1940s when Nazi terrorism intruded into every corner of everyday life. Passing references to jazz and musicians and one lovely description of a Bach fugue being converted into a rollicking "Sweet Georgia Brown." This is part of a trilogy featuring Smiricky; the other two are *The Cowards* and "The Bass Saxophone" (qq.v.).

———. *The Tenor Saxophonist's Story*. Translated by Caleb Crain, Káca Poláckova-Henley, and Peter Kussi. New York: Ecco, 1996.

Written in Prague in 1954–56, this collection of related stories depicts the totalitarian regime in Czechoslovakia after WWII. The many scattered references to jazz do not form a coherent pattern but nevertheless are associated with freedom and slavery; in fact, for the protagonist, his tenor sax hitch counterbalances "the large, shining, five-point star" of Communism.

Smith, C. W. "The Plantation Club." *Southwest Review* 62: 47–63 (Winter 1967).

Trying to be cool, two young white aspiring jazz musicians ingratiate themselves with the black musicians at the Plantation Club. When the boys are busted for possessing marijuana, they implicate one of the black musicians—a real artist—who is soon sent to jail while the boys are released, demonstrating that the so-called blindness of justice is selective.

Smith, J. P. *Body and Soul*. New York: Grove, 1987.

Polish émigré jazz pianist Jerzy Wozzeck has a gig in a rundown Paris bistro known for showcasing the best jazz this side of New York. But when a Corsican gangster takes over the club, Wozzeck is forbidden to play Charlie Parker riffs, block chords, or anything that resembles bebop. To compensate for financial woes and a job gone sour, innocent Jerzy accepts a commission to deliver a seemingly harmless package. Predictably, the contents are not as untainted as advertised, and Jerzy is implicated in crime. He flees to London but discovers his past will always be with him. Many references to jazz, especially to such luminaries as Charles Mingus, John Coltrane, Art Blakey, and Miles Davis.

Smith, Julie. *The Axeman's Jazz*. New York: St. Martin's, 1991.

Picture this: a title with a double jazz reference and a dust jacket portraying a skeleton laying down some heavy grooves on a muted trumpet. Yet this mystery, set in New Orleans yet, contains absolutely no jazz content. A novel set in New Orleans but containing references to neither food nor music is comparable to a book about Las Vegas that doesn't mention gambling. Someone should be sued for false advertising and a misleading title.

Smith, Martin Cruz. *Stallion Gate*. New York: Ballantine, 1986.

A thriller set in New Mexico in the mid-1940s involving the most secret installation of World War II, the test site for the first atomic weapon. J. Robert Oppenheimer and Klaus Fuchs are among the historical characters; the protagonist is Joe Peña, an American Indian soldier from the Southwest whose dream is to open a jazz club after the war. Joe had played piano with Charlie Parker on 52nd Street and is involved in a couple of jazz scenes, but music is clearly a background element. On the other hand, the image of Klaus Fuchs dancing a "Hapsburg ballroom number" to Joe Peña and his band's bebop clings to the memory.

Smith, Robert Paul. *So It Doesn't Whistle*. New York: Harcourt, Brace, 1941.

Although this novel contains scattered references to such musicians as Louis Armstrong, Bix Beiderbecke, Coleman Hawkins, Duke Ellington, and Bud Freeman, it is mostly about the booze life.

Smith, William Gardner. *South Street*. New York: Farrar, Straus and Young, 1954.

The story of three African American brothers whose father had been lynched when they were very young; and of Philadelphia's South Street after WWII. Scattered references to jazz and jazz musicians, a nice description of a jam session, and much attention to a blues singer, a central character; nevertheless, the novel is largely concerned with racial politics, particularly as they impinge on Claude Barrons, one of the brothers, who marries a white violinist.

Sonin, Ray. *The Dance Band Mystery*. London: Quality, 1940.

Someone's been killing the members of King Grayson's London swing band, causing Sam Underhill of the *Dance Band News* and Detective-Inspector John Adams of Scotland Yard to team up to solve the mystery. To get to the bottom of things, and also to help prevent further murders, former jazz man Underhill signs on as pianist with Grayson's orchestra. In this capacity he succeeds in uncovering the killer in a case involving the distribution of potent reefers to musicians, children's dolls imported from the U.S., and a scorned woman. According to jacket copy, author Sonin was longtime editor of the *Melody Maker*, "the world's leading dance band and light music weekly newspaper."

Southern, Terry. "The Night the Bird Blew for Doctor Warner." *Harper's Bazaar,* January 1956: 101+.

A musicologist involved in writing a comprehensive book on western music, Doctor Warner determines to do field work in bebop by procuring heroin—with predictably disastrous consequences.

——. "You're Too Hip, Baby." *Esquire,* April 1963: 68+.

An educated white man in Paris tries to make the scene by getting close to black jazz musicians, one of whom lets him know that his overtures in the direction of friendship are inauthentic. Booze and drugs are prominent.

Spicer, Bart. *Blues For the Prince*. New York: Dodd, Mead, 1950.

A hardboiled mystery in which The Prince (Harold Morton Prince)—the best jazz pianist/composer over the last twenty years—is killed and his right-hand man is charged with the crime after fraudulently claiming—or threatening to claim—that *he* had composed the music that had made The Prince famous. It turns out, of course, that nothing is as it seems. A good deal of both jazz and racial politics. In the most fully developed jazz section (chapter 17), a group of the greatest jazz all-stars gather to memorialize The Prince in a jam session.

Steig, Henry. "Gertie and the Pied Piper." *Esquire,* February 1945: 44+.

Gertie is the proprietress of the Swingland Billiard Academy in Manhattan, a snack bar and poor hall where musicians hang out. She is irritated by the musicians' nonstop chatter about jazz and other musicians. From this it is clear that her relationship with clarinetist Joe is not likely to develop into a more lasting arrangement: like his fellow jazz musicians, Joe is married to his music.

——. *Send Me Down*. New York: Knopf, 1941.

A very long, discursive but nevertheless valuable jazz novel about two working-class brothers and a buddy growing up in New York City between the wars. They study music at considerable sacrifice to their parents, become interested in jazz, and then resolve to pursue it as a career, disappointing their parents who consider such music to be trash. The brothers soon go their own musical ways, one taking to the road with a small group, the other building a big band that eventually plays Carnegie Hall. For Frank, the big band leader, success becomes a problem, but he is able to restructure his life to get back to what he most enjoys. There are references to Fletcher Henderson, Bessie Smith, and others, to the black revolution in music, and (inevitably) to the racial tensions of the time. When a black musician says to a white musician that he supposes he ought to be grateful to be in music, the white musician responds: "You certainly should . . . In almost anything else where you had a chance at all, you'd have to be five times as good as a white man. In music you only have to be, say, twice as good." A good deal about the travails of travel, the economics of the music business, and the conflict between art and entertainment. Also, significant reference to the destructiveness of marijuana in the world of swing music.

——. "Swing Business." *Saturday Evening Post,* December 19, 1936: 10+.

The difficulties of assembling a swing band and then getting bookings for it, told in irritatingly slangy language, which, apparently, is supposed to mimic the swing argot of the 1930s, as in this typical passage: "Djever gedda nextra dime oddovim for it? No! Ain'tcha got no ambition?"

Stephens, Edward. *Roman Joy*. Garden City, NY: Doubleday, 1965.

The title character of this long novel, Roman Joy, is a young, talented but undisciplined drummer during World War II. Romie briefly rises to fame with the Dave Eckhardt Band, but then crashes when he sets out on his own. This novel is saturated with jazz and swing references, from the tedium of building a big band and the hardships of life on the road to the actual making of music. Much is made of the differences between jazz and swing but the disparity is, curiously, never explained.

Stewart, John. "The Americanization of Rhythm." *The Black Scholar,* June 1975: 73–77.

A sometimes surrealistic story about a white couple in Chicago who invite a black jazz drummer to their apartment for drinks. The wife has been preoccupied with the drummer's music for some time, but when he shows up it turns out that the Jewish couple—Moses and Harriet—want to use him to start a new race.

Street, Julian. "The Jazz Baby." *Saturday Evening Post*, July 15, 1922: 6+.

A generational dispute ensues when Mrs. Merriam, an old line New Yorker, discovers that her collegiate son Lindsay has fallen in love with the saxophone, and has bought one that is "Quadruple gold plate over triple silver plate." When Mrs. Merriam reacts to these specifications by asking if it is "a fire extinguisher, or a home-brew outfit," her son replies, "No—home blew" and then proceeds to sing a chorus of "Those Home-Brew Blues" before winding up his performance with a saxophone solo. The dispute continues when Lindsay and friend take a couple of girls uptown to the Apollo to see a show called *Jazzbo* instead of going to a more culturally respected event in a more socially acceptable part of town. At one point Mrs. Merriam tries to analyze jazz, deciding it is "musical Bolshevism—a revolt against law and order in music. Apparently, too, the jazz Bolsheviks were looters, pillaging the treasure houses of music's aristocracy. One piece was based upon a Chopin waltz, another was a distortion of an aria from Tosca, another had been filched from Strauss' *Rosenkavalier*."

Suarez, Virgil. *Latin Jazz*. New York: William Morrow, 1989.

A novel of dislocation centering on a Cuban-American family trying to forge an identity. Although one of the main characters is a musician, and the novel ends with a spirited description of a salsa band in action, *Latin Jazz* contains scant reference to music of any kind. For a novel overflowing with Cuban-American music and life shortly after World War II, see Oscar Hijuelos's exuberant novel, *The Mambo Kings Play Songs of Love*. New York: Farrar, Straus, Giroux, 1989.

Summers, Barbara. "Social Work." In *Breaking Ice: An Anthology of Contemporary African-American Fiction,* edited by Terry McMillan, 601–14. New York: Viking, 1990.

Alicia has been unsuccessful in her efforts to help her lover Richard, a tenor saxophonist, overcome his drug addiction so she resolves to break with him. It was his "talent that she had fallen in love with. . . . The golden horn pumping liquid, silken sex. He wove Trane and Pharoah, Sonny Rollins, and Archie Shepp like ancestral threads into a new fabric, a new suit of clothes as sharply pressed as Lester Young, as raspy and tweedy as Ben Webster. Yet the true magic lay in removing these fine garments, that divine talent, and uncovering the naked, needy soul underneath." But apart from this resonant passage and a few more references to Coltrane, the story has little jazz content.

Sylvester, Robert. "The Lost Chords." In *Eddie Condon's Treasury of Jazz*, edited by Eddie Condon and Richard Gehman, 435–47. New York: Dial, 1956.

As Pops ("the greatest jazz trombonist of his time, which . . . meant all time") sits waiting to be interviewed for a profile in a jazz magazine, he reflects on his long involvement with the music and on the development of jazz. Bix Beiderbecke and Bunk Johnson are mentioned prominently. Although this is a well-told story, it would surely create second thoughts in anyone aspiring to a career in jazz.

———. *Rough Sketch*. New York: Dial, 1948.

Entrepreneur Tony Fenner had become such a big name that *Current Magazine* decided to do a biography of him. The reporter finally located four people who knew the mysterious Fenner. One of these is Walter "Pops" Jarman, "The Prophet of American Jazz" and the last of the riverboat jazz musicians. In this section of the novel there is much talk of the rise of jazz in the 1920s and 1930s; of the problems in leading a band; of the economics of the music industry; and of the effects of the record industry (which was just coming into prominence) on the music. Among other things, Fenner was a musicians' agent. Scattered references to early New Orleans jazz men like Muffle Jaw Chambers, Agile Bacquet, Yellow Nunez, Jelly Roll Morton, and Louis Armstrong; Bix Beiderbecke has a cameo part. Considerable talk of the effect of marijuana and booze on music.

Tate, Sylvia. *Never by Chance*. New York: Harper, 1947.

After the gal he loves dies suddenly and senselessly, Johnny Silesy learns that he didn't really know her and sets out to discover who the enigmatic woman really was. Although Johnny is apparently a ranking swing pianist, this novel has little musical content, apart from short, infrequent discussions concerning putting together charts and building a sixteen-piece swing orchestra.

Thompson, Brian. "Life's Little Mysteries." In *Blue Lightning*, edited by John Harvey, 357–75. London: Slow Dancer Press, 1998; Chester Springs, PA: Dufour Editions, 1999.

In 1961 jazz man Cliff Augur is playing in an ocean liner band, planning to defect when the ship docks in New York. On board Cliff has a brief romance with an Italian movie star, but he never loses track of his dream to seek out "Al Cohn and Zoot Sims, and blow them away." Thirty years later a young executive at Columbia records comes across an unissued 1961 recording of Cliff Augur on sax and vibes and is blown away by the music of an apparently great but altogether unknown artist.

Thompson, Robert L. "A High Type Dissertation on Skiffle." *Record Changer* 10: 10, 20 (January 1951).

More feuilleton than story proper, this piece describes in mock-serious terms the intricacies and challenges of washboard playing, the music produced by the instrument being, of course, "a very proper branch of jazziana."

Tilley, Robert J. "The Devil and All that Jazz." In *B Flat, Bebop, Scat*, edited by Chris Parker, 34–38. London: Quartet, 1986.

A fantasy reënacting the Faust theme—with a twist. In this version a trumpet player enters into the obligatory pact with the devil: his soul in exchange for surpassing talent. But this time the devil is outfoxed when the trumpeter rejects hot jazz in favor of West Coast "cool" jazz.

——. "Something Else." *The Magazine of Fantasy and Science Fiction,* 1965. In *Twenty Years of the Magazine of Fantasy and Science Fiction,* edited by Edward L. Ferman and Ralph P. Mills, 248–62. New York: Putnam's, 1970.

When Dr. Sidney Williams's spacecraft crashes on an unknown planet, he is relieved to discover that his clarinet and recording gear are in good working order. After listening to his beloved recording of Duke Ellington's "Ko-Ko," however, he is shocked to hear a facsimile of the music come back to him. He discovers that the sound emanated from an elephantine creature like nothing he had ever seen. Through the agency of jazz, they become friends, but after a while Williams is rescued and the creature dies. Several references to musicians like Art Tatum, Coleman Hawkins, and Eddie Condon.

——. "Willie's Blues." *The Magazine of Fantasy and Science Fiction,* May 1972: 54–75.

A very unusual science-fiction story told in diaristic fashion by a time-travelling jazz buff, who shuttles back to the 1930s (from 2078) to locate the jazz saxophonist who had made "Willie's Blues" famous before he died.

Tormé, Mel. *Wynner*. New York: Stein and Day, 1978.

Mel Tormé gives an insider's account of the rags-to-riches story of Martin Wynner, a young singer with a golden voice. After the musical content finally kicks in about halfway through the novel, there are many references to jazz musicians and the big band scene of, primarily, the 1930s and 1940s. At one point, Wynner sings a duet with Billie Holiday.

Updyke, James. *It's Always Four O'Clock*. New York: Random House, 1956.

After returning home to Gary, Indiana, following WWII, the narrator, guitarist Stan Powles, moves to Los Angeles, where he hangs out in nightclubs with the music fraternity, including the mysterious, eccentric Royal, the focus of the novel, an avant-garde pianist. These two, along with the bassist Walt and a female singer, form a group and attempt to forge a new kind of jazz. Music is central to the narrative, as is the stereotypically self-destructive artist-genius. Much booze and carousing and also much about the sporadic pleasures and frequent problems of trying to perform serious music in a night club.

Van Vechten, Carl. *Nigger Heaven*. New York: Knopf, 1926.

Intended to be ironic, the title refers to the far balcony in theatres where African Americans were relegated, and by extension it also obliquely connotes Harlem. It is the time-honored story of a small-town boy who falls for a big city "Lady of Pleasure" and whose character is tested in the process. An important but controversial novel that was intended to celebrate African Americans. James Weldon Johnson, among others, lauded the book; other members of the black artistic and intellectual communities excoriated it. Little jazz content.

Wain, John. *Strike the Father Dead*. New York: St. Martin's, 1962; London: Macmillan, 1962.

A British novel about the barriers—philosophical, emotional, racial—that separate people. When young Jeremy commits himself to jazz at age 17, he estranges himself from his classics professor father. Through his association with Percy, a black American hornplayer, Jeremy matures in his music and in his life. This novel takes place at the moment when the new post-World War II developments in jazz were filtering across the ocean for the first time and finding congenial accompaniment in French existentialism. Good descriptions of music-making, the jazz life, and the difficulty of simultaneously pursuing an art and trying to make a living at it. The novel also embodies the familiar Western themes of the painful complexities of family relationships and the search for a father.

Wainwright, John. *Do Nothin' Till You Hear From Me*. New York: St. Martin's, 1977; London: Macmillan, 1977.

The narrator of this light mystery is wisecracking, band-leading bassist, "Lucky" Luckhurst, whose obsessive goal in life is to put together the best big band in all of creation. Lucky's life is turned around when he receives a parcel containing a human ear and a note implying that a kidnapping is underway. Through the agency of a clarinet-playing policeman, Lucky is enlisted to help solve the crime; the denouement is improbable and unexpected. The crime/mystery dimension of this novel is pretty much submerged by Lucky's ruminations on jazz and the mechanics of building a high-quality big band.

Wallop, Douglass. *Night Light*. New York: W.W. Norton, 1953.

Young New York widower Robert Horne loses his beloved daughter to a random killing and devotes his life to uncovering the origins of the evil that resulted in her death. His quest takes him into the amoral world of jazz where excessive behavior is the norm. Limited description of bop in the making, good description of the jazz scene, scattered references to musicians—Flip Phillips, Lester Young, Dizzy Gillespie, Chu Berry, Max Roach, and Stan Getz among others. Definitely a noir novel: obsessive and feverish, like the novels of Jim Thompson.

Weatherford, Carole Boston. *Jazz Baby.* New York: Lee and Low, 2002.

A juvenile book in which, according to the Library of Congress summary, "A group of toddlers move and play, hum and sleep to a jazz beat." Not seen.

Weik, Mary Hays. *The Jazz Man*. New York: Atheneum, 1966.

A children's book about Zeke, a little boy who lives on the top floor of an old brownstone in Harlem. Zeke's imagination and spirits are lifted by the musician across the way—the jazz man. Zeke's mom leaves, his dad disappears, and so do the Jazz Man and his buddies. But Zeke's parents return and Zeke begins to regain his sense of security.

Weller, Anthony. *The Polish Lover*. New York: Marlowe, 1997.

Jazz clarinetist Danny meets a mysterious, enigmatic Polish woman, Maja, in New Zealand, enters into a globetrotting relationship with her, and then reflects bitterly, ten years after the affair has ended, on the meaning of the relationship. The jazz content is substantive—many references to musicians (including a cameo appearance by Adam Makowicz), some analytical discussions (e.g., the harmonic ideas of John Coltrane), and solid description of a recording session. In fact, the improvisational nature of jazz reflects the structure and theme of the novel. Only a pretty good novel but an excellent contribution to jazz fiction.

Welty, Eudora. "Powerhouse." *Atlantic* 167: 707–13 (June 1941).

A widely anthologized and discussed story about a mythic black pianist (loosely modeled after Fats Waller) doing a one-night gig at a white dance in Alligator(!), Mississippi. As his name implies, Powerhouse is a man of exuberance and creativity, both of which traits are in ample evidence in a story Powerhouse tells during the intermission. In fact, the improvisational story he tells, accompanied by verbal responses from his sidemen, is very much like a jam session translated into words. It is also a metaphor for the plight of the alienated artist.

Westin, Jeane. *Swing Sisters*. New York: Scribner's, 1991.

Set toward the end of the Great Depression, this 500+ page novel dramatizes the hardships of a women's swing band, emphasizing the pathos of the musicians who battle with drugs, alcohol, and passion. The narrative is speckled with references to jazz greats.

Whitmore, Stanford. *Solo*. New York: Harcourt, Brace, 1955.

A story much like Melville's "Bartleby the Scrivener." Like Bartleby, Virgil Jones is very much solo and does what he prefers to do, not what others think he ought to do; Jones changes those who come within his sphere. Ross Jaeger, an accomplished jazz pianist, wants to become the best in the world at his instrument. He soon encounters another pianist, Jones, who comes out of nowhere and plays—and lives—only for himself. Jones finally starts playing professionally and becomes famous; meanwhile, a manager and a music critic scheme to exploit him. But Jones remains true to himself and achieves whatever fulfillment life has to offer by doing so. On the other hand, Ross seeks success and musical perfection; he wants to be number one at what he does. Flip Phillips makes a cameo appearance. Much discussion of music—e.g., "When he played . . . his piano was always new, always daring yet never tangled with badly conceived innovations, always a special brand of jazz that no one could imitate."

Wideman, John Edgar. "Concert." In *The Stories of John Edgar Wideman*, 213–17. New York: Pantheon, 1992.

As the speaker attends a concert featuring a chamber jazz ensemble not unlike the Modern Jazz Quartet, the music has an hallucinatory effect on him, evoking a free association of ideas, memories, and emotions. Jazz is very much at the center of this story.

——. "The Silence of Thelonious Monk." *Esquire*, November 1997, 107–11.

A story in the form of a meditation (or is it the other way around?) regarding the relationship of the silences in Monk's music to the speaker's yearning and sense of loss: "When it's time, when he feels like it, he'll play the note we've been waiting for. The note we thought was lost in silence. And won't it be worth the wait." A reflective, deeply felt piece on the emotive value of Monk's music to the speaker's loss of a woman sometime in the past.

Williams, John A. *Clifford's Blues*. Minneapolis: Coffee House, 1998.

After being caught in a compromising situation with a young American diplomat in Germany in the 1930s, Clifford Pepperidge, a gay black American jazz pianist, is incarcerated in Dachau, where he remains throughout Hitler's reign. Told through a diary that surfaced nearly half a century after Clifford's ordeal, this novel dramatizes the resilience and resourcefulness of the human will *in extremis*. The germ of the story occurred when author Williams saw a photo of black prisoners of war in the museum at Dachau, leading him to research the history of black prisoners during WWII.

——. *Night Song*. New York: Farrar, Straus and Cudahy, 1961.

The story of Richie "Eagle" Stokes, a bop saxophonist based on Charlie Parker. When Stokes disintegrates and dies, he becomes a folk hero, with graffiti—"Eagle Lives" or "The Eagle still soars"—cropping up everywhere. The novel is dense with musical reference, including how jazz musicians are exploited by the music industry; but it is primarily interested in racial issues, as the white protagonist, David Hillary, fails Stokes by not going to his aid when cops work Stokes over.

Willis, George. *Little Boy Blues*. New York: E. P. Dutton, 1948.

The final installment in Willis' trilogy dealing with the problems of musicians. In this one, Midwestern trumpeter Low Carey aspires to have a band of his own—and meets a woman willing to bankroll him.

———. *Tangleweed*. Garden City, NY: Doubleday, Doran, 1943.

The dispiriting first volume of the author's trilogy concerning the problems faced by jazz musicians. The protagonist here, Rusty Warren, is a swing-band drummer at a dive called the Union Garden in Kansas City. Rusty and his fellow musicians are serious about their music; they wish for some kind of transcendence: "Jazz was hollow. Jazz was always just about to tell you something really important. That was when somebody else jammed. When you played for yourself, you were always just going to get it off your chest, but you never did. Somehow, the orgasm never came." Rusty's life is not only complicated in this way, but also by women, booze ("tangleweed"), the desire to compose as well as perform, and the constant pressure to commercialize the music. This book is really a collection of sketches masquerading as a novel. The author himself played drums in small jazz orchestras in the Midwest.

———. "Union Garden Blues." *American Mercury,* August 1942: 176–182.

A sad story focusing on the futility of performing in a seedy nightclub surrounded by drunks and other pathetic creatures. As in Willis's longer works, there is no joy in jazz: playing "it was like loving and hating at the same time, in an agony of eternal, unsatisfied, creative tumescence." A revised version of this story becomes a chapter in *Tangleweed* (q.v.).

———. *The Wild Faun*. New York: Greenberg, 1945.

The story of a young, good-looking pianist who prostitutes his talent by hustling the middle-aged women who hang all over him at the cocktail lounge where he holds forth. This is the second volume in what the author claimed was a trilogy: *Three Musicians*. The other two are *Tangleweed* (Garden City, New York: Doubleday, 1943) and *Little Boy Blues* (New York: Dutton, 1948), qq.v.

Wilson, Edmund. *The Higher Jazz*. Edited by Neale Reinitz. Iowa City: University of Iowa Press, 1998.

Written in the 1940s but never finished, this novel has a misleading title; in fact, the title was chosen by the editor. The novel involves a character who would like to create a new kind of music by combining the elements of the new modernistic music (Copland, Schoenberg, et al.) with American popular music.

Yates, Richard. "A Really Good Jazz Piano." *Short Story* 1. New York: Scribner's, 1958. 49–70.

Two friends who had been Ivy League undergrads together, Carson and Ken, get together in France where they befriend black expatriate pianist Sid and then reject him when they discover that he is trying to land a gig in Las Vegas in order, obviously, to make a decent living. From their privileged—and decidedly unpragmatic—perspective, the boys regard Sid's desire to forge a better life as selling out.

Yerby, Frank. *Speak Now: A Modern Novel*. New York: Dial, 1969.

As the author says, "This is a novel about miscegenation—one of the two or three ugliest words in the English language . . ." Set against the background of the Paris student riots of 1968, *Speak Now* involves black jazz musician Harry (who has an ongoing gig at *Le Blue Note*) and his white, southern sweetheart Kathy, whose life is complicated by pregnancy. But in the end their love for each other gives them the courage to face the problems of a mixed marriage. Very little musical content and even less novelistic interest.

Young, Al. *Snakes*. New York: Holt, Rinehart and Winston, 1970.

After being orphaned early and spending his early years in Mississippi, MC moves to Detroit with his grandmother, Claude, where life is a bearable struggle. After hearing Coltrane, MC is turned on to music; he forms a band, they become locally famous, the band dissolves, and MC, after getting his high school diploma, sets out for a two week vacation in New York—which, the reader suspects, will turn into a lifetime of pursuing music.

Young, Steve. "Bella by Barlight." *Brilliant Corners* 1: 45-49 (Winter 1996).

Kenneth Ayaki plays piano in an Asian jazz trio that has a running gig at a sleazy, rundown nightclub in downtown Los Angeles. Predictably, the patrons—a mix of Occidentals and Asians—want to hear only the most vapid Tin Pan Alley-type music. One night an ugly, belligerent American demands a song the trio doesn't know. When they mollify him by playing a similar tune, he introduces Ken to his Filipino wife, leading Ken to reflect on the emptiness of his own existence.

Zabor, Rafi. *The Bear Comes Home*. New York: W.W. Norton, 1997.

Several real life jazz musicians including Charlie Haden and Ornette Coleman make cameo appearances in this sprawling, exuberant novel that dramatizes the awesome challenges confronting the creative artist to be persistently spontaneous and innovative and the joy—the grace, even, and transcendence—that derives from these challenges. The protagonist is a sax-playing, talking bear—in short, an outsider's outsider—who experiences love and transcendent bliss through music; imagine the John Coltrane of *A Love Supreme*. The descriptions of music-in-the making, of the improvisational process, of life on the road with a jazz band, and of the grim financial reality of the professional jazz musician's life—all of these are richly, lovingly detailed, often technical, and consistently convincing. Often reading like an unlikely collaboration between the Saul Bellow of *Henderson the Rain King* and the Franz Kafka of "The Metamorphosis," this novel deserves a place alongside the small handful of jazz fictions that are worth rereading.

Zane, Maitland. *Easy Living*. New York: Dial, 1959.

Although this novel keeps threatening to break out into a jazz fiction, it never does so. Rather, it is the account of a porcine protagonist with a sweet tooth and his bed-hopping, hashish-smoking friends in bohemian Paris and London. One character is married to a jazz musician, there is some chatter about jazz (with specific reference to Charlie Parker), and a couple of scenes take place in jazz clubs, but generally speaking very slight musical content.

Zinik, Zinovy. "A Ticket to Spare." Translated by Frank Williams. In *B Flat, Bebop, Scat*, edited by Chris Parker, 58–70. London: Quartet, 1986.

A Muscovite, Zinovy (like the author), gets a free ticket from a friend to attend a Duke Ellington concert in Kiev. At first the concert is a resounding success with the very idea of jazz equaling freedom in the speaker's mind; but chaos soon breaks out in the concert, sending Zinovy on a surrealistic journey through the streets of Kiev on the day prayers are being held in secret for the victims of Babi Yar, leading Zinovy to question his own identity.

Please note: A 1991 book reviewed in the last volume of the Annual Review of Jazz Studies has been reissued by a new publisher:

Barbara J. Kukla, *Swing City: Newark Nightlife, 1925–1950* (New Brunswick, New Jersey: Rutgers University Press, 2002, 288 pp., $25)

BOOK REVIEWS

Richard M. Sudhalter: *Lost Chords: White Musicians and Their Contribution to Jazz, 1915–45* (New York and Oxford: Oxford University Press, 1999, 890 pp., $35.00 hardback)

Reviewed by Max Harrison

If faced with a new theory, William James always wanted to ask: would my life be better if I believed it? Confronted with a volume on jazz of 890 pages it seems reasonable to ask: if I read all this, will it make the music sound any different? One can think of few books on this subject which do that.[1]

Sudhalter goes only up to 1945 yet, given the scope and diversity of the music covered and the physical dimensions of this volume, that is far enough. One hopes that he is already at work on the Part II promised in his Preface, but one does so with no more optimism than can be extended to Part III of Gunther Schuller's parallel history. Personally, I thank Heaven that Sudhalter (and Schuller) made no attempt to deal with the so-called "New Orleans revival" performances of Lu Watters, which have long appeared to me as being—apart from 1960s British trad (Barber, Bilk, Ball, etc.)—the worst noises ever made in the name of jazz.

Yet he was, on the other hand, mistaken to omit the Charlie Barnet outfit and in particular to depend on George T. Simon's short-sighted 1939 assessment. With ocean liners and Hollywood behind him, Barnet properly started bandleading with echoes of Basie and especially Ellington. But a performance such as the 1944 "Gulf Coast Blues," composed long before by Clarence Williams and scored for Barnet by Andy Gibson and Ralph Flanagan, shows, with such features as bitonal harmony, that the band had developed a style of its own. Other pieces like "Shady Lady," "The Moose," and "West End Blues" confirm this.

A beginning is made by Sudhalter with a quotation from Lesson 2 of Stravinsky's *Poetics of Music* to the effect that the past slips away from us so quickly, that our imagination "fills the void by making use of preconceived theories."[2] Certainly anyone capable of genuine self-examination knows that autobiographical memories, for instance, are not accurate historical accounts of events as they happened at the time of encoding. Rather are they reconstructions based on a number of affective and motivational factors. Memories are contaminated with information from similar events and so change over the years as we encounter new experiences. What we remember about an event depends on when and for what purpose we are remembering, this reflecting our beliefs about ourselves and the world at present. Thus memory is continually reprocessed and reinterpreted with changing contexts and perceptions. Yet if memory is as much a product of the present as of the past, if recollections are so influenced by present-day concerns, if we cannot honestly rely on our own memories of the past, how much less can we depend on the memories of others? Seen in this light (or darkness), history becomes a highly questionable undertaking.

Of course, numerous actual facts do stubbornly survive. Books and newspapers were printed, photographs taken, recordings made at perfectly specific times. But is it likely that we experience them years and even decades later exactly as they were experienced when new?

This book is primarily concerned with music, secondarily with the music business, yet a third consideration is the society in which the music, and the musicians, found themselves. This last brings in all the highly personal factors just referred to; and others. It is a disagreeable paradox that although America, and especially the United States, has been a racial melting pot, with all that implies in cultural terms, the States in particular has been a segregated society. As we might expect of a melting pot, whites as well as blacks have always taken part in jazz. Yet as if to reverse the social effects of segregation, the slant of most commentary on jazz has been to exalt the—obviously central—contribution of blacks and diminish that of whites.

Many have seen poetic justice in this, but however much our memories and the memories of others distort the past, we should at least *try* to establish what really happened. Both in his Introduction and at many points later in this giant text Sudhalter deals with the interplay between actual events and subjective factors such as those to which I have referred. This accounts for the specific character of the book under review, its subtitle, its unusual contents.

A second beginning is made in Chapter 1 with the arrival of Tom Brown's band in Chicago during 1915, a year ahead of the Original Dixieland Jazz Band. Even this seemingly crucial event is clouded, however, by the fact some evidence implies that southern ragtime players, individually and perhaps in groups, may have gone north earlier. Of course, as the author warns us,

> Until recently, most reminiscences of New Orleans musical life in the [twentieth] century's first two decades have been highly romanticized. Emphasis was on black and Creole musicians, with whites assigned a secondary, carbon-copy role. A growing body of research has now begun to place early accounts by all parties in an accurate temporal and factual matrix. One effect has been a shift in balance: Storyville, long thought a jazz seedbed, is now seen as far less important than, for example, the turn-of-the-century brass band movement. Such figures as the cornettist Buddy Bolden, once imbued with almost superhuman powers, have been gradually stripped of their veneer of legend (5).

Yet this book pursues its main line of argument anecdotally—there remain an awful lot of stories in as inherently nomadic music as jazz, with its constant arrivals and departures. At the same time Sudhalter is always ready to break off into strict musical analysis, with notated examples whenever appropriate. Of necessity, he has listened to a vast number of records, some of them exceedingly rare, and did so with real independence, hearing many things that had been passed over until now. From this it follows that many buried careers and movements or tendencies within the music are examined, often for the first time. Among the more famous unknowns, largely because of his link with Bix Beiderbecke, is Emmett Hardy, who, although he made no records beyond the inevitably rumored cylinder, has a chapter to himself.

Two almost random instances of hitherto neglected movements are, firstly, the specifically Italo-American, and in particular Sicilian, vein in New Orleans jazz. This is typified by Charlie Scaglioni's contrapuntal, and beautiful, contribution to Johnny Bayersdorffer's "The Waffle Man's Call," although the author provides quite a list of names on page 69 and of course further recorded examples. Another case is the music of itinerant bands active through the South, Southwest and Middle Atlantic states in the 1920s and early 1930s, such as Mart Britt ("Goose Creek Stomp"), Sunny Clapp, Slim Lamar ("Memphis Kick-up"), Blue Steele, Doc Daugherty ("Alcoholic Blues"), and others. But there is a limit to what Sudhalter can tell us, and we still wonder about the true relationship of these bands' work to more familiar paths in early jazz development.

Another glimpse of the vastly complex matrix of black and white activity which lurks behind the rather simple tales that have shaped so many jazz history books thus far comes from the author's accounts of a pioneer arranger like Arthur Lange, of the roles of Art Hickman's band and the Benson Orchestra of Chicago. It seems, to judge from recordings duly cited by Sudhalter, that rather than being an independent pioneer with his scores for Fletcher Henderson, Don Redman was following a tradition already established, no doubt rather tentatively, by Ferde Grofé's arrangements for Hickman, by Roy Bargy's and Don Bestor's for the Benson Orchestra.

Returning to small groups, in fact to the "Bands from Dixieland" of Chapter 1, we soon leave Tom Brown and arrive at the Original Dixieland Jazz Band. I have always thought the demonic energy of the ODJB—what is later called its "superheated appeal" (187)—had more to do with New York, or perhaps Chicago, than with New Orleans. Though valuing the band, the author does not overrate it. Unlike most commentators, such as Wilfrid Mellers,[3] however, he has heard *all* the records and knows there is more to be said about the ODJB, for instance with regard to tempo, than is hinted at by the usual dismissals. But the fluid melodic sensibility of the New Orleans Rhythm Kings is rightly discussed in more detail, and they are given a chapter to themselves, particular attention being paid to Leon Roppolo, especially to his solos on "Tiger Rag" and the three takes of "Tin Roof Blues."

After the New Orleans Rhythm Kings and Emmett Hardy, there are chapters on "White New Orleans Jazz in the 1920s" and "White Chicago Jazz 1923–26," the latter implying that jazz would leave the South. Indeed Sudhalter asserts that "By the end of the 1930s it was clear that the days of New Orleans as a jazz gestation center belonged to the past" (84). Because he at various points in this large text justifiably reproaches several authorities for not having paid due attention to the relevant recordings, one must here turn the accusation back on him. As is proved by performances, especially on the American Music label, by Bunk Johnson, George Lewis, Wooden Joe Nicholas and others, jazz did continue developing in and around New Orleans, and on significantly new lines.

Having notionally got jazz out of New Orleans, it is excellent that the author deals with what he calls the "encyclopaedic permutations" (121) of such long-neglected bands as the Original Memphis Five, the Georgians (who, with their trumpeter, Frank Guarente, included perhaps the earliest notable jazzman born outside the USA) and the California Ramblers. Having done a little pioneering work in that direction myself,[4] it is encouraging to see it followed up in such detail and with such perceptive enthusiasm. His account of the Original Memphis Five is part of a chapter on Miff

Mole, which is this book's first major examination of one who was a central figure even if for a long time no longer recognized as such. All I will say here is that due attention should be paid to Sudhalter's comments on such Mole solos as "Rhythm of the Day" with a 1925 Ross Gorman Orchestra, "I'm Glad," also from 1925, and his 1927 and 1940 versions of "A Good Man is Hard to Find." (I meanwhile have shamefacedly noted this chapter's revelation that "Flock o' Blues," from Mole's Sioux City Six meeting with Beiderbecke, is the same piece as "Carolina Stomp": this had passed me by.)

A chapter inevitably follows on Red Nichols, who is a more complex figure than Mole, if partly for nonmusical reasons. The author explains why he was formerly overrated and ever since underrated, and there are wise words on the questions of influence and imitation in jazz. In particular he shows how differently the Nichols influence worked out in the music of several quite separate and distinct trumpeters. There is even a good contribution from Nichols himself. Concerning his relationship with Louis Armstrong in the 1920s, he says, "The jazz musicians of that day were a kind of fraternity—all working together to promote and advance the music and each other" (132). He is here speaking about Armstrong's interest in his false-fingering ideas, yet if we may judge by Armstrong's 1928 recordings with Earl Hines—the most overtly modernistic of his career—Armstrong was even more affected by Nichols's music than by technicalities of trumpet playing.

Certainly Nichols recordings like "That's No Bargain," "Washboard Blues," "Buddy's Habit," and "Get a Load of This," as Schuller belatedly acknowledged, shone with invention shaped by ideas and procedures that were new to jazz in their time. And quite apart from their immediate effect on creative virtuosos such as Armstrong and Hines, Nichols, Mole and their associates were the first, despite striking precursors like Loring McMurray and the rather separate case of Frankie Trumbauer, extensively to explore the cool vein in jazz. This had consequences which have lasted up until today.

If Nichols was, as suggested, "a more complex figure" than certain others, it is partly because of the "widespread animus" (134) which has attached to his name. This mainly was the work of supposed authorities such as John Hammond, Hugues Panassié, and the latter's many European toadies, among whom Stanley F. Dance was the most abject. These are the sort of people who typify what the author describes in a slightly different connection as the "generations of writers who would have trouble finding middle C on a keyboard" (200). He deals trenchantly and repeatedly with the deafness and ignorance they represent, which chiefly was manifest as a refusal to listen to the relevant records. (And major figures in post-World War II modern jazz would later call forth the same response, often from the same people.)

Along the way Sudhalter makes numerous and highly specific critical points, for example about Arthur Schutt's piano solo on the Charleston Chasers' "Delirium." And besides acute appreciations of Nichols, Mole, and Jimmy Dorsey, he is especially good on Fud Livingston and his "compositions for band" such as "Imagination," "Feelin' No Pain" and "Humpty Dumpty." Special note should be made of the detailed treatment of every aspect of Adrian Rollini's music, this embodying the sort of devoted attention that has seldom been applied to such jazz before.

Having dealt with New Orleans beginnings and aspects of New York sophistication, the author gives four chapters to Chicago, going well beyond what was said earlier about 1923–26 jazz activities there. In so doing he puts an unfamiliar perspective on the whole matter: we are told of so many other people beside the Austin High School Gang. He also puts paid to concepts of the 1920s, in Chicago or anywhere else, being in any sense a "jazz age." Most adults then had come of age before the postwar social rebellion and did not like jazz. Sudhalter quotes Jess Stacy saying, "Chicago was really kind of a corny town. [Customers] went for people like Ace Brigode, Wayne King, Art Kassel. There was really no audience for what we were doing" (193). Yet the mere fact that most people, then as now, did not like jazz will never stop the 1920s being called, perhaps for so long as "history" lasts, the "jazz age."

It is interesting, even amusing, that the author identifies Chicago style with "four equally demarcated steady beats" (196) in the 1920s because that, according to dogmatic commentators basing themselves on little evidence, was supposedly a feature introduced into jazz only by Count Basie a decade or so later. One of the things initially defining Chicago style was the attitude of the young-men-in-a-hurry who first played it, and played it for themselves. Their stance was quite different from the more elegant manner which prevailed with New Orleans musicians. Beyond such matters, however, Sudhalter identifies many specific musical features in careful analyses of classic recordings. And no matter how familiar we are with "China Boy," "Bull Frog Blues," "Sister Kate," "Nobody's Sweetheart" and the rest, he has found new things to say about them. He offers thoughtful remarks about Frank Teschemacher as well, especially on "Jazz Me Blues" and "I've Found a New Baby."

The diversity which this kind of jazz later took on is demonstrated in Chapter 10, "Chicago Jazz in the 1930s" and, again, many names appear. Among them is the curious figure of Boyce Brown, who is almost disconcerting in his strange originality. With his long, sometimes chromatic phrases, often employing substitute chords and altered scales, Brown was, as the author remarks, something of a proto-bopper. Here as so often, the book's anecdotal flow is relieved by a careful account of a specific recording date, in this case Paul Mares's "Reincarnation" session, in which Brown took part. Quite another aspect of this same chapter is the serious attention paid to somebody like Ted Weems, who would not normally figure—or would only figure ignominiously—in a book like this. And in this connection we hear also about another forgotten arranger, Joe Haymes, with his "unusual voicings, daring modulations" (218).

At 33 pages, Chapter 11, "Bud Freeman and the Tenor Saxophone," is one of the finest in the book, and it contains more and longer music examples than any other. At one level it is, again, anecdotal, but it is mainly a careful survey of Freeman's development, going into highly specific detail about certain crucial recordings. Thus it is fascinating to have scored one above the other his solos on the 1928, 1939, and 1957 versions of "China Boy," this providing a miniature demonstration of how a style can be renewed as it were from within. Of course there are many factors in this, and Sudhalter identifies some of them; yet instrumental tone and slight rhythmic inflections are often the most important, and they are the least susceptible to notation. Further enlightening scored comparisons involve Freeman and Lester Young on "I've Found a New Baby" and Freeman, Young, and Eddie Miller on "Honeysuckle Rose." The author's comments on the relationship between Freeman and Young as different ways of evading the once-pervasive Coleman Hawkins influence are of interest, as is his detailed comparison between Freeman and Miller, the latter being a musician not often discussed in serious contexts. Still more rarely mentioned are people influenced by Freeman like Tony Zimmers, whose contributions to Larry Clinton's "Chant of the Jungle," "How Am I to Know?" and "Dodging the Dean" merit attention. Altogether this chapter makes up for Schuller's bypassing of Freeman's "harshly gutteral" tone in *The Swing Era*.[5]

Chapter 12, "Dixieland," is in part about what that word does and does not mean. In fact, terms like "dixieland" or "bop" are a convenient shorthand, as Orrin Keepnews is here quoted as saying. We are told that although personal ties, to home and to one another, remained strong among southern black players, their musical focus had shifted north, first to Chicago and then to New

York. "In general, black musicians seemed disinclined to revisit or in any way commemorate the past—their own or that of the music they played" (276). Whatever Wynton Marsalis and his associates may say, the past was another country and they did things differently there. Budd Johnson probably spoke for most black musicians of earlier generations when he asked, "What do you want to resurrect all that old shit for?" And Tommy Benford, expected for a repertoire concert to play as he had played on Jelly Roll Morton's "Kansas City Stomps," asked, "You mean you want me to throw away all the improving I've done since then?"[6] The point is that black players outside the Marsalis orbit do not share the tendency of some of their white colleagues to romanticize the past. They have little reason to.

Beyond such matters this chapter turns first into a celebration of the Commodore catalogue, then into a celebration of the chronically neglected Brad Gowans. This latter includes, yet again, detailed comment on some of his records, in particular his solo on the 1940 "Ja-Da." Actually I would have said that Gowans's use of 9ths, 11ths, 13ths, etc., following on from Beiderbecke, looked forward to Charlie Parker and bop rather than, as Sudhalter claims, to Bob Brookmeyer. He has incidentally, in another fine bit of tune detection, traced the opening phrase of Livingston's "Humpty Dumpty" back to one of Gowans's breaks in Nichols's "Heebie Jeebies," something which, again, I had never noticed. Next we pass on to George Wettling, Lee Wiley, and others. Along the way this chapter includes many sidelights on its main story, on the unintended musical effects of the 20 percent entertainment tax levied early in World War II, for example, and why this "Americondon music" is now long gone, except on records.

A start is made in Chapter 13—"The Jean Goldkette and Ben Pollack Orchestras"—on a largely, and healthily, unorthodox view of the big bands, starting by reminding us that stereotyped attitudes by record companies sometimes led to bands not being allowed to record their best material. Additional factors were the companies' assumptions about what the tastes of record buyers were. Goldkette serves as the main instance of the resulting misrepresentation. The author supplies a great deal of background material—not just after Beiderbecke and Trumbauer had joined. And he makes interesting comments on the Goldkette-style scores written by Bill Challis for Paul Whiteman, not recorded by him but preserved in the Williams College Library in Massachusetts. The reason Goldkette's band did not last long was excellently summarized by one of its members, "Doc" Ryker, who is quoted here: "We were strictly a musicians' band. We played the way we wanted, and didn't care whether the people liked it or not"

(317). And throughout the so-called big band era these groups were touring entertainment troupes which, despite what latter-day propagandists of the "mainstream" persuasion have pretended, spent a lot of their time not preoccupied with jazz. Artie Shaw is quoted on a later page speaking eloquently of "the garbage we had to play" (153). Hence, with this band and so many others since, the records they left behind are far from being all they might have been, for, as Sudhalter tells us, "what happened in front of the microphones was little more than a faint echo of what happened every night on the bandstand" (329). But for better or for worse—often, one suspects, for worse—what is reckoned to be the history of jazz is a tale of what chanced to get on records.

With Pollack even more than with Goldkette, there is no gainsaying the favorable comments of all the people, musicians especially, who heard the band. Yet very little of its apparently singular character emerges on records. What it lacked was a composer/arranger to shape and direct it—which is what Goldkette had with Challis. I would suggest, too, that the Dorsey Brothers' Orchestra, dealt with in Chapter 15, for all its good qualities, similarly lacked a dominant composer/arranger to impart a consistent musical character. As against this we should, in Pollack's case, note a remark quoted from Ruby Weinstein, at one time the band's lead trumpeter, to the effect that it was essentially a soloist-led ensemble, and that all its good arrangements were head arrangements (330).

After Goldkette and Pollack, we at last get, in Chapter 14, a full treatment of the Casa Loma Band, hitherto usually an energetically misrepresented phenomenon. Aside from its originality, about which I have written briefly in another place,[7] there is also the matter of the Casa Loma's uncommonly wide influence. The effect of what Gene Gifford wrote for the Casa Loma Band on Jimmy Lunceford's (Will Hudson's) "Jazznocracy" and "White Heat," Henderson's "Tidal Wave," Hines's "Sensational Mood," the Blue Rhythm Band's "Blue Rhythm," Goodman's "Cokey" and "Nitwit Serenade" and other pieces is obvious. But despite the quality of its finest music, and even despite Coleman Hawkins once speaking of it as "my favorite band" (347), the Casa Loma has for several decades had a uniformly bad press. Quoted at this point in the book is James T. Maher, who is not alone among those who have actually listened to the records in finding "the anti-Casa Loma attacks in the jazz press baffling and provocative. All I can assume is that the writers were basing their criticism on a few recordings" (354). I would suggest, however, that they were writing in imitation of Hammond, Panassié, George Frazier, and other all-too-influential opinion-formers. The author deals with all this and in particular, in a long footnote, with Dance's deliberately misleading, Panassié-led assault on Hudson (791, footnote 15).

More to the point, he tackles the ways in which the Casa Loma Band's music gradually changed and developed, not only in Gifford's hands with such pieces as "Chant of the Jungle," "Avalon," and "Stompin' Around," but with other composer/arrangers approximating to his manner, like "A Study in Brown" by Larry Clinton and Larry Wagner's two-part "No Name Jive," a blues. And, besides a just tribute to Clarence Hutchenrider, we also are told of Pat Davis, Sonny Dunham, Grady Watts, Billy Rauch, and others.

The next chapter in this perhaps rather defiantly unorthodox survey of big band music is called "Dorseys and Boswells," and my earlier point about the Dorsey Brothers' Orchestra needing an arranger is here confirmed in a 1992 conversation between Sudhalter and Ray McKinley. "What they really needed," he said, "was an arranger who understood and could exploit that baritone-register sonority. But they never got it" (376). As to the jazz playing of the brothers themselves, the author mounts a staunch defense against the attacks of Schuller in particular, being especially eloquent on Jimmy's behalf as he had on earlier pages for Bud Freeman and as he would later on behalf of Artie Shaw. But even in the face of the flood tide of music examined here as in all other parts of this book, I am surprised he did not mention Jimmy's clarinet and alto work on "Aunt Hagar's Blues" and his clarinet and baritone on "Yellow Dog Blues" with the ineffable Ted Lewis.

Such favorites of mine are the Boswell Sisters—their *early* work—that, although I must resist the temptation, I am tempted to quote Sudhalter at length. Certainly the neglect of recent decades of their great and natural musicianship is—almost—inexplicable, and nearly everything in their performances is subject not to alteration for its own sake but in order subtly to improve what too often started as uninspired material. They fragment, interpolate, reharmonize, even recompose structures which end by being far less simple than they were at the beginning. As I write this I must stop and play for the *nth* time "There'll Be Some Changes Made," "Roll On, Mississippi, Roll On," "Got the South in My Soul," "Down Among the Sheltering Palms," "We Just Couldn't Say Goodbye.". . .And there are the contributions of their accompanists, Bunny Berigan on "Everybody Loves My Baby," Jimmy Dorsey on "Sleep, Come On and Take Me," Tommy Dorsey on "Hand Me Down My Walking Cane," Eddie Lang on "It's the Girl." And there are Connie's solo recordings, "Time on My Hands," "Concentratin'," "Me Minus You."

Bob Crosby's outfit grew out of the old Ben Pollack band, with arrangements by Matty Matlock, Dean Kincaide, and Bob Haggart. Maybe Luis Russell's Orchestra of a few years before was a kind of precedent and certainly the superimposing of Matlock's freewheeling clarinet over well-drilled, tightly scored imitative section readings achieved a lively evocation of a traditional form. The effectiveness of "Dogtown Blues" relies partly on rich harmonic drama, partly on the solo expression of Matlock and Yank Lawson. This is a finer distillation of early band blues than "Dixieland Shuffle," recorded over a year before and unashamedly based on King Oliver's "Riverside Blues." The Crosby account of "Royal Garden Blues" makes references to Beiderbecke's 1927 version and, although that would have been a source of pleasure to connoisseurs of jazz history, one does wonder how many people there were who could answer to such a description when Crosby recorded. The author makes useful analytical comments on, for example, "In a Minor Mood" with its debts to both Sergei Rachmaninoff and Fats Waller, and to Haggart's notable arrangement of "Between the Devil and the Deep Blue Sea."

By natural progression we move from such preoccupations to "Bix Beiderbecke and Some of His Friends," Chapter 17. Here we meet the concept of "layering," of an improvised solo speaking on several levels at once and arousing in a sensitive listener a mixture of responses. That was extremely original in the context of 1920s jazz. Certainly, and as Sudhalter remarks, the thought that Beiderbecke's vein of expression was something which came from just one musician is "hard to grasp" (416), and, however fruitlessly, one does wonder if Emmett Hardy made a significant contribution. Where *did* Beiderbecke's style come from?

We are taken, anyway, through the extremely familiar recordings—which most of us have played countless times ever since our teens. That the author still finds new things to say about them is perhaps less surprising in this case than others. Like other great artists, Beiderbecke's work is inexhaustible, and he is an inexhaustible subject for commentary. Quoted verbatim is Jay Arnold's 1944 analysis of Beiderbecke's 16 bars on "Krazy Kat," and there is a fascinating comparison between Beiderbecke and Pee Wee Russell on "Crying All Day," which was very advanced jazz thinking for 1927. Trumbauer's solo on "Singin' the Blues" from that same year is shaped by what might be described as a thoughtful *craftsmanship* in contrast with Beiderbecke's free flight of genius, even if the latter is well inside the soloistic language he had (and so quickly) established by then. We are reminded that he was only 23, and in the newsreel unearthed in the 1990s, to which Sudhalter refers, he looks even younger. Another remarkable solo, here notated, is on "Tain't So, Honey, Tain't So," which suggests that no matter how dubious the jazz value of certain of Whiteman's undertakings, he (or Challis) led Beiderbecke towards more subtle harmonic thinking.

His dissatisfaction with his own work is surely unsurprising for real artists are nearly always dissatisfied. With regard to jazz not being enough for this curiously mesmerizing figure, we are at once reminded of Parker, who expressed a comparable discontent and, to quote the author on Beiderbecke, likewise "did not avail himself of opportunities to perfect his reading, learn theory and explore composition" (432). The great altoist had a few more years than Beiderbecke, however, and *did* want to study with Edgard Varèse, *did* try to persuade Stefan Wolpe to compose some kind of concerto-like vehicle for him. This all came to nothing amid the final confusion, even chaos, of Parker's last months. Likewise it is perhaps apt that Chapter 17 is a bit episodic, shapeless; but Sudhalter does make a sensitive attempt to approach Beiderbecke the man.

There next come pages on Trumbauer which must surprise those among us who have got no further than what I have above called the "thoughtful craftsmanship" of his solos with Beiderbecke. There is considerable buried matter here, such as his solo on the Benson Orchestra's 1923 recording of "I Don't Miss the Sunshine." This had a considerable effect on other saxophonists at the time, as Benny Carter (quoted on page 448) well remembered. Also notable was his 1924 solo on the Mound City Blue Blowers' "San." The evidence of the influence of much of this work has been swept under the carpet, yet the music itself continues obstinately to exist on discs. Examples include Challis's 1928 scoring of "Singin' the Blues" for Whiteman with Trumbauer's solo written out for the whole reed section. Another is Henderson's version of "Singin' the Blues" with Rex Stewart's perceptive rendering of the Beiderbecke solo.

Trumbauer and Beiderbecke did share duets and chases, the main point of which, as the author says, is the differences between their solo styles, as in their 32 bars on Whiteman's "You Took Advantage of Me" or their 16-bar solos on "China Boy." And there is also, with Lang, their "For No Reason at All," notated in part on pages 454–56. Inevitably Trumbauer is seen to a considerable extent in the light of his association with Beiderbecke, perhaps above all on "For No Reason at All." Yet other fine Trumbauer solos, *pace* Martin Williams,[8] have now been identified, beginning with "Let's Do It," "How About Me?" "Don't Leave Me, Daddy" and a version of "Singin' the Blues" with Bee Palmer singing the words to the notes of Trumbauer's old solo. There are a considerable number of others.

Jack Purvis was a surprising choice for Chapter 19. He was an eccentric who covered his tracks with what might be called a consistent inconsistency. Yet he was an interesting, even original, musician. A title such as "Copyin' Louis" is partly misleading and perhaps deliberately so. Armstrong's influence is plain, yet the detail is different and often arresting in its aggressive elegance, the degree of rhythmic freedom being rather unusual for the period. Purvis had abundant agility and power, and the stinging attack of his trumpet galvanizes the ensembles of, say, "Dismal Dan" or "Be Bo Bo." Many of the themes he recorded were his own, and they show he possessed considerable flair for composition and arrangement. Some of Purvis's recordings are, characteristically, rather obscure, as Sudhalter acknowledges, and I regret that I have not heard them.

It is curiously apt that we pass from the almost invisible Purvis to one who was born for fame. Not that Bunny Berigan (Chapter 20) is the easiest person to get into sharp focus. A doctor can bury his failures, an architect can advise discontented clients to plant trees, but a jazzman, living or dead, has no protection against reissue programs, and evaluation of Berigan has been made difficult by the little matter of what performances have and have not been put back into circulation. The fact remains that almost every recorded solo by this great romantic trumpeter is concise, exactly to the point notwithstanding a virtuosity that allows him to send phrases soaring complexly across the entire range of his instrument, their effect heightened by variety of timbre and attack, and a fine harmonic sense.

During the long years of work on this book the author located all the great Berigan performances even if some of them have not of late been widely circulated, and one could do worse than append a partial list: "Troubled" with Trumbauer, "Nothing but the Blues" and "Squareface" with Gene Gifford, "In a Little Spanish Town" with Glenn Miller, "Jingle Bells" and "Sometimes I'm Happy" with Goodman, "Keep Smilin' at Trouble" with Freeman (whose dry, laconic phrases are a particularly apt foil to the trumpet's more expressionistic manner), "Mr Ghost Goes to Town" with Tommy Dorsey; and Berigan under his own name: "The Wearing of the Green," "Russian Lullaby," "Jelly Roll Blues," "Candlelights," and the earlier 1936 Vocalion "I Can't Get Started." The absolutely wholesale enthusiasm for Berigan's playing expressed by virtually all the musicians who worked with him and are frequently quoted in Chapter 20 can arouse one's suspicions yet almost any reservations are soon quieted by jazz like this.

Moving on, we reach Benny Goodman, who both as a musician and as a man was both very fortunate and very unfortunate. As a musician he apparently saw himself above all as a clarinetist, with jazz as one of a number of possible lines he could follow. This led to his adventures with the classical repertoire (Mozart, Weber, etc.) and modern "straight" repertoire (Bartók, Hindemith, Copland, Malcolm Arnold, etc.), which, particularly in the 1930s and 1940s, jazz fans and even some jazz musicians found so mystifying. One has no patience with that kind of parochialism and can only pass on to his personal quirks, which are what seem to interest so many folk. Certainly he appears to have drawn a rigid line, as Sudhalter tells us, between the way he dealt with people whom he admired and considered to be his peers, and his treatment of his sidemen. Since Goodman's death in 1986 an increasing number of his former employees have gone into print with stories about his meanness, his unawareness of the feelings of others, his gaucherie. For instance, one magazine, which has always been too much centered round its editor's personality, devoted most of four issues to a peculiarly sustained attack on Goodman.[9]

And yet we are also told of Goodman walking nine blocks down New York's Second Avenue one morning and during those ten minutes being stopped by no fewer than four strangers who recognized him and vigorously shook his hand (554). They varied in age from near contemporaries to youngsters born long after Goodman's period of maximum fame, yet they all had much the same thing to say, namely "I can't imagine my life without you and your music . . ." This is the other side of the coin from his former employees' resentment. I am in no position to suggest that their complaints are not truthful, but Goodman reached a vast number of people, perhaps more than Ellington, perhaps even more than Armstrong. Rather typical was the Carnegie Hall occasion marking the 40th anniversary of his 1938 triumph there: it was sold out within 24 hours.

The author does not follow his usual procedure of taking us through carefully chosen recordings and identifying their outstanding musical features. This is most disappointing, not least because I was allotted so very little space to say anything about Goodman in the appropriate chapter of the recent *Oxford Companion to Jazz*.[10] Instead Sudhalter provides a question-and-answer sequence with Goodman, which is not without value yet is on a different level from the rest of this book. A few points of interest do emerge but also further disappointments. Anyone who has repeatedly listened to Goodman records over a long period of years can only be discouraged by the great clarinetist's obvious preference for stale arrangements by Henderson, Jimmy Mundy, etc., over scores from Eddie Sauter which still sound as fresh as when they were recorded.

It is no great surprise that this book's treatment of Goodman is followed by one of Shaw, except that the latter is the subject of two chapters which are richly detailed and far superior to what was done for his rival. Thus we are taken through Shaw's early records from 1934 onwards, with "Interlude" (1936) as the first to show real independence. In another sense, however, most of them show independence, being a reaction against what most other bandleaders were playing. Shaw much later wrote, "I thought Fletcher Henderson's was one of the most boring bands in the world. You knew exactly what was going to happen unless somebody like Coleman [Hawkins] or Louis [Armstrong] was in there doing something."[11] At this much later date one can only agree, although it is far more to the point that a few other bandleaders such as Red Norvo and Bob Haggart agreed at the time. Besides being a reaction against music like Henderson's, some parts of what Shaw would do were a continuation of lines Whiteman had earlier undertaken. See the long footnote 21 on page 821, which indicates that the so-called "King of Jazz" remains a largely unexplored subject. Also see footnote 10 on page 830 concerning his role as a talent scout.

Meanwhile Shaw's musical convictions were seconded by clarinet playing which by now had only one rival, and its most distinctive feature was its tone. As the author says, it was "centered in all registers, its sweetness balanced by a minty astringency of attack and warmed by a violin-like vibrato; it is almost from date to date ("My Blue Heaven" is particularly good) an increasingly personal expressive vehicle" (579). Yet however consistent his clarinet work, Shaw contradicted himself when it came to words rather than notes. Thus at the start of Chapter 23 he is quoted as making fun of Goodman for being "too hung up on the goddam clarinet" (569) while a few pages later saying the instrument "calls for total concentration . . . . I used up a large part of my life developing and honing my technique" (579).

The various Shaw outfits' use of strings was the most musical in jazz since that of Whiteman's arrangers and remained the best at least until Robert Graettinger started writing for Kenton's Innovations in Modern Music band. Of course, the string scoring, by Shaw or Jerry Gray, is never "Stravinsky-esque" (578) and, as elsewhere in this volume, there are plenty of assertions with which to disagree. For example I would suggest that Sammy Weiss's drumming is far more offensive in "It Ain't Right" than in "Japanese Sandman" and that the treatment of "Skeleton in the Closet" is hardly "dixielandish" (578). However, I agree with Sudhalter that this score is likely to be where Shaw got his idea for "Nightmare." Concerning Shaw's reported pompous remarks on "Cream Puff"—where he almost compares himself with Mozart! (580)—it was presumably beneath his dignity to acknowledge that this *important* composition was actually composed by someone else, namely by Franklyn Marks (who later won greater fame with Kenton's Innovations band).

Some of these early Shaw recordings, like "Darling, Not without You," are very soft-centered, but every performance is most carefully rehearsed, and the clarinet playing is every bit as good as nearly everyone always said it was. The author is excellent on the specific qualities of the RCA Victor band and grows positively eloquent about Shaw's solos both on studio recordings and various air shots: "Lover, Come Back to Me," "Out of Nowhere," "Just You, Just Me," "Deep Purple," "Say It with a Kiss," "It Had to Be You" (compare this with the Goodman version set down only a week earlier), "Carioca," and "Begin the Beguine."

Shaw was so very much in control of his bands—the *way* as well as *what* they played—that some people would say the result was not quite jazz. Faced with such achievements as his wonderful "Stardust"—the 1938 air shot as well as the 1940 studio recording—I disagree. However, I am glad that he had the grace to admit that his tawdry "Concerto for Clarinet" was "a fraud, a pasteup" (593). Yet this lapse can be forgotten in view of such absorbing later Shaw ventures as the unlikely four tracks with Henry Allen, J.C. Higginbotham, and Benny Carter; Fred Norman's "Solid Sam"; Ray Conniff's "Just Kiddin' Around" (alias "Savoy Jump") and "Lament" (a great improvement on "Concerto"); Margie Gibson's "Deuces Wild"; Thomas Griselle's "Nocturne"; Paul Jordan's "Suite No. 8," "Evensong" (alias "Dusk"), "Carnival," and "Two in One Blues." And beside such "poems for band" there were "Through the Years," where Shaw's playing is so touching, and the two-part "Saint James Infirmary." Several of these essays have a rather Ellingtonian orientation, for however much Shaw was the boss with the master plan, he persuaded some other people to write extremely well for him.

Comparing his solos on the 1939 and 1945 recordings of "The Man I Love" is a quick way of grasping how Shaw's sensibility had changed during those years, and such pieces as Coniff's "Lucky Number" indicate that he was aware of what had been going on elsewhere in jazz. This led beyond the Gramercy Five's tightly pattered mosaics in "The Sad Sack," "The Gentle Grifter," well beyond "Summit Ridge Drive"—that absolute contradiction in terms, a million-seller which also was good music—to a band that had a more intelligent relationship with the new music than those led by Goodman or Barnet. Like theirs, Shaw's attempt at fronting a "bop band" did not last for long, but it recorded some highly intriguing scores, such as Gene Roland's "Aesop's Foibles," Tadd Dameron's "So Easy," and, perhaps above all, George Russell's "Similau."

Whether Shaw recognized it or not, that was a sort of climax and not very much lay beyond it except a final edition of the Gramercy Five, which managed to discover new facets even in such things as "Begin the Beguine." Much later Shaw said of these final performances, "That isn't *jazz*, that's *music!*" (615). Though many features of his public career and, one suspects, of his private life suggest that he was utterly lacking any sense of humor, Shaw may have been the rare case of a musician who was too intelligent for jazz. At least, unlike Kenton, Herman, and several others, he avoided becoming a prisoner of his own past.

The last section of this book, "The Fine Art of *Sui Generis*," consists of four chapters, two on Red Norvo and Mildred Bailey, one on either side about Bobby Hackett, and a final one about Pee Wee Russell and Jack Teagarden. Sudhalter is astute on the qualities of such things as Hackett's 1938 "Small Fry" solo, his "Embraceable You" of the following year, his 1945 "Body and Soul," his "I'm Comin', Virginia" in Condon's *Bixieland* set of a decade later. Indeed we are given a full account of the many facets of Hackett's subtle art; one has only to disagree with his asserting that Armstrong and Billy Butterfield were the only trumpeters "who can play up high and always make it musical" (645). Dizzy Gillespie and Fats Navarro could do this as well. Along the way there are also words on such neglected figures as Butterfield and Ernie Caceres. Speaking of the latter, there also is interesting detail on the independently instrumented group which Hackett led at the Voyager Room during the mid-1950s, and rather than the Capitol LP we are led to the three-LP set of its broadcasts on Shoestring. This was a descendant of the group Norvo fronted at the Famous Door in the 1930s, which also had an unusual instrumentation and, more to the point, was among the great bands of the swing era though still not generally recognized as such.

Spread over two chapters, we are given all necessary details on Norvo's and Bailey's records, centering on such items as Norvo's nearly atonal "Dance of the Octopus," a rather astonishing jazz composition for 1933 even if only half of it got on disc. Perhaps Sauter's 1937 scoring of "Smoke Dreams" for Norvo's band was no more than a curiosity, but elsewhere I have described his "Remember" as "cool big band jazz a decade before Gil Evans's work for Claude Thornhill."[12] Particularly welcome in this chapter—in this book, in *any* book—is Norvo's detailed putdown, quoted on pages 697–8, of the grotesquely overrated Billie Holiday. He rightly preferred Ethel Waters, Mildred Bailey, Lee Wiley, Connie Boswell.

There is also, as there should be in a book like this, a full account of Teagarden's unique music and, in the end, rather sad career. As the author says, the vocalization of the trombone was a central factor in the character of Teagarden's work and something which set him apart from Jimmy Harrison. The latter's supposed influence on Teagarden and alleged superiority to him have been the subject of much ill-informed partisanship, but the matter is dealt with sensibly here, as is the question of Teagarden's period with Whiteman. Beyond such topics, a few peaks of trombone jazz from Teagarden are duly cited, like "Whoopee Stomp" (the 1928 Harmony recording), Condon's "That's a Serious Thing," "Tailspin Blues" with the Mound City Blue Blowers, "Indiana" with Red Nichols, the twelve bars in "Basin Street Blues" with the Louisiana Rhythm Kings (again Nichols), all from 1929, and later high points such as "Texas Tea Party" with Goodman, and "Jack Hits the Road" with Freeman. Regarding both Teagarden and Pee Wee Russell, Sudhalter is enlightening on the matter of "wrong" notes which are musically right, an important question in improvised music, not only in the jazz idiom.

On Russell he has some interesting thoughts too, for instance about the clarinetist's virtual "deconstruction" of the usual way of going about making an improvised solo grow. In part this seemed to arise out of an unusually sensitive response to Beiderbecke's ideas. He refers to Russell as being, like Henry Allen, "an architect of wonderfully asymmetrical musical structures," as in their jousting on the Rhythmakers' "Who's Sorry Now?" The way they both play here manages, as Charles Fox said, to avoid the ensemble patterns established both in Chicago and New Orleans.[13] Meanwhile the author identifies several of the well-known Russell occasions, such as "Love is Just Around the Corner" on Commodore, "Fidgety Feet" with the 1940 Summa Cum Laude band, the following year's "The Last Time I Saw Chicago," "Sunrise Serenade" with Hackett's big band, his 1944 quartet recordings with Stacy like "Take Me to the Land of Jazz." And Sudhalter even roots out the little-known Russell solos with Louis Prima, above all "Cross Patch," besides taking in the altogether exceptional renewal of the clarinetist's last years, when he performed and recorded such items as Strayhorn's "Chelsea Bridge," Dameron's "Good Bait," and Coltrane's "Red Planet."

That is the kind of happy note upon which my brief account of what the author calls "this vast and sprawling chronicle" (744) should end. Yet along with being vast and sprawling it is also original and above all independent, and these latter qualities, especially the last, will ensure that it receives much adverse comment in the expected places from the expected people. Indeed, I should like, however belatedly, to get in on this act myself.

The book is naturally written from an American viewpoint, yet Sudhalter should have realized that such a volume will reach an international readership. He assumes knowledge which no doubt is shared by countless citizens of the U.S.A. but may be quite unfamiliar to people elsewhere. Thus he writes of Venice Beach as "a kind of southern Californian equivalent of Atlantic City." What does that mean? What is the significance of Atlantic City? Someone is called "Harry Reser-like" (341). Who is this Reser? Who are Edward Hopper and Thomas Hart Benton (687–98)? And on page 403 he writes "thumb and pinky." Pinky? And entertaining though she sounds, I have no idea of who Betty Boop (661) is, or was.

The correct year for Milhaud's "La Création du Monde" is 1923, and on page 428 better instances of the influence of jazz on modern classical music would have been the slow movement, actually titled "Blues," of Ravel's Violin Sonata (1923–27) and Antheil's Jazz Symphony (1925). On page 429, Sudhalter notes that there is no improvisation in Bloom's "Soliloquy," but neither is there improvisation in Ellington's "Reminiscing in Tempo" or Dameron's "Fontainebleau," yet each is just as "unmistakeably a jazz composition."

Misinformation continues to spread about Reginald Foresythe (223) despite his fascinating, almost unknown music. Rather than a West Indian, his father was West African (a barrister) and his mother German.

On another non-American, it is a pity no mention was made in Chapter 21 of Django Reinhardt's status as a composer nor of his big band music, particularly as most of this was several years ago reissued on CD, at least in Scotland, on the Hep label.

Further on non-American activities, it is yet again claimed for Commodore that it was "The first label wholly devoted to recording hot jazz of *any* sort" (281, author's italics). The label which actually was first was Swing, in Paris.

Still further on non-Americans, I am twice given credit which is not due to me. It was Charles Fox who wrote those nice words about Lee Wiley attributed to me (294),[14] and it was Eric Thacker (585), not I, who in the same place[15] spoke up for Artie Shaw. Each piece in that book is clearly initialled so there is no excuse for misattributions.

Yet, Reinhardt's music aside, these are small failures of scholarship. Scholarship is about information and knowledge whereas criticism, like poetry, is about something else. This book fuses together information, knowledge, criticism and even wisdom to a degree that will surely remain uncommon. And—to return to my initial question—reading it twice, including the 93 pages of footnotes, and listening repeatedly to as many of the relevant recordings as possible, *has* made the whole of jazz sound rather different.

NOTES

1. One of the very few, though evidently ignored by most American readers, is André Hodeir, *The Worlds of Jazz* (New York: Grove Press, 1972).
2. Igor Stravinsky, *Poetics of Music in the Form of Six Lessons* (New York: Vintage Books, 1956), 26.
3. Wilfrid Mellers, *Music in a New Found Land: Themes and Developments in the History of American Music* (London: Barrie & Rockliff, 1964).
4. Max Harrison, Charles Fox, Eric Thacker, *The Essential Jazz Records, Vol. 1: Ragtime to Swing* (London: Mansell Publishing, 1984), 26–29, 152–54.
5. Gunther Schuller, *The Swing Era: The Development of Jazz, 1930–45* (New York and Oxford: Oxford University Press, 1989), 601.
6. These quotations from Johnson and Benford occurred in a personal communication from the author to me, dated May 16, 2001.
7. Harrison et al., *The Essential Jazz Records Vol. 1*, 267–69.
8. Martin Williams, *The Jazz Tradition* (New York and Oxford: Oxford University Press, 1983), 72.
9. Bill Crow, "To Russia without Love: the Benny Goodman Tour of the USSR," *Jazzletter* (August, September, October, November 1986). The two following issues, December 1986 and January 1987, plus May 1987, carried letters from readers mostly saying how marvelous this attack was, admittedly with a few saying the opposite.
10. "Swing Era Big Bands and Jazz Composing and Arranging" in Bill Kirchner (ed.), *The Oxford Companion to Jazz* (New York and Oxford: Oxford University Press, 2000), 277–91.
11. Artie Shaw, *The Trouble with Cinderella* (New York: Farrar, Straus & Young, 1952).
12. Harrison et al., 439–41.
13. Ibid., 123–24.
14. Ibid., 447.
15. Harrison et al., 330–32.

Lewis Porter, *John Coltrane: His Life and Music.* (Ann Arbor: The University of Michigan Press, 1998, 409 + xvii pp., $29.95 hardcover; $17.95 paperback)

Reviewed by Alexander Stewart

Jazz musicians, educators, scholars, and listeners have had to wait nearly twenty-five years for a reliable, newly researched biography of John Coltrane, "one of the great musical artists of the twentieth century" (1). In 1975, eight years after the saxophonist's death, two books appeared, both useful and interesting, but each fraught with errors and lacking documentation.[1] In *Coltrane: His Life and Music* Lewis Porter has filled this long-lasting void.

As he states in his preface, although Porter originally intended to limit his scope to an in-depth survey of Coltrane's musical accomplishments, a project that began with the author's doctoral work in 1980, he "eventually realized that a new biography was also required" (ix). To some extent Porter still relies on these earlier biographies, whenever possible rechecking their information. He conducted numerous interviews with musicians, family members, and others intimately involved with the saxophonist, but he places particular weight on Coltrane's own words, derived from numerous recorded and/or published interviews with his subject (many freshly transcribed by the author). A primary resource remains, of course, Coltrane's music: his compositions and his extensive recorded output (commercially released, "bootleg" and home recordings). In an appendix he presents a detailed chronology of the saxophonist's life, much of it reconstructed by scouring newspapers, national magazines and jazz journals from North America and abroad, as well as studio and jazz club logbooks. His work also benefits from the research of other scholars in recent years, which he generously acknowledges throughout his text.

Porter's primary concern is discovering Coltrane's musical influences and resources. Coltrane's insatiable musical curiosity and obsessive work habits led him constantly to seek new ideas from a wide range of sources. Porter compiles and illuminates Coltrane's borrowings from Negro spirituals, "world" music (particularly South Asian), classical music (such as Ravel), and even piano etudes, as well as his deep rooting in the jazz tradition. He also explores Coltrane's profound interest in composing and its inextricable relationship to his playing.

After presenting an extensive genealogy of the Coltrane family, Porter explores Coltrane's youth and early career, as always, with an eye toward possible musical influences. Biographical chapters are interspersed with interludes titled Musical Education I, II, and III that look at his training and musical growth in detail. The Coltranes' home in the small town of High Point, North Carolina, was not devoid of music. His mother, Alice, played piano and his father, John R., the violin and ukulele. His father's favorite song, "The Sweetheart of Sigma Chi," was "the kind of romantic melody," Porter notes, ". . . that Coltrane could pull off in later years with that intense nostalgic calm of his" (26). When he was twelve, in the space of only a few months, the deaths of an aunt, his grandfather, and, most devastating, his father brought major upheaval to the family. They were forced to rent out much of their house, and his mother took work as a domestic.

His father's death, writes Porter, brought him "pain that he never seems to have allowed himself to fully explore except through music " (17). Conjecturing that music became a father substitute for him, Porter feels that ballads, in particular, "somehow . . . brought back his father to him" (26–27). Interestingly, as the author points out much later (127), Coltrane's lyrical and tender approach to ballads, typically involving less improvisation and more melodic embellishment, contrasted with the rapid fire formulas and "sheets of sound" for which he became better known.

Coltrane's first instrumental training, on alto horn, began not long after his father's death. As soon as an instrument became available he switched to clarinet and eventually to alto saxophone. Two of his friends at the time reported that tunes he was most fond of playing were "Tuxedo Junction," Hoagy Carmichael's "Blue Orchids" (both recorded by Glenn Miller), and "Margie" (recorded by Jimmy Lunceford).

In 1945, after his family moved to Philadelphia, Coltrane entered the navy. Stationed with a black unit in Hawaii, he played in a band called the Melody Masters. Thanks to a lead provided by Phil Schaap, Porter was able to track down eight tunes recorded by Coltrane with an integrated sextet that had gotten together to jam on an ad hoc basis (the navy was still segregated). These sides, with their obvious bebop leanings (at least four of them are tunes associated with Parker and Gillespie), reveal that Coltrane was no prodigy. The most obvious flaw in his playing is his rhythmic weakness, also apparent to a somewhat lesser extent in recordings a few years later with Hodges and Gillespie (all available on a recent compilation assembled by Porter, *The Last Giant*). Porter attributes this "awkwardness" to possible mechanical problems with his instrument and the general difficulty that "young players all over the country" were having assimilating the demanding new style of bebop (50). He credits the collegial atmosphere among Coltrane's peers in the emerging Philadelphia jazz scene (Benny

Golson, Jimmy Heath, and others), as well as the saxophonist's work ethic and relentless practicing, as helping this "late bloomer" overcome his deficiencies. Rather than being, as Porter describes it, part of a "normal process" of development that is common to everyone, Coltrane's spectacular improvement seems to me more likely to be a result of his extraordinary ability to evaluate his own strengths and weaknesses (probably aided by his habit of recording himself and, later, constant presence in the studio). Indeed, Porter emphasizes his humility and "self-effacing" personality. In interviews Coltrane frequently talked about his own shortcomings, even specifically mentioning that he was "better equipped" harmonically than rhythmically or melodically.[2]

Taking advantage of his veteran's benefits, Coltrane studied at the Granoff School in Philadelphia. His teacher, Dennis Sandole, recalls that the saxophonist worked hard, often taking two lessons a week. He was exposed to "exotic" scales and "advanced harmonic techniques" (51).

One of Porter's most valuable contributions to the understanding of Coltrane's music and to jazz studies in general is his reconstruction of the saxophonist's practice regimen. Fellow saxophonist Jimmy Heath, who frequently practiced with Coltrane, demonstrated numerous exercises and patterns that Porter has transcribed and reproduced in the text. Testimony from other musicians and teachers has enabled the author to uncover several rather surprising sources of Coltrane's material. For example, James "Hen Gates" Forman, a pianist with the Gillespie band, recalled that Coltrane, always looking for material to practice, borrowed some Hanon and Czerny piano exercise books. Porter persuasively links these exercises (many of which are extremely difficult on saxophone) to devices in Coltrane's later recordings such as the expanding intervallic leaps from a fixed pitch in "My Favorite Things" and the neighbor-tone figures in his composition "Like Sonny." Because "Coltrane collected materials freely from all sources," Porter concludes, he "began to develop a new kind of jazz style, new in part because it didn't rely exclusively on traditional jazz materials" (83).

From the time he left the navy in 1946 until he joined Miles Davis in 1955, other than brief stints with Johnny Hodges and Dizzy Gillespie, Coltrane earned his living mostly in the burgeoning R&B scene, in units led by King Kolax, Eddie Vinson, Earl Bostic, and other more obscure artists. On such gigs saxophonists were often expected to "walk the bar" while playing. Porter recounts the by-now-familiar story of Coltrane's embarrassment at being caught in the act by colleagues such as Benny Golson. Coltrane later acknowledged, as Porter notes, the great respect Coltrane had for Vinson and Bostic and their technical mastery of the saxophone. Despite his apparent discomfort with some aspects of performance, in my view Coltrane's years in R&B bands had a far-reaching impact on his style, which is particularly evident in his early recordings and in the "shrieks and hollers" of his later work. Coltrane's style has proven particularly adaptable to funk, as can be readily heard in the playing of Michael Brecker and numerous other contemporary players. Porter mentions Coltrane's experience with the blues (25), but in discussing Coltrane's later playing, does little to follow up on Billy Taylor's suggestive comment that Coltrane had learned to "scream" in rhythm-and-blues bands (288).

Coltrane's association with Miles Davis proved a critical turning point in the saxophonist's career and personal life. Although only a few months younger than Davis, who was already an established artist, as Porter points out, Coltrane was perceived as an emerging young talent. Even more open-minded critics such as Nat Hentoff were not initially impressed. Still quite unsure of himself, Coltrane received little help from Davis, who later complained in his autobiography that "Trane liked to ask all these motherfucking questions" (100). By the time of the release of *'Round About Midnight* in March 1957 on Columbia, some critics, such as Ira Gitler, had come to his support. Still, Coltrane's drug and alcohol problems, afflictions shared with so many other players of his generation, remained an obstacle. Davis, who had successfully battled his own heroin addiction, finally lost patience and fired Coltrane (along with his drummer, Philly Joe Jones) in April.

With the help of his first wife, Naima, Coltrane determined to go "cold turkey" and experienced what he later described as a "spiritual awakening." He had already been practicing and hanging out with Monk. Porter's account, based largely on Coltrane's own words derived from previously unavailable interviews, depicts the nurturing and fertile environment Coltrane found playing with Monk. In contrast with Davis, Monk actually liked to discuss music! Monk asked Coltrane to join him in an engagement at the Five Spot, which "turned out to be a significant career move for both of them" (109).

In May 1957 and a few months later in September, during this now legendary summer and fall residency at the Five Spot, Coltrane recorded his first two albums as a leader: *Coltrane,* on his regular label, Prestige, and *Blue Train* on Blue Note. Both recordings showcase Coltrane's talents as a composer. Tunes such as "Straight Street," "Moments Notice," and "Lazy Bird" reveal his fascination with intricate harmonies, particularly chromatic ii7–V7 progressions. Porter does not engage in a detailed analysis of any of Coltrane's solos from this period; instead, he simply states that Coltrane "relied heavily on a personal collection of formulas, or licks" (121) and, occasionally, development of short motives. A series of examples (122–23 and 134–35) illustrate some of Coltrane's favorite devices (but without giving any discographical references).

After the Five Spot gig (Porter's evidence indicates January 1958), Coltrane rejoined Davis. He now played, in Porter's words, "with charisma and authority" and "a renewed vision of what he could accomplish in life" (131). He also became increasingly aware that, like his predecessor in the Davis quintet, Sonny Rollins, he was now in a position to lead his own group. Recognition did not necessarily mean approval, however. His playing continued to shock many listeners. In Paris he was booed and some critics still perceived his sound as "angry." Rather than simply dismissing Coltrane's detractors, Porter does his best to understand their reaction in historical context. Speaking of Coltrane's solo on "Bye Bye Blackbird," recorded live at Paris's Olympia Theater, he confides, "To be fair, the whole thing *is* outrageous and 'torrential' and full of 'anguish.' I happen to love it, but I can see that many would not" (144). He speculates that, despite Coltrane's denials ("The only one I'm angry at is myself when I don't make what I'm trying to play"), "it may be angry at some level, and it may be the intense shouting of a man in pain, of a man who had something important to say, something he desperately needed to say" (139).

The midpoint of this book, chapter 13, examines Coltrane's role in what might be considered the two most important albums of 1959: Davis's *Kind of Blue* and his own first record as a leader for Atlantic, *Giant Steps.* The saxophonist was being drawn down two divergent musical paths: just as his exploration of complex harmony reached an apex through his use of third-related chord changes, Davis was leading the way toward simpler, static harmonies in "modal jazz." Porter contrasts these two approaches by examining Coltrane's solos on "Giant Steps" and "So What." Following Barry Kernfeld in his 1983 article "Two Coltranes," Porter distinguishes between a formulaic and a more developmentally minded Coltrane.[3] For "Giant Steps," the author again emphasizes Coltrane's heavy reliance on formulas and describes his solo as constructed "largely out of four-note patterns that could be easily transposed to fit each chord" (151).

Like Kernfeld, Porter valorizes "organic unity" and sees Coltane's playing as evolving away from formulaic or "lick" playing to greater thematic coherence. He discusses how Coltrane builds a "tightly unified solo" by developing a few "abstract" melodic motives in "So What." "By spending so much time on each chord and mode," Porter concludes, "he was able to grow in his ability to develop musical ideas while improvising" (165).

"Jazz musicians . . . define modes," says Porter, "in a somewhat oversimplified manner, as types of scales." His reiteration of Kernfeld's suggestion that "we do away with the label *modal jazz* altogether" (159) seems, at the very least, unrealistic in light of its common use by jazz musicians all over the world. He is more to the point when he observes that "modal jazz" indicated a "repertory of pieces that was different from other jazz of the time . . . in the use of unusual scales, in staying on each one for many measures at a time, and in leaving the choice of chords open and free" (160). He also points out that Coltrane and other players still imposed harmonic progressions and "stacked chords" on top the static harmonies. In Coltrane's words, " The [modal] approach allowed the soloist the choice of playing chordally (vertically) or melodically (horizontally)" (160).

As Coltrane grew musically he devoted more of his energies to composing. His playing and writing developed hand in hand; as his obsessive practicing and exploration of wide-ranging musical resources yielded distinctive and virtuosic improvisations he needed appropriate vehicles on which to base them. Earlier in his career, according to Jimmy Heath, "he said he had no time for that [writing]—he used his time for practicing" (69). Forming his own quartet allowed him to concentrate more on his own music, and by the time he left Davis he had "dedicated himself in earnest to developing as a composer" (170).

Coltrane's interest in complex harmony culminated in his use of third-related harmony in his compositions. Porter lists exhaustively Coltrane's possible sources for the "Giant Steps" changes: (1) the bridge of "Have You Met Miss Jones" (believed by many musicians); (2) the turn-around to Tadd Dameron's "Lady Bird" (Brian Priestley's suggestion); (3) the last four measures of Vinson's "Tune Up" (from Carl Woidek); (4) his teacher in Philadelphia, Dennis Sandole (looked into by David Demsey); and (5) Nicolas Slonimsky's *Thesaurus of Scales and Melodic Patterns* (also explored by Demsey). Additionally, Porter mentions the possible influence of classical composers who used modulations to mediant harmonies. During 1959 and 1960, Coltrane applied these changes to a host of standards, jazz tunes, and originals, among them: "But Not For Me," "Body and Soul," "Tune Up" ("Countdown"), "Hot House"/"What Is this Thing Called Love" ("Fifth House"), "How High the Moon" ("Satellite"), and "Confirmation" ("26-2").

On Tuesday, May 3, 1960, Coltrane's first quartet opened at Joe Termini's Jazz Gallery on St. Mark's Place. Because Elvin Jones and McCoy Tyner were not available (Jones was serving time in Riker's Island for drug violations, and Tyner was unable to get free from Golson's Jazztet),

Coltrane used Steve Kuhn and Peter Sims "LaRoca" on piano and drums. The group's repertoire comprised much of the original material that Coltrane had been recording for Atlantic (which, unlike Prestige, allowed him to retain the publishing rights).

All indications are that Coltrane had been thinking about the personnel for his group for many years. Tyner acknowledges that they had a "verbal understanding," and Porter quotes a little-known interview in which Coltrane told a French journalist "I noticed him [Tyner] when I was in Philadelphia and promised myself to call him if I formed my own group one day" (177). About six weeks later Tyner was able to extricate himself from his obligations and, finally, probably in late September, Jones joined the group in Denver.

The overlap of recording contracts led to "a confusing variety of material coming on to the market each year" (191). On the Impulse album *Coltrane Jazz,* the "classic quartet" appeared for the first time on record (minus Jimmy Garrison, who didn't join until late in 1961). Listeners who had not yet heard the group in performance must have been struck by the contrast between the single track on which they appear, a minor blues titled "Village Blues" (October 1960), and the rest of the album (recorded in 1959). Tyner's "particular type of voicing in fourths that was to characterize the sound of the quartet" (177) is already evident, as is Jones's strength and "powerful interest in complex rhythms" (179).

Porter observes that "Coltrane was a serious blues player, and his blues pieces reflect a desire to get back to a primal mood, and away from the harmonically more complex blues of the boppers" (184). He provides a transcription of Coltrane's solo on another minor blues, "Equinox," in which the ten choruses are vertically aligned to facilitate comparison of the soloist's ideas and their placement. Coltrane may have been criticized for lengthy, note-filled solos, but to Porter "this solo provides a good illustration of how concise Coltrane's improvising became in the 1960s" (185). His solo is built from "just a few motives" mostly "deriv[ed] from the theme itself." He reaches an "emotional climax" in the eighth chorus, saving the two remaining choruses to "create a sense of repose and finality" and "set[ting] the stage for Tyner" (188).

In December 1964 Coltrane recorded his first extended suite, *A Love Supreme.* His notes and an original poem that appeared on the album jacket linked the music to the pivotal moment of his life: his spiritual awakening in 1957. It became his best-selling album—over 500,000 copies by 1970. Music was becoming a very personal expression of his spiritual beliefs. Porter quotes a 1966 interview for *Newsweek* in which Coltrane states, "My goal is to live the truly religious life and express it in my music. If you live it, when you play there's no problem because the music is just part of the whole thing. . . . My music is the spiritual expression of what I am—my faith, my knowledge, my being" (232).

Porter traces the underlying architecture of the four-part work, praising its symmetry and unity. Most of Coltrane's material, from the key relationships of the four sections (F, E♭, B♭, C) to the motivic ideas developed in his solos, is derived from the cells in Example 1. Porter looks closely at the last part of the first movement, which is based entirely on a figure derived from cell a. His transcription shows how "Coltrane transposes it to every one of twelve keys and utilizes the middle and low registers" (242). The outer sections are "more exploratory and open-ended" while the central movements have chord progressions and chorus structures. The four sections, "Acknowledgement," "Resolution," Pursuance," and "Psalm," "suggest a kind of pilgrim's progress," writes Porter, "in which the pilgrim acknowledges the divine, resolves to pursue it, searches, and, eventually, celebrates what has been attained in song" (232). Porter hears Coltrane's (and Garrison's?) incantation of the words "a love supreme" at the end of Part I as a "reverse development," an "exposition" which has been purposely delayed so as to become more like a "revelation." Porter writes, "He's telling us that God is everywhere—in every register, in every key—and he's showing us that you have to discover religious belief" (242). In the final movement his improvisations are a "wordless 'recitation'" of Coltrane's poem (244).[4]

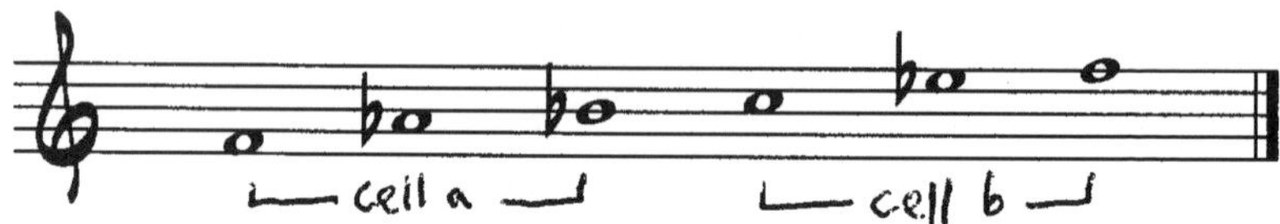

Example 1: Cells in *A Love Supreme* from Porter, 234

After devoting a chapter to *A Love Supreme*, in what has almost become obligatory in jazz (auto)biographies, Porter interrupts his narrative with a chapter (18) that consists almost entirely of testimonials. "The Man: 'A Quiet, Shy Guy'" quotes Coltrane's friends and colleagues on topics ranging from his personality, sense of humor, and health regimen to his views on politics. Porter concludes that, as Coltrane became "a spokesperson for the younger generation . . .[,] this new following brought with it an intense fervor, even a cultism, that was unfamiliar to jazz fans. At the same time, Coltrane's music began to change in ways that alienated some of his former audience. The passions around the man and his music were raised to a fever pitch" (261).

By 1965 Coltrane's career had reached a peak. *Down Beat* named *A Love Supreme* album of the year and Coltrane "Jazzman of the Year." At the same time Coltrane was becoming "something of a father figure to the growing avant-garde" (262). His success allowed him to reach out to less fortunate players. His earlier collaborations with Eric Dolphy led to associations with Pharoah Sanders, Archie Shepp, Marion Brown, and others. He recommended many artists to his label, Impulse, and welcomed younger players to "sit in with his group at performances" (262).

Many listeners who appreciate Coltrane's earlier style(s) have long been bewildered about how he could work so long and hard at playing over complex harmonic structures only to abandon them as he became interested in freer forms in the early 1960s. "I haven't forgotten about harmony altogether," he told a Belgian interviewer, Benoît Quersin (probably in 1961, according to Carl Woidek), "but I'm not as interested in it as I was two years ago."[5] He openly expressed his admiration for Ornette Coleman. Porter quotes this revealing passage:

> I love him [Coleman]. I'm following his lead. He's done a lot to open my ideas to what can be done. . . I feel indebted to him, myself. Because actually, when he came along, I was so far in this thing ["Giant Steps" chords], I didn't know where I was going to go next. And I don't know if I would have thought about just abandoning the chord system or not. I probably wouldn't have thought about that at all. And he came along doing it, and I heard it, I said, "Well that must be the answer" (203).

Coltrane recorded several of Coleman's tunes in June and July of 1960 with the altoist's sidemen (Don Cherry, Charlie Haden, and Ed Blackwell) for an album, *The Avant-Garde John Coltrane & Don Cherry*, that wasn't released until 1966. "It is revealing that," Porter concludes, "perhaps feeling he was not ready for free improvisation, Coltrane chose for his session some of Coleman's earliest compositions that do have prearranged chord progressions. And he certainly didn't play like Coleman—Coltrane's own musical personality was too well established to incorporate Coleman's saxophone style" (204).

One thing that tended to keep Coltrane more grounded in harmony, unlike Coleman, was the continued presence of a pianist in his group. With the "open" quality of his fourth-chord voicings and his uncanny ability to follow Coltrane's freer harmonic explorations, Tyner was particularly well suited for this role. Tyner might also lay out or "stroll," as would Garrison on occasion, during extended drum and saxophone duets.

As Coltrane ventured away from set chord changes, he also began to experiment with freeing up rhythm. He tried a second bassist and hired a second drummer, Rashied Ali. It is difficult to imagine a powerful drummer such as Jones sharing his role with another drummer, and there were bad feelings between the two drummers practically from the beginning. The volume level rose as each drummer tried to outplay the other. Jones and Tyner were increasingly unhappy with this situation and complained that they couldn't hear themselves or, for that matter, anyone else playing. More fundamentally, they "were unhappy with the group's moving away from a steady beat. As daring as they are, the one thing they both relied on was a steady and propulsive beat to work off" (266). Tyner left in late 1965 to be replaced by Coltrane's second wife, Alice, and Jones departed in early 1966 to take a short-lived gig with Ellington.

Ekkehard Jost used the term "rubato ballads" for these late works in which Coltrane abandoned a traditional groove and meter for a more flowing sense of time.[6] Porter, however, points out they are essentially "unclassifiable because they move quickly away from a ballad pace" as they build in intensity (276).

He also stresses that, despite his experimentation, Coltrane *didn't* abandon his harmonic approach. The author presents David Demsey's evidence of "Giant Steps" chordal superimpositions in "Impressions" and his own close reading of an extended solo, "Venus." A duet with Ali recorded only a few months before the saxophonist's death, this piece illustrates "the new context of Coltrane's last music [which] changed the meaning of his dissonance" (277). To Porter, Coltrane's ideas are similar to the ones in his work before 1965, such as "the little cell that runs through *A Love Supreme*" (276). But now his "dissonant formulas" suggest "changing key centers instead of serving to enrich a tonal center already established. . . . In practice, he tended to create some tonal structure in his improvisations" but he was free to "move from one key to any other at will" (277). Coltrane's music, states Porter unequivocally, remained "perfectly coherent on all his late recordings" (266), unlike, by implication, many of the younger "avant-garde" musicians with whom he associated.

Porter describes the opening theme (Example 2) as being "based on the notes E and G of a C major arpeggio" with the seventh (B) sometimes added even though "there is never a pause on the tonic C." After reiterating this theme seven times, Coltrane constructs a solo of "changing key" passages that are "quite different than the theme" (280). Though recognizing that "the key areas are sometimes ambiguous," Porter hears movement to third-related keys (as in "Giant Steps") followed by chromatically ascend-

Example 2: Opening theme, "Venus," from Porter, 283 (transcription, p. 1, line 1)

ing tonal centers. Coltrane builds a solo of increasing density, playing faster and faster while reaching for ever higher notes in his chromatic ascent. After this "explosive climax," Coltrane "avoids arpeggios with tonal implications"as his explorations dissolve into a wash of "atonality," before finally returning to an "expanded recapitulation" (282).

Although I agree with Porter's description of the work in general terms, I have problems with some of the details of his analysis. First, it seems a distortion to impose the idea of C major on the piece. In the theme, C is seldom played and almost all of its occurrences are as a neighbor to D and, occasionally, B. In Example 3, I have mapped Coltrane's set of pitches along with their resolutions. Coltrane builds his theme from a hexatonic scale based on G.

Example 3: Pitch collection, "Venus"

Porter also depicts the theme's restatement at the end as a "return to the simple C major pedal point of the theme." His later mention of an "implied dominant pedal in C" (282) seems more precise. Both the opening and final pitches are G and there is never a convincing resolution to C. It is not a simple G major tonality; the seventh (F), though rare, is minor. Like many Latin and Spanish pieces in the mixolydian mode, "Venus" never "resolves" to the tonality a fifth below. The "restlessness" Porter hears "that pervades this whole opening" never finds resolution, even in the final restatement of the theme.

Further, in his transcription Porter's use of accidentals is inconsistent and somewhat misleading. He speaks of "arpeggios in the key of B" and, a little later on the same page, of a strong implication of B-major tonality (281), but he spells both passages in C-flat (p. 2, line 1, and p. 4, line 11, of his transcription). By making the questionable statement that "Coltrane mixes flats with sharps" during the "most truly atonal" section of the piece, he probably means that the figurations are not analyzable as being in any particular key. However, he notates the entire passage (over 300 notes), with well over one hundred flats and only six sharps. No one can know whether Coltrane was thinking in sharps or flats; it is largely an issue of notational convenience.

Porter is on firmer ground when he discusses Coltrane's movement among third-related keys. His analysis, however, is somewhat limited by its reliance on "traditional" theory and might benefit if informed by post-tonal techniques. Coltrane's solos on tunes with "Giant Steps" changes were built almost entirely from four-note patterns that fit within the two-beat duration of each chord. On the other hand, the "Venus" hexachord has properties that make it particularly adaptable to the free structure of his late works. Coltrane's pitch class set is [0, 2, 4, 5, 7, 9], which corresponds to Forte's prime set 6-32.[7] This hexachord has some interesting properties. It is inversionally symmetrical: the intervals read the same from left to right as from right to left. Inversion yields the same pc set at T_4 (a minor third above) and it maps onto itself at T_9I. The set also has a high degree of "combinatoriality"—it can easily be combined with "one or more transposed or inverted forms of itself to create an aggregate" (all twelve pitch classes).[8] Combinatoriality allows for smooth transitions between sets: the common-tone links that Porter hears connecting the phrases. The absence of the seventh degree of the diatonic scale allows Coltrane to disregard whether the seventh is major or minor as in regular "Giant Steps" changes. He is free to navigate his way around the tonal areas of G, B♭, E♭, G♭, and C♭ (and occasionally A♭ and E) without having to consider dominant seventh resolutions. Because he wants to introduce "outside" pitch classes, he almost never performs the operations T_7, T_2, or T_{10} (transposing his pitch collection to the nearby keys on the fifth [D], the second [A] or seventh [F]). Just a few phrases into his improvisation, when he lays on the F# in line 9 of the transcription, he has already sounded the aggregate.

Though Porter describes the beginning of his improvisations after his opening statements as "quite different than the theme," they are constructed from transposed versions of exactly the same pc set or one of its subsets such as [0, 2, 4, 5, 7].[9] The 6-32 set appears in various forms repeatedly throughout the solo. One important example is page 2, line 10, of the transcription where Porter notes that "Coltrane briefly relaxes the tension with a tonal phrase in the key of A♭" (281). The hexachords *can* be tonally ambiguous because each is held in common by two different major scales, but if this phrase is reduced to its "normal form" it can clearly be seen to be a transposition of Coltrane's hexatonic collection down a major third (T_9), not to A♭, but to E♭ (see Example 4).[10]

Example 4: Excerpt, "Venus," from Porter, 284 (transcription, p. 2, line 10)

In a 1962 interview with Quersin in Paris he hinted at his approach to atonality. Though he had not studied 12-tone music, he said "I do like to play passages which do contain twelve tones, but I build them in my own way of structure, sequential structure."[11] The complex organizational rules of serial music largely preclude their use in improvisation. Coltrane's "combinatorial" method permits him to exploit the aggregate, like many twelve-tone composers, by "modulating" from area to area.[12]

Jazz solos are not easy to capture in notation. Late Coltrane is particularly elusive, and Porter has made a noble effort. His transcription, however, is difficult to follow because he does not always indicate Coltrane's phrasing consistently. Generally (but not always), Coltrane's phrases are indicated by breaks in the beaming. Perhaps rests or breath marks could have provided more clarity. The lack of a definite meter makes it difficult to notate rhythms, but Porter's long strings of 16th- and 32nd-notes gloss over many notes of unequal values. Though he often depicts Coltrane's use of harmonics and multiphonics, Porter's transcription omits pitch bends, subtleties of intonation, and timbral effects. For example, the section of the solo that Porter characterizes as the most atonal, in the middle of page four, is notated in several long series of discrete pitches. To my ear, much of the wild effect Coltrane produces here is a result of false fingerings and overtones, which are not indicated in the transcription.

Analysis of "Venus" leads seamlessly into a discussion of Coltrane's failing health and untimely death (288–92). Though his liver cancer was still undiagnosed, he canceled a European tour and other gigs. Having another horn player in the band relieved some of his load in performances. The presence of Pharoah Sanders, he told Kofsky, "helps me stay alive sometimes, because physically, man, the pace I've been leading has been so hard. . . . I feel that I like to have somebody in there in case I can't get that strength" (288). When Coltrane did find out the seriousness of his illness, apparently he shared the information with no one, not even his family. His death on July 17, 1967, two months before his forty-first birthday, in Davis's words (avoiding the profanity), "shocked everyone, took everyone by surprise" (290).

A brief epilogue discusses Coltrane's spiritual and musical legacy, the distribution of his estate, and the fate of his family members. Alice Coltrane has continued her spiritual pursuits and overseen the release of previously unissued recordings. Their son Ravi "has become a regular fixture on the New York jazz scene" (294).

While controversies may rage over canonization of a small, select pantheon of "jazz giants" (witness the recent Ken Burns film, *Jazz*), no other jazz musician has been worshipped in the spiritual sense like John Coltrane. When asked by a reporter in a press conference during his triumphant tour of Japan in 1966 what he would like to be in ten years, Coltrane replied cryptically, "I would like to be a saint." Porter, attempting to reconcile this comment with Coltrane's universally acknowledged humility, states that "it can only be interpreted one way; that he wanted to be saintly, that is, a virtuous person. Clearly he did not mean that he wanted to die and be canonized!" (260). Nevertheless, during his life the unique spiritualism that infused his music inspired a cult-like following that only became greater after his death. The One Mind Evolutionary Transitional Church of Christ, eventually renamed St. John's African Orthodox Church, was established in 1971 in San Francisco by some of his followers. Members worship to the music of *A Love Supreme.*

Although we can be grateful that Porter has not "fully explained how [he] arrived at each sentence in the book" (x), as a matter of convenience he might have provided a bit more discographic and bibliographic detail. Most of his music examples of formulas provide no discographical information. Though he claims that these ideas pervade most of Coltrane's work in any given period, references would have made listening to these snippets in context much easier. The interviews listed in the biography give only the dates of publication, requiring the reader to wade laboriously through the forty-page chronology to find the actual date of the interview.

Unlike most previous works on Coltrane, Porter never loses the balance between the requirement to remain objective and his obvious deeply felt passion for the man and his music. Still, I can't agree with Carl Woidek that Porter's volume renders earlier biographies obsolete.[13] Despite its many errors and occasional excesses, Thomas's book offers a compelling narrative of the saxophonist's life, particularly through the first-hand accounts of average listeners, the diaries of the mysterious "Trane's lady," and Thomas himself.[14] But this long overdue volume has done much to set the record straight and stands unquestionably as the authoritative chronicle of Coltrane's life and music.

NOTES

1. J.C. Thomas, *Chasin' the Trane: The Music and Mystique of John Coltrane* (New York: Doubleday and Company, 1975; reprinted New York: Da Capo, 1976) and Cuthbert Ormond Simpkins, M.D., *Coltrane: A Biography* (New York: Herndon House, 1975; reprinted Black Classic Press, 1989).
2. See Carl Woidek, *The John Coltrane Companion: Five Decades of Commentary* (New York: Schirmer Books, 1998), 119.
3. Barry Kernfeld, "Two Coltranes," *Annual Review of Jazz Studies* 2 (1983): 7–66.
4. Interestingly, *A Love Supreme* can be seen as related to "Giant Steps." The motive built from cell "a" is based on a rising minor third and perfect fourth—the same interval classes as the root motion in "Giant Steps." That Coltrane was aware of these relationships seems almost certain. A "mandala" on the circle of fifths drawn by Coltrane and reproduced in Fujioka shows his fascination with symmetrical interval and key relationships. See Yashuro Fujioka with Lewis Porter and Yoh-ichi Hamada, *John Coltrane: A Discography and Musical Biography* (Lanham, Maryland, and London: The Scarecrow Press, 1995), 67.
5. In Woidek, 117–18, 120.
6. See Ekkehard Jost, *Free Jazz* (New York: Da Capo, 1994 [1974]), 102–103.
7. Two analyses that have used pc set analysis with interesting results are: Steven Block, "Pitch-Class Transformation in Free Jazz," *Music Theory Spectrum* 12, no. 2 (1990): 181–202; and Jeff Pressing, "Pitch Class Set Structures in Contemporary Jazz," *Jazzforschung* 14 (1982): 133–72.
8. This set is actually one of only six hexachords that are *all-combinatorial,* i.e., it can combine with a transposed (P), inverted (I), retrograde (R) or retrograde inversional (RI) form of itself to create an aggregate. Joseph N. Straus, *Introduction to Post-Tonal Theory,* 2nd Edition (Upper Saddle River, New Jersey: Prentice Hall, 2000), 184–89.
9. As in his reiterations of the theme, occasionally a seventh sneaks in (usually minor).
10. David Demsey also discusses Coltrane's apparent "knowledge and use of pitch-class set organization techniques" in his article, "Chromatic Third Relations in the Music of John Coltrane," A*nnual Review of Jazz Studies* 5 (1991): 171–74; 180.
11. In Woidek, 127.
12. See Straus, 189.

13. Woidek, 251.
14. Porter confirms that "during his first Jazz Gallery stay, at the end of May 1960, John began a relationship with a white woman that was to continue, on and off, for the next three years." He finds the excerpts from the diary "convincing because the dates tie in with John's known movements" (270).

Linda Dahl, *Morning Glory: A Biography of Mary Lou Williams* (Berkeley: University of California Press, 2000), 463 pp., $16.95 (paperback)

Reviewed by Ted Buehrer

Mary Lou Williams enjoyed the "firsts" in her life. Even late in her life, she could vividly recall her first professional gig as an adolescent pianist, performing for a mortician in her hometown of East Liberty, Pennsylvania. She relished the opportunity to become the first female pianist/arranger for Andy Kirk's Clouds of Joy in 1931. Later in her career, Williams became the first African-American woman to produce a jazz festival and the first jazz composer to be commissioned to write sacred jazz for a festival, both in 1964. Throughout her career, Williams often found herself at the forefront of jazz music's latest developments.

Though regarded by her fellow jazz musicians as a key figure and a major contributor to each of the jazz styles that evolved from the 1930s to the 1950s, including swing and bebop, over the years jazz scholars have often focused on the innovations offered by such jazz legends as Duke Ellington, Dizzy Gillespie, Charlie Parker, and Miles Davis. Interest in the life and music of Mary Lou Williams has been, until recently, largely overlooked. However, the publication of another "first" for Williams, Linda Dahl's *Morning Glory: A Biography of Mary Lou Williams* should do a great service to spark interest in the study of Williams's career as a jazz pianist and composer. Without diminishing the important contributions of these other, much-celebrated giants of jazz, Dahl demonstrates, often persuasively, Williams's impact on the development of jazz music by placing her with these innovators at the time that new styles were emerging, arguing that Williams deserves some of the credit.

But this is not the focus of Dahl's book as much as it is a byproduct. She has no axe to grind. Rather, Dahl weaves together from a variety of sources an interesting narrative describing Williams's life in music, from her early childhood in East Liberty, a suburb of Pittsburgh, through her long career that spanned almost 60 years until her death in 1981. These sources include, among others, a series of autobiographical articles written by Williams and edited by Max Jones that appeared in the British magazine *Melody Maker* in 1954,[1] numerous published interviews, the Mary Lou Williams Archive housed at the Institute of Jazz Studies (Rutgers University), and Dahl's own interviews of family members, friends, and her personal manager. In addition, the author draws from some 37 additional writings that are either about or involve Williams; Dahl lists these in her "Selective Bibliography" at the back of the book. Although this may seem like a significant number, it is important to note that many of these citations do not amount to more than a short magazine article or a book chapter (or even less) on Williams.[2] While there are a few feature articles (or book chapters) and even a handful of research papers and/or theses on Williams that are listed, Dahl's book provides the first thorough treatment of Williams's biography. Although there are criticisms to be made about the book, which I will point out during the course of this review, it is, overall, a welcome and much-needed addition to an existing body of jazz scholarship that has neglected this deserving musician for far too long. For those readers who are unfamiliar with the details of Williams's life, I begin my review with a brief outline of her career based on Dahl's work; my commentary follows this biographical sketch.

Dahl begins her biography with Williams's birth in 1910 in Atlanta, Georgia,[3] chronicles her family's journey north to East Liberty in 1915, and describes many of her childhood experiences there. Mary's mother, Virginia Burley, was her first musical influence and the first to encourage her to pursue her musical talents that were evident from the time she was three or four years old. Interestingly, despite Virginia's encouragement, Mary was not taught to read music and instead relied solely on her ear. As Dahl states, "she came to place enormous importance on her ear training and it became part of her credo that real jazz—improvisation with feeling—could not be systematically taught. Nor is it too much to say that in Mary's mind, at a fundamental level, playing music and improvising were synonymous" (16). Before she was even a teenager, she was playing multiple gigs (at churches, at afternoon teas, at other private parties) and using the money she earned to help support her family. One of her stepfathers, Fletcher Burley, bought the family a player piano, giving Mary her first opportunity to hear such pianists as Jelly Roll Morton and James P. Johnson, two musicians who, along with local pianist Jack Howard, proved to be important influences on her playing style during her early years. In addition to these influences, she was also exposed to (and learned to play by ear) several classical pieces, light opera arias, and waltzes. These musical skills were entirely self-taught during these early years, a point that Dahl reinforces time and time again.

Mary left her home for life on the road after school let out in the summer of 1924. At just 14 years of age, she joined Buzzin' Harris and His Hits 'n' Bits, a show that traveled the black vaudeville circuit. Life on the road was hard, but it was on these travels that Mary first met and heard other important jazz musicians: Earl Hines, Louis Armstrong, and Buck Washington.

Though some in the group were skeptical because she was a young girl, she soon became a favorite of band members and audiences alike, not only because of her ability to "clown around," that is, to play with her elbows, feet, spinning on a stool, while blindfolded, and so on, as was expected of her, but also because she could play entire shows by ear and imitate any style she heard. Dahl relates bandmember (and Mary's first husband) John Williams's first impression of her:

> There wasn't no band pianists that were women. I'd made this trip and here was this little girl—she was only fourteen at the time—playing piano. When they had the first rehearsal, I was very disgusted when I saw it was a girl. I'd played with women piano players and they'd be just tinkling. Women really couldn't handle it at the time—I'm not lying. . . . [But] Mary was already playing for this show when I joined. Well, then she hit on the piano and I'd never heard nothing like that in my life. Terrific. She outplayed any piano player I'd ever played with. She played note for note anything that she heard, Earl Hines, Jelly Roll Morton, and heavy like a man, not light piano. At fourteen (44).

The Hits 'n' Bits folded in 1925, but John Williams retained most of the band's members and formed a group of his own called the Syncopators, managing to hold them together with frequent strings of one-nighters and occasional longer runs in cities such as Memphis. Mary, married to John in 1926, stayed with the group as the pianist until this band finally fell apart in 1928. It was not until 1931 that Mary, who had been traveling with John as an unemployed spouse while John worked as a member of Andy Kirk's Clouds of Joy, got her first big break when Kirk's regular pianist was fired and she was hired to fill his spot.

But Mary Lou Williams was more than a pianist for the Clouds of Joy. During the prior three years while traveling with the band, she showed an increasing interest in and aptitude toward composing and arranging. Kirk himself helped her to learn music theory and basic skills of instrumentation and arranging. By the time she was hired in 1931, she had already written numerous tunes for the band, many of which were recorded, among them "Messa Stomp," "Cloudy," and "Froggy Bottom." She thus assumed the role of chief arranger and composer in addition to her duties as a pianist. Dahl states that Mary "was never a consistently prolific composer, but had periods of high creativity, including the unrecorded period in the thirties when the band spent so much time hanging out in Kansas City" (89). This unrecorded period, lasting from 1931 until 1936, was due primarily to the toll taken by the Great Depression; times were hard for everyone, and the band had difficulties even stringing together one-nighters. But with Kansas

City serving as home base, Williams flourished musically as both a pianist and a composer.

The Clouds' fortunes turned in 1936 when they began to record again. Although the band began to achieve success unlike what they had known before, tensions began to mount between the band's leader and its pianist-composer-arranger. This rift can be attributed to two related factors. On one hand, Kirk wanted to play sweet arrangements that featured the band's vocalist, Pha Terrell, while Williams wanted to continue to write her own music: more straight ahead, hard-swinging jazz. On the other hand, her reputation as an arranger had begun to grow, and other bandleaders were beginning to contact her, asking her for arrangements. She obliged several of them, including Benny Goodman, for whom she wrote several arrangements in the late 1930s.[4] This practice incensed Kirk, and by May of 1942, the relationship between the two had deteriorated so much that Williams walked off a gig in Washington, D.C., leaving the band after almost twelve years and in spite of the band's recent successes.

The 1940s were a tumultuous time for Williams. Having divorced her first husband and left the Clouds of Joy, she first returned home to Pittsburgh, where she pulled together a combo of local musicians (among them a young Art Blakey on drums and trumpeter Shorty Baker, who left the Clouds around the same time as she did and who was to become her second husband). Though this group performed locally, it never recorded, and it was relatively short-lived: in September of 1942, Shorty Baker left the group for Duke Ellington's band. She soon joined Baker on the road, and they were married in December. But she found herself, once again, traveling as an unemployed spouse of a bandmember. This time it was worse, however, because Williams had acquired a reputation and a following of her own. She soon began arranging for the Ellington band, writing numerous arrangements, among them Ellington's hit "Trumpets No End."

Although her marriage to Baker ended in the spring of 1944, she continued to write for Ellington (though not exclusively) throughout the 1940s and into the 1950s. Through the middle of the 1940s, Mary found work primarily as a combo leader and as a composer. As a leader, she recorded quite frequently with various sidemen for Moe Asch on Disc records. She also performed frequently throughout New York City; in addition to the dates she played with a combo, she also had a regular solo gig at the Café Society Downtown, the first racially integrated club. For a brief time, she hosted a weekly half-hour radio program on which she would play some of her music and invite guest musicians to accompany her. She also was offered a featured role in a Broadway revue called *Blue Holiday*. And she wrote her most ambitious composition to that point in her career: her *Zodiac Suite* (1945), a set of twelve pieces, one for each sun sign. Though most of the individual pieces in this suite were originally conceived for solo piano or for trio, Mary came up with the idea of scoring the suite for chamber jazz ensemble. The suite was premiered in this form in December of 1945, and met with enough success that six months later, three of the movements were scored for piano and symphony orchestra and performed at Carnegie Hall. Citing all of this activity, Dahl emphatically states, "she was at the peak of her New York fame" (154).

But perhaps the most important events to happen in Williams's life during this time were not those just cited, but rather her interactions with the musicians who were responsible for the birth of bebop. In her mid-thirties, Williams was considered a member of the "old guard," but she embraced bop's new, complex melodic and harmonic language. Many of her compositions from this period reflect this new style: "Kool," "In the Land of Oo-bla-dee," "Just You, Just Me," and a reworking of her earlier "Mary's Idea." More significantly, she befriended many of the musicians who were developing this new style, among them Thelonious Monk, Dizzy Gillespie, Bud Powell, and Tadd Dameron. She was a regular at Minton's Playhouse and Monroe's Uptown House, where most of these musicians liked to play, and she frequently invited these musicians to her apartment, where they would continue to play all night. Billy Taylor comments that Mary's influence on Monk and Powell can be directly heard in their recordings:

> Mary Lou Williams took Monk and Bud up to her house and really worked with them. . . . She made them both more aware of touch. And you could hear the difference in the early Powell records and the later Powell records in terms of just the touch. You can hear the same with Monk, when Monk was recording for Blue Note and labels like that—it was one touch. And then later he began to record for other labels, it just wasn't the change in sound, he changed. And you could hear a more pianistic approach. This was, in my opinion, a result of his close association with Mary Lou.[5]

She even joined Benny Goodman's combo for a brief time in 1948 (by this time, Goodman had abandoned his big band and had put together a smaller combo dedicated to playing the "hotter" style of bebop).

But Williams's career suffered some setbacks in the late 1940s, which, combined with some difficulties in her personal life, sank her into a state of depression, what she herself called the "toughest time of my entire life" (218). When an offer for a nine-day tour of England materialized in 1952, with Williams as the headline attraction, she accepted. But she stayed in

Europe more than nine days; she stayed for two years, and was an active performer not only in England but also in Germany and France, particularly Paris. Despite her professional successes while in Europe, however, her life hit its lowest point, and she turned to Christianity for help. She gained spiritual strength, and in 1954, returned to New York, determined to "give up music, night life and all else that was sinful in the eyes of God" (243).

Williams was true to her word. Though she lacked specific guidance in the tenets of Christianity and was not a member of any particular church, she spent hours each day in prayer, began her new work caring for those in need, and virtually eliminated all performances. She cared for several of her family members in her New York apartment for about a year. In 1958, she established the Bel Canto foundation, a nonprofit organization dedicated to helping musical performers who were in need. But without a steady income other than a quarterly ASCAP check and occasional royalties, she was desperate for money. She tried unsuccessfully to obtain copyrights on tunes she had written but of which others had claimed authorship.

She was drawn back to her music by a Catholic priest (and a jazz lover), who encouraged her to use her God-given talents to help further the causes important to her. As she put it, she began "praying through her fingers," and resumed her performance career around 1958. Additionally, she also began composing "spiritual jazz," bridging the gap between sacred and jazz music. Among her compositions in this genre are *St. Martin de Porres* (also titled *Black Christ of the Andes*) for mixed-voice choir (premiered in 1962), *Mass* (1967), *Mass for the Lenten Season* (c. 1968), and *Music for Peace* (also called *Mary Lou's Mass*), her best-known work in this genre (c. 1969–70).

If the late 1950s and 1960s saw Williams's focus and attention shift toward Roman Catholicism (she converted in 1957) and the composition of music for the church, one of the chief reasons was her relationship with Father Peter O'Brien. O'Brien, who met her in 1964 while he was a seminary student, befriended her and, according to Dahl, "was to become arguably the most important person in Mary's life" (284). He provided hours and hours of counsel to Mary who had questions about the Catholic Church and about Christianity in general. Their relationship developed into a deep friendship. Dahl asserts that others who knew Williams at this time felt that her relationship with O'Brien was more harmful than productive; these others felt that "O'Brien manipulated Mary's credulity and peripheralized her other relationships" (286). Many found the relationship between a young white priest and an older black woman peculiar at best; some even suspected that the two of them were having an affair. Nevertheless, her relationship with O'Brien continued, lasting for the rest of her life. O'Brien assumed the role of her personal manager in 1971, the first time in her career that Williams was represented by someone other than herself.[6]

With O'Brien's help, Williams entered a fruitful time in her career in the early 1970s. She began an important long-term association with a restaurant in New York called The Cookery, where she held many long engagements until 1978. She played other important gigs at Blues Alley (Washington, D.C.), London House (Chicago), and the Newport Jazz Festival. She began recording again, including a recording called the *History of Jazz,* in which she plays examples from various eras. She organized and played an important engagement with fellow pianist Cecil Taylor at Carnegie Hall in 1977, a concert that highlighted the contrasting styles of Taylor's avant-garde approach and Mary's more traditional style. Titled *Embraced*, this concert was significant because Williams had been an outspoken critic of jazz's avant-garde for some time, and this was her attempt at reconciliation for some of the things she had said. Though it was an interesting idea, the concert did not go as planned, and according to Dahl, most everyone involved—audience members, reviewers, and the musicians themselves—was disappointed with the outcome.

A new opportunity presented itself in 1977: she was offered the position of artist-in-residence at Duke University. She accepted the offer and moved into a house in Durham, North Carolina. At Duke, she taught the history of jazz, jazz improvisation, led the university jazz ensemble, and presented four concerts a year. O'Brien quit his job as a priest in New York to move to Durham, and he helped out as a teaching assistant (though unpaid for a while) and continued his duties as her manager. Williams was a success in her new environment, well liked by students and the administration alike. She signed a three-year contract extension in her second semester at Duke, and she maintained a busy schedule of classes and professional engagements until 1979 when her health took a turn for the worse. She was diagnosed with bladder cancer, and though her doctors treated the disease aggressively, including radiation and surgery, the cancer progressed quickly, and by January of 1980 it had spread into her body. Throughout her illness, and even as her health declined, she managed to perform and to teach many of her classes. She also continued to compose and arrange works, but her productivity gradually slowed and eventually stopped by the winter of 1981.

Mary Lou Williams died in her home on May 28, 1981. O'Brien flew her body back to New York, and a funeral was held there on June 1, attended by many jazz musicians and fans. The next day, a Mass of Christian Burial was held in Pittsburgh attended by family and friends, and she was buried there at Calvary Cemetery.

Dahl convincingly tells the story of William's life. Her meticulous research is to be commended, as every story and anecdote are told with sufficient amount of detail. Dahl's prose is, for the most part, clear and effectively written. One especially useful technique that helps to unify the book is the return to certain themes that often resurface in Williams's life. By returning to these recurring themes, the reader is helped to understand the things that were important to her and how her thoughts about these things might have evolved over the years.

Two examples will help to illustrate my point. The theme of race and racism surfaces frequently throughout the book and in different guises. From her childhood in East Liberty, where her family lived in a house between two white families, to her life on the road with the Syncopators and then the Clouds of Joy, where racism and racial segregation varied from geographic region to region, to her engagements at the racially integrated Café Society, to her romantic relationship with Jack Teagarden and, later, white artist David Stone Martin, the reader learns not only that her encounters with issues of race were ongoing throughout her life—hardly a surprise—but also that she fought hard against racial prejudice and that she did not allow it to affect her relationships with others, white or black. Another recurring theme is the issue of gender, as Williams worked hard throughout her career to succeed in the male-dominated field of jazz. Dahl points to an early critic of Williams's playing style, who noted that while her style was derivative of the stride piano of James P. Johnson and Fats Waller, it was also "much more fantastic and ardent," and that her playing was "like that of a man; one would never guess that it was a woman playing" (77). Williams herself proudly proclaimed throughout her career that she "played heavy like a man," but also believed that gender should not matter when it comes to playing jazz: "You've got to play, that's all. They don't think of you as a woman if you can really play."[7]

Despite the book's compelling narrative, it is not without its problems. One weakness is Dahl's descriptions of Mary's music, her playing style, or musical style in general, which are often poor, uninspired, or require further explanation. For example, early in the book, Dahl describes the influence that both ragtime and the stride style had on Williams's playing without bothering to define either term or differentiate them from one another (26–27, 64). Later, while talking about a recording of her tune "Cloudy," Dahl notes that "the final chorus of the first 'Cloudy,' which opened and closed with a *hair-raisingly weird full-band chord*, was dropped in the 1936 version" (98, emphasis mine).

In her discussion of two tunes composed for the Clouds of Joy in 1938, Dahl remains typically vague: "Especially in 'Mr. Freddie' and 'Patunia,' there are hints of the modern jazz to come in the next decade, of harmonic inversions and complex chords" (112). Dahl argues that Williams was looking ahead to bop's harmonic complexities long before other musicians began to work them out for themselves, but she continues to refer to Williams's "complex chords" even after other jazz musicians had fully incorporated them into their own music. Regarding a 1951 recording, Dahl writes: "Here were her advanced harmonies, her trademark ethereal-sounding chords ('Yesterdays' and 'People Will Say We're in Love') . . ." (217).

Dahl reveals her unfamiliarity with musical terminology even further when, describing an LP of Williams's sacred music, she writes, "Besides *St. Martin*, there was Mary's modern gospel piece 'Anima Christi' and 'Praise the Lord,' set to Psalm 150" (278). Likely, the text of Psalm 150 is set to "Praise the Lord," not the other way around. These are just a few of many poor musical descriptions that appear throughout the book. Often, Dahl avoids her weakness in this area by relying on quotations by Williams or other musicians or musical scholars to describe the music or the performance style, an effective technique, but there remain too many of the author's own inadequate descriptions.

Another problem that the reader encounters throughout the book is the lack of a clear chronology, due primarily to the fact that Dahl simply does not provide enough date references. The lack of certain dates might be understandable during certain times in Williams's life, for example, her early childhood, where very little was written down and few records were kept. But this pattern of making relatively few references to specific dates (or even specific years) continues throughout the book, however, making it increasingly problematic and frustrating for the reader. This problem is exacerbated by Dahl's decision to organize succeeding chapters of her book as chronological spans of years (a logical choice) but use a writing style that often departs from strict chronology within a given chapter's time span. This style may allow Dahl certain freedoms in her storytelling, but when combined with an inconsistent use of dates to keep the reader oriented, it becomes very easy for the reader to get lost and constantly ask oneself "now what year is this?"

As a work of scholarship, one that includes thorough notes and bibliography, Dahl's book is a mixed blessing. On the one hand, the book includes, as an appendix, a wonderful (though incomplete) discography. It includes a *complete* chronological listing (from date of recording) of all of Williams's music that is available on compact disc, followed by a *selective* listing (again, chronological) of vinyl and tape recordings of her music. Dahl herself acknowledges that the discography is meant to be "user-friendly rather than scholar-oriented and all-inclusive"(400). Nevertheless, the discography exceeds 30 pages, and includes, in addition to the date and location of each recording session, the musicians playing on the session, the tunes recorded at the session, and the label and number of the session. As another appendix, the book contains a listing of Williams's compositions and arrangements, subdivided into those composed or arranged for Andy Kirk and the Clouds of Joy, for Duke Ellington, for Benny Goodman, and for other big bands. A separate master list, titled "Selected Compositions by Mary Lou Williams" is also included in this appendix, but again, this list is incomplete. Finally, the book contains a thorough, easy-to-navigate index, which makes searching for specific topics quite easy.

On the other hand, one would expect to find in a book of this sort extensive footnotes or endnotes that cite the sources used for each quotation or other piece of information. Regrettably, this is not the case. There is no system of numbering for footnotes or endnotes used in the book, so when one wishes to check a reference to a quotation, one must note the page number, turn to the "Sources and Notes" appendix (organized by chapter) and hope to find the relevant quotation listed there along with a citation. Unfortunately, I found that there were a number of quotations that appear in the text *not* cited in this appendix, making it impossible to determine the source from which these quotes were obtained. Related to this, several of the sources that are cited in the "Sources and Notes" are not included in the "Selective Bibliography." These two factors combined make the work of future Mary Lou Williams researchers that much more difficult should they wish to use Dahl's book as a resource.

The most significant shortcoming of Dahl's book, however, is the general lack of serious study of Williams's improvisational and compositional style. Perhaps, given Dahl's aforementioned musical descriptions, this is understandable; that is, perhaps she did not feel qualified to undertake such a study. Perhaps it simply lay beyond the scope of her work. If this is the case, then perhaps it is an unfair criticism of the book. However, Dahl does devote an entire chapter in her book to a more in-depth look at the *Zodiac Suite* that begins to approach the kind of analytical study that I have in mind, but even this chapter falls well short of the attention her music deserves. As interest in Mary Lou Williams's music and approach to improvisation grows, she deserves the same scrutiny that has been given to fellow composers (e.g., Morton, Ellington, Strayhorn, Dameron, etc.) and improvisors (e.g., Parker, Coltrane, Davis, etc.). Of particular interest would be to examine how Williams's composition and arranging style evolved over the course of her career by investigating the handful of tunes to which she returned numerous times on recordings for different instrumentations and group sizes, such as "Froggy Bottom," which she recorded at least eight times over a span of forty years for groups as varied as the Clouds of Joy (big band) and her own piano trio. Countless other projects loom as possibilities as well, enough to keep a number of scholars busy studying and analyzing this music well into the future.

Mary Lou Williams was a successful African-American woman in the male-dominated field of jazz. She was widely respected by her peers as a composer, arranger, and performer. As one of the significant figures in the history of jazz, Williams also stands among the leaders of America's cultural development. Her work, long recognized by other jazz musicians for its originality and freshness, is beginning to attract attention in wider circles. Linda Dahl's effort in this biography goes a long way to further this cause. The book is solidly researched, and Dahl tells her story using a very approachable style. The shortcomings of the book that I have mentioned may be overlooked when one considers the important role this book will play as scholarly interest in Williams's music is revived. Thorough while at the same time leaving the door open to several paths of scholarship, this biography will remain the cornerstone upon which future Mary Lou Williams research is built.

NOTES

1. These autobiographical articles have been reprinted in Robert Gottlieb's (ed.) *Reading Jazz* (New York: Pantheon Books, 1996), Max Jones's *Talking Jazz* (New York: W.W. Norton and Co., 1988), and Nat Shapiro's and Nat Hentoff's (eds.) *Hear Me Talkin' to Ya* (New York: Holt, Rinehart, and Winston, 1955).
2. By comparison, a *WorldCat* search revealed that there are over 300 books on (or books containing information about) Duke Ellington. This search does not even take magazine or journal articles into account.
3. Mary Lou Williams was actually born Mary Elfrieda Scruggs, and her surname changed more than once in her childhood as she took the name of her stepfathers: Mary Lou Winn, Mary Lou Burley. She took the name Williams upon marrying her first husband, John Williams, and kept the name for the rest of her life. Throughout the book, Dahl refers to her simply as Mary.
4. Among those arrangements made for Goodman's band was "Camel Hop," the theme song of Goodman's radio program (sponsored by Camel cigarettes), and "Roll 'Em," one of her best known tunes. Goodman even asked Williams

to write exclusively for his band and offered her the piano chair in his small band when Teddy Wilson left. She refused both offers.

5. Billy Taylor, in Ira Gitler (ed.), *Swing to Bop: An Oral History of the Transition in Jazz in the 1940s* (New York: Oxford University Press, 1985), 103.
6. Williams did have an on-again, off-again working relationship with Joe Glaser, the agent who was so influential in the career of Louis Armstrong, among others. The details of this relationship are well documented in the letters and correspondence kept in the Williams Archives, and Dahl revisits this ongoing story often during the course of her biography. Glaser was never officially hired to represent Mary as O'Brien was, however.
7. Marian McPartland, "Mary Lou Williams: A Return," *Down Beat* 24, no. 21 (October 17, 1957): 12.

Jeroen de Valk, *Ben Webster: His Life and His Music* (Berkeley, California: Berkeley Hills Books, 2001, 280 +xi pages, $15.95)

Reviewed by Jay Sweet

First published in its original Dutch, Jeroen de Valk's biography, *Ben Webster: His Life and His Music*, lays claim as the first biography written about the famed jazz tenor saxophonist. Unlike his contemporaries Lester Young and Coleman Hawkins, jazz scholarship has generally classified Ben Webster as a jazz stylist and not as an innovator. As a result of his stylist classification, serious discussion of Webster's music has been lacking. Admittedly, I was initially excited to finally find a biography dedicated to Ben Webster.

While first previewing Ben *Webster: His Life and His Music* I was immediately struck by the layout of the work. Deciding that the publisher might be responsible for the large type, the generous spacing, and the wide margins, I assumed that the substance was more important than presentation and pressed ahead. After reading de Valk's short preface and very limited three-page chronology (which leaves gaps of over ten years), I was surprised by the tone of de Valk's first chapter, "The Brute and The Beautiful," which is intended to introduce the contents of the book. Chapter 1 is not at all complimentary and paints a picture of Webster as a spoiled, violent, and aggressive alcoholic—a theme that de Valk frequently returns to.

In his very first paragraph, de Valk classifies Webster as one of the seven greatest jazz tenor players along with Hawkins, Young, John Coltrane, Dexter Gordon, Stan Getz, and Sonny Rollins. Following past criticism, the author states that, as compared to the other saxophonists, Webster was not a revolutionary and belongs in the group because he "possessed a distinctive, immediately recognizable way of playing"(1). This subjective classification is not at all useful, since even an early beginner has a recognizable way of playing. This extreme subjectivity and obsession with ranking unfortunately set the tone for the entire text.

When discussing recordings and performances in the text and in his own select discography, de Valk often places his own value judgements about the quality of a performance. In his select discography de Valk gives short reviews and a star rating system for each recording. Comments and value judgements such as "The result was far from satisfactory" (167), "Unfortunately, [Dick] Katz is suffering from an over-active left hand—he doesn't seem to realize there is a bass player present" (230), and "Webster doesn't need strings; he is mellow enough on his own" (263) fill the entire work.

While I do not suggest that de Valk should completely silence his opinions about the quality of Webster's works, I find such a focus on reviews to be educationally limiting in a biographical format. If it is an author's intention to review an artist's work, it should be clearly stated in the preface of the text. In this case, de Valk's fragmented opinions seem to offer little in terms of analysis or serious discussion.

The author also falls short in his attempt to provide a comprehensive chronological biography. Curiously, de Valk seems to rush through Webster's life to focus on his later years in Europe, which lasted from 1964 until his death in 1973. It is a major miscalculation to spend over half of the text on his later career. While as a European, de Valk had convenient access to European musicians and materials, the focus of Webster's later life leaves the biography seriously unbalanced and misdirected. Much more focus and discussion could have been spent on Webster's early musical development in Kansas City, his movement through the different popular jazz orchestras of the 1930s, his inspirational work with Duke Ellington's Orchestra in the 1940s, and his work as a bandleader and as a featured soloist.

The biography is most irresponsible in its treatment of Webster's personal life. The author often makes bold statements, regarding Webster's relationships and habits, then proposes them as fact. At the same time, de Valk continually brings up Webster's sexual activity, alcoholism, and violent nature without documentation. For example, de Valk claims that in 1936, Webster pushed a woman out of a window in a moment of blind rage. This incident is not at all documented and quite possibly never occurred:

> Ben never talked about the incident. Aside from Harley and Joyce, nobody else I spoke with—even Jimmy Rowles and Harold Ashby, Ben's best friends in the States—had heard of it. Dan Morgenstern of the Institute of Jazz Studies agreed to ask a few Ellington researchers, but his inquiries didn't yield any results. There are no documents, either, that even mention it. Perhaps Ellington and Ben's family succeeded in keeping the matter out of the papers (38).

The author also speculates on a short-lived affair with Billie Holiday in which Webster was physically abusive (42). There appears to be no evidence supporting the affair.

Such unproven theories and undocumented speculations have little value in attempting to recognize the truth about Webster's life and music. This style of writing is speculative, irresponsible, and provides little lasting value.

Despite its many shortcomings, *Ben Webster: His Life and Music* does provide some areas of interest. Although it is somewhat confusing and possibly mistranslated, de Valk provides a family history that is said to involve Abraham Lincoln as an ancestor. While the family history is interesting, there are no genealogical research references or documentation to support events. It appears that de Valk relies heavily on information provided to him by Webster's cousin, Harley Robinson, and his second cousin, Joyce Cockrell, who was 103 years old at the time the book was written. Other areas of interest include a long letter written by Cockrell describing Webster's youth and early musical development, a photo of Webster as a baby, and a chapter about the fate of Webster's favorite tenor saxophone, Ol' Betsy, which changed hands frequently after Webster's death.

At the conclusion of each chapter, de Valk provides bibliographical references in a section he titles "notes," which indicate that de Valk gathered most of his data by looking at jazz articles, liner notes, preexisting jazz literature and other secondary sources. In fact, de Valk seems to rely heavily on films: *The Brute and the Beautiful* by John Jeremy (1989), Big *Ben* by Johan van der Keuken (1967), and *Ballad for Ben* by Per Møller Hansen (no date given). It should also be noted that de Valk provides no musical examples, samples of published music, or transcriptions of Webster's playing.

While *Ben Webster: His Life and his Music* does not appear to be intended for a scholarly jazz readership, de Valk's irresponsibility should in no way be dismissed. Although it is gratifying to see Ben Webster acknowledged, we unfortunately must await a more complete and well-researched study of Webster's life and music in order to gain a deeper understanding of his talents.

Geoffrey C. Ward and Ken Burns, *Jazz: A History of America's Music*. (New York: Alfred A. Knopf, 2000, 490 pp., $65.00)

Reviewed by Edward Berger

Reaction to the recent controversial Ken Burns documentary, *Jazz*, seems to correlate with the viewer's previous exposure to jazz. Novices were generally positive and, judging from the huge sales of the various *Jazz* CD configurations, many have been enticed into exploring the music further. The overall response of the jazz community, on the other hand, has been negative. Although some of the criticism is deserved, many jazz experts saw the film as an assault on their territory and seized upon any omission or minor factual error as proof of the project's abject failure. Perhaps such a proprietary reaction is inevitable in any popular treatment of a complex art form with a passionate following.

Jazz, the book, while not without flaws, is a remarkable accomplishment and far more than a coffee table bauble aimed at those who enjoyed *Jazz*, the film. Written by Burns collaborator Geoffrey C. Ward, the book bears much in common with the film—in organization, approach, and tone. But it also differs in some ways. First, it includes several of the figures whose absence from the film so disturbed many critics and fans. In addition, the talking heads, who played so prominent a role in the film and, justifiably or not, raised a number of ires, play a diminished role in the book. While there are many contributions by Messrs. Marsalis, Giddins, Crouch, and Early, they are in separate essays or interview segments, or confined to short quotes within the text. Some of the film's more expendable pundits, including Matt Glaser (who contributed the surreal interpretation of Armstrong's "Up a Lazy River"), have been omitted. Furthermore, the print medium carries less of the "gravitas" of the spoken narration, which grew increasingly self-important over the course of the nineteen-hour film production.

The film's successes, notably the stunning visual images which bring to life the kaleidoscope of events and personalities of jazz, translate surprisingly well into book form. Burns's staff has done a thorough job of photo research, unearthing many significant new images and incorporating them (in superb reproductions) in a dramatically effective way. Again, the book manages to eschew some of the film's excesses (e.g., frequent repetition of the same still images or film footage of street scenes).

But the major strength of the book is Ward's ability to relate the story of jazz in a genuinely interesting way. He is a master storyteller, skillfully weaving the narrative threads into an entertaining historical tapestry. Perhaps it takes the enthusiasm of someone like Ward, a lifelong jazz listener but not a professional jazz historian or critic, to achieve the fresh and entertaining narrative style that eludes many surveys written by those in the jazz field. As in the film, Ward follows the careers of his protagonists—particularly Armstrong and Ellington—against the unfolding backdrop of jazz's (and America's) chronology, rather than relegating them to a single period, as standard jazz histories do. Ward's approach is more difficult to bring off but successfully conveys the continuity of the idiom and the tremendous stylistic and generational diversity that coexists within the music at any given time.

Race is a leitmotif permeating both the film and the book. (Even the spine of the dust jacket juxtaposes a "White" sign, presumably indicating a segregated facility, with a "Black Swan" Records label.) As Burns writes in his introduction: ". . . And so jazz necessarily becomes a story about race and race relations and prejudice, about minstrelsy and Jim Crow, lynchings and civil rights"(vii). All true, but jazz is also about music, a fact that is frequently eclipsed by the emphasis on historical, social, and economic factors. As one veteran black musician said after viewing the film: "Of course race is important, but not everything we played was influenced by it. We're musicians—sometimes we just make music!" Music often takes a back seat to vivid descriptions of the dress, mannerisms, and personal idiosyncrasies of jazz's more colorful practitioners. For example, we are constantly told how radical a departure bebop was but precious little about *how* it differed from what preceded it. Yet Charlie Parker's gruesome final days are rehashed in great detail.

Occasionally, in his pursuit of a good story, Ward resorts to hyperbole or oversimplification. For example, in attempting to show how Ellington's 1956 Newport triumph revitalized his career, the author writes, "In the summer of 1955, Duke Ellington was reduced to accompanying ice skaters at a Long Island rink" (399). This is misleading on several counts. First, it was not a public rink but an ice show, along the lines of the Ice Capades, and even received favorable coverage in the New York press. Furthermore, Ward's statement implies that this was the only type of engagement Ellington could get at the time, but only a couple of months earlier, Ellington premiered "Night Creature" and "New World A-Comin'" with the Philadelphia Orchestra and at Carnegie Hall with the Symphony of the Air. And *after* his success at Newport (and the *Time* magazine cover it spawned), Ellington continued to accept all sorts of one-nighters in such venues as the Wabash Valley Fair in Terre Haute, Indiana (see Klaus Stratemann, *Duke Ellington : Day by Day and Film by Film*).

At times, the generally engaging literary style descends to the *Reader's Digest* level of mawkish first person sentimentality. Ward is also quite taken by the pithy quotation, sometimes isolated on a separate page. But not every casual remark uttered by a musician or critic is as profound as such treatment implies (e.g., Interviewer: "What Is Jazz?" Louis Armstrong: "Jazz is what I play for a living") (169). In addition, many of the chapter and section headings are obscure and silly.

Supplementing Ward's text are interviews with Wynton Marsalis and Albert Murray (although the latter is not listed in the table of contents), and essays by Dan Morgenstern, Gerald Early, Gary Giddins, and Stanley Crouch. The Marsalis material is culled from interviews done for the film, and contains the customary Marsalis mix of insight, homily, and conjecture presented as fact. Morgenstern contributes a warm personal reminiscence of his own introduction to jazz in pre-World War II Europe and his first-hand observations and experiences after coming to United States in 1947. Giddins contributes a useful survey of the avant-garde, and Crouch an intriguing if somewhat amorphous memoir of the 1970s New York scene.

Gerald Early's essay, "White Noise and White Nights: Some Thoughts on Race, Jazz, and the White Jazz Musician," is a major disappointment, especially in light of his often perceptive comments in the film and his cogent writing elsewhere. He paints with a broad brush and tosses off reductive stylistic terms without attempting to define them:

> . . . it is noteworthy that, of the jazz movements that have sprung up since World War II, the ones most denigrated or dismissed by critics and looked upon with the greatest suspicion by most of the jazz-loving public are the ones most dominated by or identified with whites: cool or progressive or West Coast or third-stream jazz, as well as fusion or jazz-rock, genres generally held in lower esteem than the once-controversial avant-garde of the 1960s. To be sure, a good deal of the music made within these movements hasn't aged well, but a lot of hard bop and soul jazz is just as dated and unlistenable today (324).

Early then turns to Richard Sudhalter's *Lost Chords*, which he calls "a long mess of a book that is neither serviceable nor kind to its reader. . . . To write a book such as Sudhalter's . . . that is a defense of white people in their whiteness, is, for many, racism trying to disguise itself as an exploration of diversity" (324–325). One may certainly take issue with many of Sudhalter's conclusions—indeed, with his entire premise—but at least he, unlike Early, offers some concrete musical evidence for his arguments.

Much of Early's piece is devoted to a misplaced and self-contradictory attack on Stan Kenton, whom he excoriates for his right-wing politics ("a jazz record producer told me that Kenton's records still have enormous appeal to members of the NRA" [325]. And later: ". . . it isn't likely that many blacks joined the Stan Kenton Fan Club in those days; it put 'KKK' on all its letters, which stood for 'Keep Kenton Kicking'" [326]).

Although Early acknowledges that Kenton did hire black musicians, he quickly adds: "But blacks never had a real presence in his bands nor any impact on the nature of the music. The *character* of the band was always overwhelmingly white, inasmuch as it is legitimate to describe the character of a band in racial terms" (326). This comes dangerously close to Roy Eldridge's claim that he could distinguish between black and white soloists. (He failed miserably in a 1951 *Down Beat* Blindfold Test.) And even if the "character" of Kenton's band was white (whatever that means), so what? Much of contemporary European jazz has also strayed from the music's black roots. Is this racism or artistic preference?

Incidentally, although he lists several black musicians who worked with Kenton, Early is apparently unaware of the bandleader's close friendship with bassist/arranger George Duvivier, whom he encouraged to write. Duvivier's Kentonesque arrangements were used with great success by such black R&B-influenced bands as those led by saxophonists Joe Thomas and Arnett Cobb in the late 1940s and early 1950s.

Although relatively short, Early's peculiar polemic can do a lot of harm, given the prominence of race in Ken Burns's overall treatment and the fact that this may prove to be the only book on jazz ever to reach a mass audience.

Returning to the work as a whole, it is a brilliant synthesis of much of the existing jazz literature. The author has clearly read widely, extracted the essence of many varied sources, and reorganized these nuggets into an informative and captivating whole. One only wishes he were as diligent in acknowledging these sources. At least a quarter of the text is comprised of direct quotations from musicians, which certainly lends authenticity and vitality to the narrative. Unfortunately, none of the sources of this material is acknowledged, apart from the inclusion of a bibliography. Some of these quotes are, of course, taken from interviews conducted specifically for the Burns project, but the majority are not. This is not a "scholarly" book, and the author/publisher may consider footnotes a cumbersome academic exercise. Nonetheless, I believe they are obligated to clearly identify the sources of direct quotations taken verbatim from other works, if not out of intellectual integrity, then at least to allow readers to gauge the veracity and accuracy of these statements. Although the failure to identify sources will irritate scholars, it should not affect the general audience, for which this is one of the most appealing overviews of jazz ever produced.

Robert Walser, editor. *Keeping Time: Readings in Jazz History.* (New York and Oxford: Oxford University Press, 1999. 450 pp., $35.00 cloth, $22.95 paperback)

Reviewed by Sam Miller

In recent years, the anthology has become increasingly common among the many books about jazz being published. There has been a wide variety of different types of anthologies: those dedicated to a particular musician, collections of an individual author's works, collections of interviews, anthologies of writing genres (record liner notes and fiction/poetry, for example), anthologies of newly commissioned works, and more general anthologies.[1] Robert Walser's *Keeping Time: Readings in Jazz History* is a welcome addition to the latter category. One of the advantages of an anthology is that it allows the editor to incorporate writings from a wide variety of perspectives, and therefore to appeal to a diverse audience. In this regard, Walser's work is quite successful. The book will be of interest to students just now getting familiar with jazz, jazz fans and musicians, and to jazz scholars.

Keeping Time is organized into chapters by decade. The overall organization is good, but each chapter includes both writing about the decade and writings from the decade, which I found to be occasionally misleading (by the author's own admission, the book is "roughly organized"). The reader should check the citation at the bottom of the first page of each excerpt to be sure of the date it was written. Each selection is numbered according the order it appears in the book, from one through sixty-two. This is particularly helpful to the classroom teacher, as readings can be easily assigned. Walser also provides a short introduction to each selection.

Walser's motivations and goals for *Keeping Time* are clearly outlined in his thoughtful preface. "It is often said that recordings are the primary documents of jazz history, but written documents can help us understand the disparate reactions of those who heard those recordings as contemporaries, so that we do not take our own reactions to be the only rational ones" (vii). The overemphasis on studying recorded materials has certainly been a major shortcoming of previous works on jazz, such as those of Gunther Schuller. The many excerpts from newspapers and from periodicals ranging from *Downbeat* to the *Ladies Home Journal* to *Playboy* that appear in *Keeping Time* help to place jazz in its proper historical context. Some, such as Walter Kingsley's often cited 1917 article on the origin of jazz from the *New York Sun*, are printed in complete for the first time since their original publication (6–7).

Walser outlines four themes that guided him when putting together the book. First, he wanted to present jazz as both an art form and a significant social practice. Second, he tried to emphasize the insider perspective. Thus, many of the excerpts are written by jazz musicians, with an emphasis on writings by African Americans. Third, he hoped to focus on the nature of the music itself, emphasizing critical musicological analysis as well as writings by musicians discussing why they made musical choices. Fourth, Walser wanted to create an anthology that would be effective for educators in the classroom. It is in this last regard that *Keeping Time* is most successful.

"First I wanted to present jazz not only as a virtuosic art form, but as a social practice of great significance. Jazz musicians have produced not only great music, but great understandings—of culture, race, gender, nation, the body, creativity, tradition, individuality, co-operation and community" (vii–viii). Walser has chosen excerpts by authors from diverse disciplines to help illustrate this. Included here are works by sociologist Howard Becker (179–91), psychoanalyst Miles D. Miller, M.D. (234–38), and an excerpt from African American Studies professor Hazel Carby that takes a feminist approach to interpreting blues singing (351–64). An excerpt from Ben Sidran's *Black Talk,* titled here *Oral Culture and Musical Tradition,* situates jazz as an African American tradition. Sidran makes excellent observations about the differences between the nature of the oral culture and tradition of Africa and that of the literate Western culture (297–301). Later excerpts in *Keeping Time* build upon these themes and apply them to specific jazz performances. Samuel Floyd Jr.'s 1991 article *Ring Shout! Literary Studies, Historical Studies and Black Music Inquiry*, makes use of Henry Louis Gates's theory of "signifyin'" to locate elements of oral culture in Jelly Roll Morton's 1926 recording of "Black Bottom Stomp" (401–10).

In putting together *Keeping Time,* Walser has made a point of including as much insider perspective as possible: "Second, this anthology includes a wide range of voices beyond the jazz critics who (however vigorous their disagreements at times) have dominated published discussion of the music. . . . In particular, I have foregrounded the voices of African Americans; nearly half of the excerpts included here are statements by black musicians or writers" (viii, my ellipses). Indeed, *Keeping Time* includes excerpts written by some of the most important musicians in the history of jazz. Those chosen are by musicians from the earliest years of the music to the present, including Sidney Bechet, Jelly Roll Morton, Louis Armstrong, Billie Holiday, Duke Ellington, Dizzy Gillespie, Charles Mingus, Leo Smith, Miles

Davis, and Wynton Marsalis. While many of these excerpts will no doubt be familiar to jazz scholars, I found this to be invaluable in teaching. Having so many statements from the musicians themselves greatly helped to enrich my undergraduate jazz history class. Some lesser-known musicians, such as Johnny Otis, also appear. *Keeping Time* helps to disprove the common misconception that African American authors have not written prolifically about jazz. The excerpt by Will Marion Cook (15–16) and an editorial from the black newspaper *Chicago Defender* (15–16), both originally published in 1919, prove that African Americans have written about jazz from the earliest days of the music. Several celebrated African American authors appear in *Keeping Time*, including Langston Hughes, Ralph Ellison, and Albert Murray.

Although Walser expresses a desire to provide alternative points of view to those of critics, their voices are here as well. This does not detract from the book, but rather helps maintain a balance in perspective. The best of the critical essays are musicological in nature and serve the third purpose Walser states in the preface. "Third, I have focused, as much as possible, on the music—on the specific choices, techniques, and rhetoric upon which everything else depends" (viii). Of interest here are André Hodier's analysis of Ellington's "Concerto For Cootie"(199–212) and Gunther Schuller's famous analysis of Sonny Rollins "Blue Seven" (212–22). Both Hodier and Schuller take a similar approach, using methods of analysis traditionally reserved for Western art music and applying them to jazz. Walser provides insightful commentary in his introduction to the Schuller article: "Schuller's analysis was an important milestone for jazz scholarship in that it dealt specifically and rigorously with the details of an improvised solo. Yet its lack of cultural context meant that it illuminated only his own delight in the music, without necessarily explaining why other listeners may have enjoyed Rollins's performance (such as the bohemian intellectuals who heard him, around the same time, at the Five Spot in New York)" (213). The focus on the music extends to excerpts written by the musicians themselves. For example, the only passages that Walser chooses from Miles Davis's autobiography are those where Davis specifically discusses his music. Again, many readers will have already read the complete original text, but in a surprisingly effective condensation, we get a real sense of *why* Davis made changes in his music, from the early "cool" period to his pioneering work in jazz-rock fusion (365–76).

Walser is associate professor and chair of musicology at the University of California, Los Angeles. Perhaps this guided him in assembling *Keeping Time* in a manner that is complimentary to use in education: "Fourth, I wanted to find writings that would be enjoyable to discuss. This drew me to excerpts that took a stand on what jazz is and why it matters. Thus, although it is aimed at a broad readership, this book should prove useful in classrooms" (viii). Since anthologies lack a strong overall narrative, it is difficult to recommend *Keeping Time* as a primary text for a jazz history course, but it does serve as an excellent supplemental text. Seeking to understand, analyze, and compare the different views in the book will help the student to develop valuable critical thinking skills. Some of the latter selections in the book, such as Carby's aforementioned article on female blues singers (351–64), Wynton Marsalis's article "What Jazz Is and—Isn't" (titled here "The Neoclassical Agenda," 334–39), and Scott DeVeaux's excellent survey and criticism of approaches to jazz historiography (416–24), will certainly provoke discussion. The sixty-two selections in *Keeping Time* provide us with many considerations, and best of all, inspire further study.

NOTE

1. A complete list of recent anthologies is beyond the scope of this review; a partial list might include the following:

Collections dedicated to a particular musician:
Lewis Porter's *A LesterYoung Reader* (Washington: Smithsonian Institution Press, 1991), Mark Tucker's *Duke Ellington Reader* (New York: Oxford University Press, 1993), Carl Woideck's *John Coltrane Companion* (New York: Schirmer Books; London: Prentice Hall International, 1998.), Todd Selbert's *The Art Pepper Companion* (New York: Cooper Square Press, 2000), and Gerald Early's *Miles Davis and American Culture* (Columbia, MS: University of Missouri Press, 2001).

Collections of a particular author's work:
Thomas Brothers's *Louis Armstrong in His Own Words: Selected Writings* (New York: Oxford University Press, 1999), Whitney Balliett's *Collected Works: A Journal Of Jazz 1954–1999* (New York: St. Martin's Press, 2000), and Robert G. O'Meally's *Living With Music: Ralph Ellison's Jazz Writings* (New York: Modern Library, 2001).

Collections of interviews:
Arthur Taylor's *Notes and Tones* (Expanded Edition, New York: Da Capo Press, 1993), Mario Luzzi's *Uomini e avanguardie jazz* (Milano:

Gammalibri, 1980), and Wayne Enstice and Paul Rubin's *Jazz Spoken Here: Conversations with Twenty-Two Musicians* (Baton Rouge: Louisiana State University Press, 1992).

Anthologized liner notes:
Tom Piazza's *Setting the Tempo: Fifty Years Of Great Jazz Liner Notes* (New York: Anchor Books, 1996).

Jazz Fiction and poetry:
Art Lange and Nathaniel Mackey's *Moment's Notice: Jazz In Poetry and Prose* (Minneapolis: Coffee House Press, 1993) (with works by Langston Hughes and Jack Kerouac among others).

Newly commissioned essays:
Bill *Kirchner's Oxford Companion To Jazz* (New York: Oxford University Press, 2000).

General anthologies:
Robert Gottlieb's *Reading Jazz* (New York: Pantheon Books, 1996) and Andrew Clark's *Riffs And Choruses: A New Jazz Anthology* (London and New York: Continuum, 2001).

Manfred Selchow, *Ding! Ding!: A Bio-Discographical Scrapbook on Vic Dickenson* (Westoverledingen: Published by the author, 1998, 947 pp., 82 euros)

Reviewed by Dan Morgenstern

This monumental tome (available only from the author, Eekeweg 14, D-26810 Westoverledingen, Germany) is a notable entry in the burgeoning genre of jazz bio-discography. The term (and concept) was introduced in 1955 by the late Walter C. Allen for his and Brian Rust's *King Joe Oliver* (Allen's 1973 *Hendersonia* remains a landmark in the field) and then taken up by D. Russell Connor for his 1958 *B.G. Off the Record* (revised and expanded several times, with changing titles). Other significant works are Laurie Wright's on Oliver and Fats Waller, Yasuhiro Fujioka's on John Coltrane (with Lewis Porter and Yoh-ichi Hamada), Ben Young's on Bill Dixon, and, by no means least, Manfred Selchow himself (with Karsten Lohman) on Edmond Hall.

It was for this work (*Profoundly Blue*) that Selchow created the variant "Bio-Discographical Scrapbook" title, since he had access, via Hall's widow, to his subject's scrapbooks, as he did, by way of Dickenson's niece, for *Ding! Ding!* (the title inspired by the trombonist's favorite expression, in greeting or approval). However, this does not substantively distinguish these works from, for example, *Hendersonia*, which also included reproductions of flyers, advertisements, and photographs—categories of ephemera found in scrapbooks—as well as record labels. Yet *Ding! Ding!* is particularly rich in materials that enhance the text (literally from birth to death certificates), among them letters (the earliest, to Dickenson's mother, from 1926), music (complete songs with lyrics to brief sketches), reviews (from newspapers and jazz periodicals), and even school documents (with declensions of Latin verbs in Dickenson's hand—sic transit gloria mundi!).

Though Selchow did not meet the great trombonist until just 17 months prior to his death (on November 16, 1984), he'd long admired his playing, and once they met, they got along famously. The book, more than a decade in the making, is a prime example of dedicated amateur scholarship infused with genuine and often touching affection for its subject, as man and artist. His disclaimer: "With regard to syntax, choice and spelling of words, and the general simplicity of language in this book, the reader is kindly requested to bear in mind that whatever mistakes occur are attributable to the fact that English is not the author's native tongue," notwithstanding, Selchow is never a less than clear and succinct guide through the amazing amount of material he has assembled, and the occasional malapropism actually lends a certain charm to the text.

Every possible nugget relevant to Dickenson's long and rich life and career has been mined by the author from a multitude of sources, including interviews with the trombonist by himself and others (among them the lengthy one conducted by this writer in 1976 for the Jazz Oral History Project of the National Endowment for the Arts), and with a myriad of musicians and others who worked with or knew the man. The narrative, which begins with family history, is strictly chronological and interspersed with details of all known engagements and, of course, recordings—studio and live, issued and unissued. Comments on solos by Dickenson and other performance aspects are often included. Many of the live performances, which often exist on private tapes only, have never before been documented, and whenever possible, Selchow has auditioned them personally, or, when that was impossible, relied on authoritative sources.

The result of this impressive labor of love, in the true sense of that term, is a matchless documentation of the life and times of a musician whose active career spanned seven decades, included experience with both little-known and famous bands, and intersected with some of the greatest names in jazz, crossing stylistic and generational boundaries, and covering the entire Golden Age of the music. There is a wealth of information about venues, remuneration, the trials and joys of life on the road, relations between colleagues, journalistic coverage of jazz through the decades, circumstances of recording, and the overcoming of illness and other tribulations.

All this would be of interest even if Albert Victor Dickenson had not been one of jazz's true originals, both as a player who invented his own style (and a sometime singer of great charm and composer of more than a handful of good tunes), and as a man whose human qualities were such that, in his own quiet but determined way, he commanded respect and affection throughout his life.

As one who had the pleasure and privilege of knowing Vic well, I can say without the slightest hesitation that this is a work that does him justice. Ding! Ding!

JAZZ RESEARCH BIBLIOGRAPHY (1999–2000)

Keith Waters and Jason R.Titus

In response to the rapidly growing body of jazz scholarship, the *Annual Review of Jazz Studies* will be providing a jazz research bibliography as a feature. The articles contained in the bibliography are scholarly essays contained in journals that are not specifically devoted to jazz. The items included are intended as an aid for jazz researchers. Essays in this issue's bibliography were published between 1999 and 2000. Thanks to Roberto Agostini, Fred Bashour, Barbara Bleij, Monica J. Burdex, Mark Burford, Krin Gabbard, John Hasse, Evan Jones, Bill Kirchner, Steve Larson, Henry Martin, Tom Owens, Bruce Boyd Raeburn, Robert Rawlins, Richard M. Sudhalter, Dmitri Tymoczko, Kristin Wendland, J. Kent Williams, Stefano Zenni, and others for their invaluable suggestions on items for inclusion.

Suggestions of academic articles published in nonjazz journals after 2000 may be emailed to Keith Waters (waters@stripe.colorado.edu) or Jason R. Titus (JRTitus1@aol.com). Complete citations (date, volume and number, pages) would be appreciated.

Albjerg, Erik. "From Mellow-textured Mood Music into Dissonance: Gil Evans's 1948 Arrangement of Moon Dreams." *Tijdschrift voor Muziektheorie* 5/1 (2000): 1–15. (In English.)

Anderson, T.J. "Body and Soul: Bob Kaufman's Golden Sardine." *African American Review* 34/2 (Summer 2000): 329–46.

D'Andrea, Franco. "Il pianismo di Ellington: un'analisi." *Musica Oggi* 19 (1999): 23–29. (In Italian with abstract in English.)

Bashour, Frederick. "A Different View: 'On Miles and the Modes.'" *College Music Symposium* 39 (1999): 124–129.

Bayles, Martha. "What's Wrong with Being Classical?" *The Antioch Review* 57/3 (Summer 1999): 318–326.

Brown, Lee B. "Afrocentrism Old and New: The Critical Theory of Jazz." *The Journal of Aesthetics and Art Criticism* 57 (1999): 235–246.

Brown, Lee B. " 'Feeling My Way': Jazz Improvisation and Its Vicissitudes—A Plea for Imperfection." *The Journal of Aesthetics and Art Criticism* 58/2 (Spring 2000): 113–124.

Comeglio, Gabriele. "Appunti sulla 'Such Sweet Thunder.'" *Musica Oggi* 19 (1999): 30–35. (In Italian with abstract in English.)

Day, William. "Knowing as Instancing: Jazz Improvisation and Moral Perfectionism." *The Journal of Aesthetics and Art Criticism* 58/2 (Spring 2000): 99–111.

DeVeaux, Scott. " 'Nice Work if You Can Get It': Thelonious Monk and Popular Song." *Black Music Research Journal* 19/2 (Fall 1999): 169–186.

Early, Gerald. "Ode to John Coltrane: A Jazz Musician's Influence on African American Culture." *The Antioch Review* 57/3 (Summer 1999): 371–385.

Feinstein, Sascha. "Misterioso." *Black Music Research Journal* 19/2 (Fall 1999): 201–206.

Frost, Richard. "Jazz and Poetry." *The Antioch Review* 57/3 (Summer 1999): 386–401.

Gabbard, Krin. "Evidence: Monk as Documentary Subject." *Black Music Research Journal* 19/2 (Fall 1999): 207–226.

Gabbard, Krin. "Innocence Lost: American Movies Revisit Jazz." *Chronicle of Higher Education* 46/2 (Sept. 3, 1999): B10–11.

Gabbard, Krin. "Ken Burns's 'Jazz': Beautiful Music, but Missing a Beat." *Chronicle of Higher Education* 47/16 (Dec. 15, 2000): B18–19.

Gould, Carol S. and Kenneth Keaton. "The Essential Role of Improvisation in Musical Performance." *The Journal of Aesthetics and Art Criticism* 58/2 (Spring 2000): 113–23.

Harker, Brian. " 'Telling a Story': Louis Armstrong and Coherence in Early Jazz." *Current Musicology* 63: 46–83.

Jenkins, Willard. "Where's the Jazz Audience?" *The Antioch Review* 57/3 (Summer 1999): 355–362.

Johnson, Jerah. "Jim Crow Laws of the 1890s and the Origins of New Orleans Jazz: Correction of an Error." *Popular Music* 19/2 (2000): 243–251.

Joyner, David. "Analyzing Third Stream." *Contemporary Music Review* 19/1 (2000): 63–87.

Kanner, Melinda. "Reading Jazz: Recent Books." *The Antioch Review* 57/3 (Summer 1999): 432–440.

Kaplan, Erica. "Melba Liston: It's All from My Soul." *The Antioch Review* 57/3 (Summer 1999): 415–425.

Kelley, Robin D.G. "New Monastery: Monk and the Jazz Avant-Garde." *Black Music Research Journal* 19/2 (Fall 1999): 135–168.

Larson, Steve. Reviews of *The American Popular Ballad of the Golden Era, 1924–1950*, by Allan Forte; *The Music of Gershwin*, by Steven Gilbert; and *Charlie Parker and Thematic Improvisation*, by Henry Martin. *Music Theory Spectrum* 21/1 (1999): 110–121.

Larson, Steve. "Swing and Motive in Three Performances by Oscar Peterson." *Journal of Music Theory* 43/2 (Fall 1999): 283–314.

Levine, Mark. "Notes on Ellington: the Clave and Piano Strategies." *Musica Oggi* 19 (1999): 18–22. (In English.)

London, Barbara. "Jazz Theory Education in the USA: From Our Perspective." *Tijdschrift voor Muziektheorie* 4/3 (1999): 241–250. (In English.)

Lopes, Paul. "Diffusion and Syncretism: The Modern Jazz Tradition (The Social Diffusion of Ideas and Things)." *The Annals of the American Academy of Political and Social Science* 566 (Nov. 1999): 25–37.

Lowney, John. "Langston Hughes and the 'Nonsense' of Bebop." *American Literature* 72/2 (June 2000): 357–359.

Magee, Jeffrey. "Fletcher Henderson, Composer: A Counter-Entry to the *International Dictionary of Black Composers*." *Black Music Research Journal* 19/1 (1999): 61–69.

McNeilly, Kevin. "Word Jazz 1." *Canadian Literature* 164 (Spring 2000): 179–84.

Modirzadeh, Hafez. "Spiraling Chinese Cyclic Theory and Modal Jazz Practice Across Millenia: Proposed Sources and New Perceptions for John Coltrane's Late Musical Conceptions." *Journal of Music of China* 2/2 (2000): 235–264.

Monson, Ingrid. "Monk Meets SNCC." *Black Music Research Journal* 19/2 (Fall 1999): 187–200.

Moreno, Jairo. "Body'n'Soul?: Voice and Movement in Keith Jarrett's Pianism." *Musical Quarterly* 83/1 (Spring 1999): 75–92.

Nettelbeck, Colin. "Jazz at the Theatre Graslin: A Founding Story." *French Cultural Studies* 11/ 2 (June 2000): 201–17.

Newberry, Elizabeth. "Prodding the Spirit: The Searching Words of Ben Harper." *Sojourners* 29/2 (March/April 2000): 58–60.

Panetta, Vincent J. "'For Godsake Stop!' Improvised Music in the Streets of New Orleans, ca. 1890." *Musical Quarterly* 84/1 (Spring 2000): 5–29.

Porter, Eric. "Dizzy Atmosphere: The Challenge of Bebop." *American Music* 17/4 (Winter 1999): 422–446.

Porter, Horace. "Jazz Beginnings: Ralph Ellison and Charlie Christian in Oklahoma City." *The Antioch Review* 57/3 (Summer 1999): 277–295.

Pritchard, William H. "All That Jazz." Review of *Visions of Jazz: The First Century*, by Gary Giddins; and *Lost Chords: White Musicians and Their Contributions to Jazz, 1915–1945* by Richard M. Sudhalter, *Hudson Review* 52/2 (Summer 1999): 332–338.

Ramalho, Gerber L., Pierre-Yves Rolland, and Jean–Gabriel Ganascia. "An Artificially Intelligent Jazz Performer." *Journal of New Music Research* 28/2 (June 1999): 105–129.

Sadoff, Ira. "Inside/out." *The American Poetry Review* 29/2 (March/April 2000): 9–12.

Sterritt, David. "Revision, Prevision, and the Aura of Improvisatory Art." *The Journal of Aesthetics and Art Criticism* 58/2 (Spring 2000): 163–172.

Strunk, Steven. "Chick Corea's 1984 Performance of 'Night and Day.'" *Journal of Music Theory* 43/2 (Fall 1999): 315–348.

Thomson, William. "Response to Frederick Bashour." *College Music Symposium* 39 (1999): 130–35.

Tucker, Mark. "Mainstreaming Monk: The Ellington Album." *Black Music Research Journal* 19/2 (Fall 1999): 227–244.

Tucker, Sherrie. "Telling Performances: Jazz History Remembered and Remade by the Women in the Band." *Oral History Review* 26/1 (Winter/Spring 1999): 67–84.

Tucker, Sherrie. "The Prairie View Co-eds: Black College Women Musicians in Class and on the Road During World War II." *Black Music Research Journal* 19/1 (Spring 1999): 93–126.

Tymoczko, Dmitri. "The Consecutive–Semitone Constraint on Scalar Structure: A Link Between Impressionism and Jazz," *Intégral* 11 (1997): 135–179.

van der Blick, Rob. "A Selection of Monk Sources." *Black Music Research Journal* 19/2 (Fall 1999): 245–252.

Visconti Prasca, Marco. "Le meravigliose trasgressioni del Duca." *Musica Oggi* 19 (1999): 36–42. (In Italian with abstract in English.)

Waters, Keith. "Introducing Pitch-Class Sets in the Music of Coltrane and Harbison." GAMUT 9 (1999): 83–90.

Willard, Patricia. "Dance: the Unsung Element of Ellingtonia." *The Antioch Review* 57/3 (Summer 1999): 402–414.

Williams, Richard. "Gifted." *Granta* 69 (Spring 2000): 231–255.

Yaffe, David. "Special Pleading and Counter–Intuition: Hart Crane's Swinging Muse." *The Antioch Review* 57/3 (Summer 1999): 327–332.

Young, James O. and Carl Matheson. "The Metaphysics of Jazz." *The Journal of Aesthetics and Art Criticism* 58/2 (Spring 2000): 125–33.

Zenni, Stefano. "La reinvenzione della musica: tra improvvisazione e composizione jazz." *Musica/Realtà* 61 (March 2000): 187–192. (In Italian.)

Zhang, Weihua. "Notes on the Current Jazz scene in China." *Journal of Music of China* 2/2 (2000): 265–272.

BOOKS RECEIVED

Compiled by Vincent Pelote

The following list recently published or republished books added to the archives of the Institute of Jazz Studies. Books are listed alphabetically by title, with the primary title in full capitals.

AFRO-CUBAN JAZZ, by Scott Yanow (Miller Freeman Books, 2000)

ARRANGING THE SCORE: Portraits of Great Arrangers, by Gene Lees (Cassell, 2000)

THE ART PEPPER COMPANION: Writings on a Jazz Original, ed. by Todd Selbert (Cooper Square Press, 2000)

BACKWATER BLUES: In Search of Bessie Smith, by Sara Grimes (Rose Island, 2000)

BEBOP, by Scott Yanow (Miller Freeman, 2000)

BEFORE MOTOWN: A History of Jazz in Detroit, 1920–60, by Lars Bjorn with Jim Gallert (University of Michigan Press, 2001)

BEN WEBSTER: His Life and Music, by Jeroen de Valk (Berkeley Hills Books, 2001)

THE BIG BAND READER: Songs Favored by Swing Era Orchestras and Other Popular Ensembles, by William E. Studwell and Mark Baldin (Haworth Press, 2000)

BILLIE HOLIDAY, by Chris Ingham (Unanimous, 2000)

BING CROSBY: A Pocketful of Dreams: The Early Years 1903–1940, by Gary Giddins (Little, Brown, 2001)

BIRTH OF THE COOL: Beat, Bebop, and the American Avant-Garde, by Lewis MacAdams (Free Press, 2001)

BLACK BOTTOM STOMP: Eight Masters of Ragtime and Early Jazz, by David A. Jasen and Gene Jones (Routledge, 2002)

BLUE NIPPON: Authenticating Jazz in Japan, by E. Taylor Atkins (Duke University Press, 2001)

BLUES FACES: A Portrait of the Blues, by Ann Charters and Samuel Charters (David R. Godine, 2000)

BRILLIANT CORNERS: A Bio-Discography of Thelonious Monk, compiled by Chris Sheridan (Greenwood, 2001)

CARMEN McRAE: Miss Jazz, by Leslie Gourse (Billboard Books, 2001)

CHARLIE BARNET: An Illustrated Biography and Discography of the Swing Era Big Band Leader, by Dan Mather (McFarland, 2002)

CLASS ACT: The Jazz Life of Choreographer Cholly Atkins, by Cholly Atkins and Jacqui Malone (Columbia University Press, 2001)

CLASSIC JAZZ, by Scott Yanow (Backbeat Books, 2001)

CLASSIC JAZZ: A Personal View of the Music and the Musicians, by Floyd Levin (University of California Press, 2000)

COLLECTED WORKS: A Journal of Jazz 1954–2000, by Whitney Balliett (St. Martin's, 2000)

DEAD MAN BLUES: Jelly Roll Morton Way Out West, by Phil Pastras (University of California Press, 2001)

DUKE ELLINGTON AND HIS WORLD: A Biography, by A. H. Lawrence (Routledge, 2001)

EDDIE CONDON ON RECORD, second edition, by Giorgio Lombardi (Italian Jazz Institute, 2001)

88: THE GIANTS OF THE JAZZ PIANO, by Robert L. Doerschuk (Backbeat Books, 2001)

ELLA FITZGERALD: An Annotated Discography; Including a Complete Discography of Chick Webb, compiled by J. Wilfred Johnson (McFarland, 2001)

FAKEBOOK: Improvisations on a Journey Back to Jazz, by Richard Terrill (Limelight Editions, 2000)

GIL EVANS: Out of the Cool: His Life and Music, by Stephanie Stein Crease (Acappella, 2002)

GOING FOR JAZZ: Musical Practices and American Ideology, by Nicholas Gebhardt (University of Chicago Press, 2001)

HARLEM IN MONTMARTRE: A Paris Jazz Story Between the Great Wars, by William A. Shack (University of California Press, 2001)

IF YOU CAN'T BE FREE, BE A MYSTERY: In Search of Billie Holiday, by Farah Jasmine Griffin (Free Press, 2001)

IN A SILENT WAY: A Portrait of Joe Zawinul, by Brian Glasser (Sanctuary, 2001)

JAZZ: A History of America's Music, by Geoffrey C. Ward and Ken Burns (Knopf, 2000)

JAZZ: The First 100 Years, by Henry Martin and Keith Waters (Wadsworth, 2002)

JAZZ COUNTRY: Ralph Ellison in America, by Horace A. Porter (University of Iowa Press, 2001)

JAZZ CULTURES, by David Ake (University of California Press, 2002)

JAZZ HARMONY AT THE PIANO, Vol. 1, by Frans Elsen (self-published, 2001)

JAZZ IN AMERICAN CULTURE, by Peter Townsend (Edinburgh University Press, 2000)

JAZZ IN THE BITTERSWEET BLUES OF LIFE, by Wynton Marsalis and Carl Vigeland (Da Capo, 2001)

JAZZ ON THE ROAD: Don Albert's Musical Life, by Christopher Wilkinson (University of California Press, 2001)

JAZZOGRAPHY: Profiles of Regional Jazz Musicians Who Perform in San Francisco, by Mars Breslow and Dan Guaraldi (Larkdale, 2000)

THE KING OF ALL, SIR DUKE: Ellington and the Artistic Revolution, by Peter Lavezzoli (Continuum International, 2001)

KISS AND TELL: Autobiography of a Traveling Musician, by Martin Taylor with David Mead (Sanctuary, 2000)

LESTER LEAPS IN: The Life and Times of Lester "Pres" Young, by Douglas Henry Daniels (Beacon, 2002)

LIVING THE JAZZ LIFE: Conversations With Forty Musicians About Their Career in Jazz, by W. Royal Stokes (Oxford University Press, 2000)

LIVING WITH MUSIC: Ralph Ellison's Jazz Writings, ed. by Robert G. O'Meally (Random House, 2001)

THE LOUDEST TRUMPET: Buddy Bolden and the Early History of Jazz, by Daniel Hardie (toExcel, 2000)

THE MAN BEHIND THE HORN: Leon Merian, by Leon Merian & William Bridges, Jr. (Diem, 2000)

MASTERS OF JAZZ SAXOPHONE: The Story of the Players and Their Music, ed. by Dave Gelly (Belafon, 2000)

MILES AND ME, by Quincy Troupe (University of California Press, 2000)

MILES BEYOND: The Electric Explorations of Miles Davis, 1967–1991, by Paul Tingen (Billboard, 2001)

MILES DAVIS AND AMERICAN CULTURE, ed. by Gerald Early (Missouri Historical Society, 2001)

MILES TO GO: Remembering Miles Davis, by Chris Murphy (Thunder's Mouth, 2001)

THE MILLER COMPANION TO JAZZ IN CANADA: And Canadians in Jazz, by Mark Miller (Mercury, 2001)

MORE BLUES SINGERS, by David Dicaire (McFarland, 2002)

THE NAT HENTOFF READER, by Nat Hentoff (Da Capo, 2001)

A NEW HISTORY OF JAZZ, by Alyn Shipton (Continuum International, 2001)

NEW YORK IS NOW!: The New Wave of Free Jazz, by Phil Freeman (Telegraph, 2001)

OPEN THE DOOR: The Life and Music of Betty Carter, by William R. Bauer (University of Michigan Press, 2002)

PENGUIN GUIDE TO JAZZ ON CD, Fifth Edition, ed. by Richard Cook and Brian Morton (Penguin, 2000)

PERRY ROBINSON: The Traveler, by Perry Robinson and Florence Wetzel (Writers Club, 2002)

RHINO'S CRUISE THROUGH THE BLUES, by Barry Hansen (Miller Freeman, 2000)

SHACKLING WATER, by Adam Mansbach (Doubleday, 2001)

SHOUT, SISTER, SHOUT!: Ten Girl Singers Who Shaped a Century, by Roxane Orgill (Margaret K. McElderry, 2001)

SIDEMAN: Stories About the Band, by Paul Tanner (Cosmo Space, 2000)

SOMETHING TO LIVE FOR: The Music of Billy Strayhorn, by Walter van de Leur (Oxford University Press, 2002)

SONGS OF THE UNSUNG: The Musical and Social Journey of Horace Tapscott, by Horace Tapscott (Duke University Press, 2001)

SONNY ROLLINS: The Definitive Musical Guide, by Peter Niklas Wilson (Berkeley Hills, 2001)

SWING, by Scott Yanow (Miller Freeman, 2000)

SWING IT! An Annotated History of Jive, by Bill Milkowski (Billboard, 2001)

SWING, THAT MODERN SOUND, by Kenneth J. Bindas (University Press of Mississippi, 2001)

TAJ MAHAL: Autobiography of a Bluesman, by Taj Mahal with Stephen Foehr (Sanctuary, 2001)

THAT DEVLIN' TUNE: A History, 1900–1950, by Allen Lowe (Music and Arts Programs of America, 2001)

THE THELONIOUS MONK READER, edited by Rob van der Bliek (Oxford University Press, 2001)

TRUMPET KINGS: The Players Who Shaped the Sound of the Jazz Trumpet, by Scott Yanow (Backbeat, 2001)

WALTZING IN THE DARK: African American Vaudeville and Race in the Swing Era, by Brenda Dixon Gottschild (St. Martin's, 2000)

YOU CAN'T STEAL A GIFT: Dizzy, Clark, Milt, and Nat, by Gene Lees (Yale University Press, 2001)

ABOUT THE EDITORS

EDWARD BERGER, associate director of the Institute of Jazz Studies, writer, is active as a record producer and photographer. He is coauthor of the recently revised and updated *Benny Carter: A Life in American Music* and author of two other works in the Scarecrow Press Studies in Jazz series.

DAVID A. CAYER was a founding coeditor of the *Journal of Jazz Studies,* the predecessor of *Annual Review of Jazz Studies,* in 1973 and has been affiliated with the Institute of Jazz Studies since 1965. In 1991, he retired from Rutgers University as associate vice president for academic affairs.

HENRY MARTIN, associate professor of music at Rutgers University–Newark, is a composer and music theorist. He is also founder and chair of the Special Interest Group in Jazz Theory of the Society for Music Theory. His *Charlie Parker and Thematic Improvisation* is no. 24 in the Studies in Jazz Series. Wadsworth/Schirmer recently issued his jazz history text (coauthored with Keith Waters), *Jazz:The First Hundred Years.*

DAN MORGENSTERN, director of the Institute of Jazz Studies, is a jazz historian and former editor of *Down Beat.* His many publications include *Jazz People,* and he has won six Grammy awards for album notes. He has been a vice president of the National Academy of Recording Arts and Sciences, a jazz panelist for the Music Program of the National Endowment for the Arts, and a teacher of jazz history at Brooklyn College, New York University, the Peabody Institute, and Rutgers.

ABOUT THE CONTRIBUTORS

TED BUEHRER is an assistant professor of music at Kenyon College, where he teaches courses in music theory, jazz, and composition. He has published articles and reviews in *Indiana Theory Review* and *CHOICE*. Outside of his continuing research on Mary Lou Williams, his interests include Duke Ellington, music theory pedagogy, and the analysis of pitch-centric twentieth-century music.

ELLEN CASWELL received her B.A. in creative writing from Lycoming College in Williamsport, Pennsylvania. Her poems have appeared recently in *High Plains Literary Review*, and several others are under consideration at various journals. She is currently working toward an M.F.A. at the University of Arizona and hopes to work in editing or publishing.

DAVID DIAMOND is currently a teaching assistant in the Jazz Division at the University of Illinois, where he is pursuing a D.M.A. degree in trumpet performance. He studies trumpet with Ray Sasaki, improvisation with Ron Bridgewater, and trumpet and jazz writing with Thomas Wirtel. He received his master's degree in trumpet performance from the University of Colorado at Boulder.

CLIVE DOWNS plays alto saxophone and flute (currently in a semiprofessional big band) and has researched the music of, and literature on, Charlie Christian for some years. His main jazz research interest (apart from Christian) is in the music of Eric Dolphy. Current academic affiliation: Oxford Brookes University, Oxford, England.

MAX HARRISON studied with Anthony Milner, Iain Hamilton, and finally with Mátyás Seiber. He worked for many years in classical music publishing in London as an editor, arranger, and orchestrator, but writing about music finally took over. He produced hundreds of reviews of classical concerts for the *Times* and of classical recordings for *The Gramophone*, as well as other publications in Britain and on the Continent. He has also written extensively about jazz, most recently as coauthor of *The Essential Jazz Records, Volume 2: Modernism to Postmodernism.* He is currently working on a biography of Rachmaninoff.

TAD HERSHORN, archivist at the Institute of Jazz Studies since 1999, began taking photographs in his hometown of Dallas, Texas, in 1969. His work as appeared in such publications as *JazzTimes* and *Swing Journal*, and on record covers of such jazz figures as Ella Fitzgerald, Count Basie, and Dizzy Gillespie. He is currently completing his biography of jazz impresario, record producer, and civil rights activist Norman Granz.

SAM MILLER has a degree in ethnomusicology from the University of California at Los Angeles, where he studied with jazz guitarist Kenny Burrell. He is currently a student in the M.A. program in jazz history and research at Rutgers University in Newark, where he is preparing a thesis on jazz saxophonist and composer Hank Mobley.

DAVID MORGAN is a jazz bassist and composer. He is assistant professor of jazz studies at Youngstown State University. He received his doctorate from the University of Texas at Austin. His compositions for large ensemble are featured on the 1999 Jazz Unit recording, *Choices.*

VINCENT PELOTE is the head of collection service/sound archivist at the Institute of Jazz Studies. He has compiled discographies of Billie Holiday, Lionel Hampton, and the Commodore label; lectured on Louis Armstrong, women in jazz, Eubie Blake, and the International Sweethearts of Rhythm. He has contributed to the Oxford Companion to Jazz and to LP and CD notes on jazz guitar, Mary Lou Williams, Benny Carter, and others.

DAVID J. RIFE is the John P. Graham Professor of Teaching at Lycoming College in Williamsport, Pennsylvania, where he has taught American literature and modern fiction, among other subjects, since 1970. His writing on a variety of topics have appeared in *American Literary Realism, Annual Review of Jazz Studies, Dictionary of Literary Biography, Journal of Modern Literature,* and *The Oxford Companion to Crime and Mystery Writing,* among others. He is Associate Editor of *Brilliant Corners: A Journal of Jazz and Literature.*

ALEXANDER STEWART is assistant professor of music at the University of Vermont. He holds a Master of Music from Manhattan School of Music and a Ph.D. from the Graduate Center of the City University of New York. His dissertation explores the compositions and performance practices of some of the over eighty big bands he identified as currently active in New York. His articles and entries appear in *Popular Music, Yearbook of Traditional Music,* and *Encyclopedia of Popular Music of the World.* A saxophonist, he his performed, recorded, and toured with many artists, including Lionel Hampton, Ray Charles, and David Liebman.

VICTOR SVORINICH received his master's degree in jazz history and research and his bachelor's degree in music performance at the Newark campus of Rutgers, the State University. He is a lecturer of music theory at Rutgers and a guitar instructor at the Calderone School of Music in Millburn, New Jersey.

JAY SWEET works frequently as a performing bassist and bandleader in the New York area. He is a graduate of the Berklee College of Music and is currently working on a Master of Arts in jazz history and research at Rutgers University in Newark.

JASON R. TITUS holds degrees in music from the Eastman School of Music, Indiana University of Pennsylvania, and Louisiana State University. He is currently a Ph.D. student in music theory at Eastman. His research interests include the chord voicings of Thelonious Monk and the modal jazz of Miles Davis.

KEITH WATERS is assistant professor of music theory at the University of Colorado at Boulder. He has published articles pertaining to jazz improvisation and analysis, and his book, *Jazz: The First Hundred Years*, coauthored with Henry Martin, was recently published by Wadsworth/Schirmer. As a jazz pianist, he has performed throughout the U.S.A., Europe, and in Russia, and has performed in concert with James Moody, Bobby Hutcherson, Chris Connor, Sheila Jordan, Buck Hill, and others. He has been featured in *Jazz Player* magazine. His most recent recording is with the Jon Metzger Quartet for VSOP Records.

ABOUT THE INSTITUTE OF JAZZ STUDIES

The Institute of Jazz Studies of Rutgers, the State University of New Jersey, is a unique research facility and archival collection, the foremost of its kind. IJS was founded in 1952 by Marshall Stearns (1908–1966), a pioneer jazz scholar, professor of medieval English literature at Hunter College, and the author of two essential jazz books: *The Story of Jazz* and *Jazz Dance*. In 1966, Rutgers was chosen as the collection's permanent home. IJS is located on the Newark campus of Rutgers and is a part of the John Cotton Dana Library of the Rutgers University Libraries.

IJS carries on a comprehensive program to preserve and further jazz in all its facets. The archival collection, which has more than quadrupled its holdings since coming to Rutgers, consists of more than 100,000 sound recordings in all formats, from phonograph cylinders and piano rolls to video cassettes and laser discs; more than 5,000 books on jazz and related subjects, including discographies, bibliographies, and dissertations; and comprehensive holdings in jazz periodicals from throughout the world. In addition, there are extensive vertical files on individuals and selected topics, a large collection of photographs, sheet music, scores, arrangements, realia, and memorabilia.

IJS serves a broad range of users, from students to seasoned scholars, authors, and collectors. The facilities are open to the public on weekdays by appointment. In addition to students, scholars, and other researchers, IJS routinely assists teachers, musicians, the media, record companies and producers, libraries and archives, arts agencies, and jazz organizations.

For further information on IJS and its programs and activities, write to:

Institute of Jazz Studies
Dana Library, Rutgers, the State University
185 University Avenue
Newark, NJ 07102

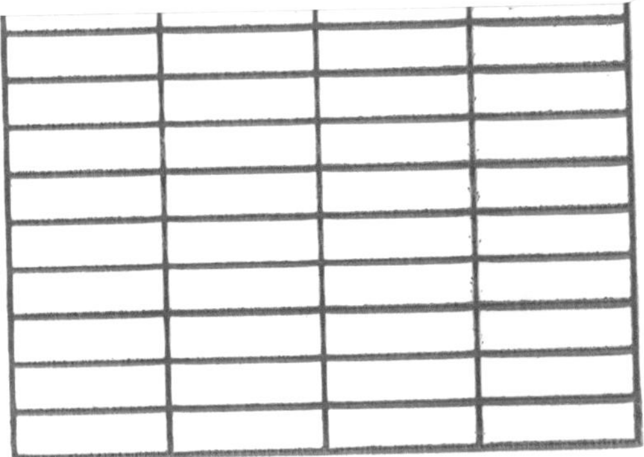